Sets in Motion

Sets
in
Motion

Art Direction
and
Film Narrative

Charles Affron
and
Mirella Jona Affron

Rutgers University Press
New Brunswick, New Jersey

Library of Congress Cataloging-in-Publication Data

Affron, Charles.
    Sets in motion : art direction and film narrative / Charles
Affron and Mirella Jona Affron.
        p.   cm.
    Includes bibliographical references and index.
    ISBN 0-8135-2160-2 (cloth) — ISBN 0-8135-2161-0 (pbk.)
    1. Motion pictures—Art direction.   2. Motion pictures—Setting
and scenery.   I. Affron, Mirella Jona, 1937–   .   II. Title.
PN1995.9.A74A35   1995
791.43′0233—dc20   94-39443
                                                    CIP

British Cataloging-in-Publication information available

For Elda Gentilli Jona and Renato Jona
In memoriam

"E le morte stagioni, e la presente
E viva . . ."
Giacomo Leopardi, "L'Infinito"

Contents

Illustrations

Photo Credits

Photos 1, 9, 24, 26, 27, 29, 30, 36, 37, 38, 42, 43, 50, 57, 60, 61, 62, 66, 72, 74, 75, 76, 82, 83, 90, 91, 92, 94, 95, 100, 101, 103, 105 courtesy of the Museum of Modern Art/Film Stills Archive; photos 2, 3, 6, 10, 11, 12, 16, 17, 18, 19, 20, 21, 22, 25, 28, 31, 44, 45, 46, 48, 49, 52, 53, 55, 56, 58, 63, 64, 67, 68, 71, 77, 81, 85, 86, 87, 88, 93, 96, 97, 99 courtesy of Photofest; photos 4, 33, 34, 35 courtesy of the Cineteca Italiana; photos 7, 8, 13, 39, 40, 54, 59, 65, 108, 111 courtesy of Jerry Ohlinger's Movie Material Store; photos 5, 15, 32, 51, 69, 70, 73, 78, 79, 89, 98, 106, 107, 109, 110, 112 courtesy of the National Film Archive, London; photos 14, 23, 41, 47, 80, 84, 102, 104 authors' collection.

Acknowledgments

We are delighted to be able to thank those who have so generously facilitated our research and writing.

We are grateful, first and foremost, for the support we received for this project from the National Endowment for the Humanities Interpretive Research/Projects, and in particular from its then director, Dorothy Wartenberg. We are also grateful to the PSC–CUNY Research Award Program, to the Research Challenge Fund of New York University, and to the American Council of Learned Societies for their grants-in-aid. The grants officers at New York University, Marti Dunn and Nancy Greenberg, and at the College of Staten Island/CUNY, Marie Miller, also have our gratitude.

Among the archivists and librarians without whom this work would not have been possible are the staff of the British Film Institute Library; Noëlle Giret, Directeur de la Bibliothèque-Musée La Cinémathèque Française, Paris, and her colleagues Marianne de Fleury and Dominique Brun; Walter Alberti, Conservatore, Cineteca Italiana, Milan; Guido Cincotti, Curator, Cineteca Nazionale, Rome; Ned Comstock and Ann Schlosser of the Doheny Library, Special Collections, University of Southern California, Los Angeles; Sam Gill and Howard Prouty of the Margaret Herrick Library, the Academy Foundation, Los Angeles; Mischa Schutt and Lisa Davis of the Louis B. Mayer Library, American Film Institute, Los Angeles; Donald Albrecht of the Museum of the Moving Image, New York City; Brigitta Kueppers, Ann Caiger, Carol Turley of The University of California at Los Angeles, Research Library, Special Collections; Leith Adams, archivist, the Warner Brothers Collection, University of Southern California. We are especially indebted to the staff of the College of Staten Island/CUNY Library and Media Services: Rebecca Adler, Jeanette Cohen, Walter Dornfest, Jerome Mardison, Raja Jayatilleke. Finally, we want to acknowledge the extraordinary assistance we received from Francesca Dragone Bandel and Emilia Bandel in securing otherwise inaccessible Italian materials.

To the distinguished art directors who gave of their time and their inspiring memories we have a special debt: Gene Allen, Robert Boyle, Edward Carfagno, Max Douy,

Harold Michelson, Alexandre Trauner, Maurice Zuberano. Director Luigi Comencini was especially gracious in granting us an interview.

We thank George Custen for his acute and informed reading of the manuscript, Matthew Affron for his numerous bibliographic and iconographic contributions, Beatrice Jona Affron for her transcriptions of taped interviews and unfailingly pertinent suggestions, and Sara Jona Levy for her patience and support. Finally, we thank our editors at Rutgers University Press: Marilyn Campbell and India Cooper for the scrupulous attention they devoted to this manuscript and, above all, Leslie Mitchner for her perceptive counsel, invaluable encouragement, and her friendship in this and so many other projects.

Cragsmoor, New York   June 1994

Sets in Motion

Introduction

"It is not generally recognized by the public that the most genuinely creative member of a film unit, if the author of the original story and screenplay is excluded, is the art director. . . . In the film world the producer and director and cameraman are so full of themselves that it is not sufficiently acknowledged that the art director is the creator of those miraculous images up there on the big screen."[1] From his own lofty perch as director, accustomed to commanding—and receiving—attention and recognition, Michael Powell acknowledges the neglect of the art director. Like editors and costume designers, and occasionally writers, set designers are expected to lend their skill and talent to the film enterprise in faceless silence. Producers, directors, and cinematographers are free to imitate the ostentatious behavior of movie stars; art directors should be seen but not heard. Most designers do not quarrel with this characterization. They understand and accept their role as model citizen, appropriately self-effacing collaborators in the collective undertaking of creating movies. In interview after interview, set designers insist that their job is to provide the physical setting that shows off character and story to greatest advantage, without advantaging their own craft or their own talent. Michael Powell's rare formulation is that much more significant and, more important, correct. Neither art directors, the film world, nor the viewing community at large give adequate credit to those artists who are largely responsible for the "miraculous images up there on the big screen."

The purpose of this book is to define the status of art direction in cinema: to identify the functions of decor within the film narrative and to recover the movie set—and the work of the art director—from its present position as a widely neglected object. The design of a set reflects industrial as well as narrative pressures. We begin with issues of systems, specifically the relationship between art direction as subsystem and the larger system of film production, in order to provide a frame in praxis for our theoretical and analytical discussion of decor and narrative, a subject that has received little attention from historians, theoreticians, critics, and practitioners of set design. The central five

1

chapters of our study are devoted to a taxonomy of decor within film narrative. We conclude with questions of reception and evaluation.

Apart from crucial allusions to German cinema of the 1920s, we focus primarily on the United States and, to a lesser degree, on Great Britain, France, and Italy. Hollywood has, after all, dominated exhibition in North America and Europe since the end of World War I; the three other national cinemas have, at different times, exerted significant influence over praxis and taste. Although we draw our examples from films as early as *Cabiria* (1914) and as late as *The Cook, the Thief, His Wife, and Her Lover* (1990), our sample and our analysis is concentrated in the period that begins with the introduction of talking pictures in the late 1920s and ends circa 1960, a year of turning points in the four cinemas under discussion.[2] In the United States, 1960 closes the decade-long decline of the studio system that had ruled production since the early 1920s. In Europe, it marks the transformation of narrative practice through a critique of conventional narrative logic and modes of production. This rupture is announced by the films of the Free Cinema Group (Lindsay Anderson, Karel Reisz, and Tony Richardson) in Great Britain, by those of the *Cahiers du Cinéma* critics/directors (Jean-Luc Godard, François Truffaut, Jacques Rivette, Claude Chabrol, and others) in France, and by the release of Michelangelo Antonioni's *L'avventura* and Federico Fellini's *La dolce vita* in Italy. The new filmmakers in Great Britain and France make explicit declaration of their independence from the conventions of decor that had dominated their national cinemas. Finally, our choice of temporal and national boundaries has been guided by what we took to be the likelihood of reader familiarity with the film texts to which we refer.

Our study attends, with very few exceptions, to constructed decor. The decors of cinema are everywhere, not on sound stages alone but in city streets and natural landscapes as well, and the "real" locations the art director has the responsibility of choosing attain, within narrative film, the same fictional status we ascribe to constructed decor. We have opted, however, to consider decor in the widely accepted sense of scenic elements created for the illusionary representations of cinema. Among these are playing areas constructed in three dimensions: private rooms, offices, lobbies, streets, railway stations, nightclubs, ocean liners, arenas. Many are not constructed to scale but rather in miniature, or painted on glass, and photographed so as to create the impression of substance and depth. During the course of our analysis, we do not generally distinguish between the constructed set and the model or matte shot. We consider all scenic elements as the textual domain of art direction. This is, after all, how the viewer is meant to perceive them. But if we do not differentiate among these elements, we do not mean thereby to negate the distinct and unique contributions of the design specialists responsible for their creation. As we make clear in our discussion of systems and praxis, while the unit art director controlled the general design of the film during the studio era, sketch artists, draftspersons, set decorators, and other practitioners were entrusted to conspire in the creation of the "miraculous images" we identify as decor.

A final cautionary word about the taxonomy of design intensities—denotation, punctuation, embellishment, and artifice—plotted and then detailed in the book's second chapter. These are our categories, not industrial or conventionally critical ones. The lines we draw between the categories are meant to be neither strict nor unambiguous borders; in many cases, we know them to be fluid, sometimes fluctuating divides. The levels that comprise our taxonomy are intended as benchmarks around which to organize the discussion of the complex relationships between decor and narrative, as useful indices, we hope, by which to analyze and assess the value of decor among the factors that determine readings of film.

Chapter 1

Systems
and
Praxis

It all starts with the story. Design decisions follow, their purpose, in general, to support the narrative. Art directors speak again and again of the need to serve the story. They are, of course, not the only film practitioners devoted to the production of narrative. Their contributions are shaped by the generalities of collaboration and the particularities of working conditions, tastes, and talents. Purely schematic accounts of the process that turns story first into design and then into movie set—tables of organization, for instance—elide those particularities and the degree to which they determine what finds its way onto the screen. What are the practices of art direction, this enterprise that proclaims its fealty to narrative? Who are the art directors? How do they characterize their own work? What do others think of it? How does it fit into the system of moviemaking?

Most writing on art direction is related to these questions. Many of the writers are themselves practitioners. From this body of evidence, published materials and unpublished interviews, a double problematic emerges: the standing of art directors in the industry and their claim to authority and authorship. Not unexpectedly, available documentation focuses on the Hollywood system, dominant and most prosperous in world cinema. European set designers share some of the concerns voiced by their American counterparts: the status of art direction in cinema and the status of the individual art director in the creation of the film text.

After examining the publicity value of set design, an index of its weight in the marketing of the cinematic product, we discuss the widely held contention that the corporate system neglects the contribution of the art director. Of particular interest to this discussion are the hierarchical organization of art departments, the power wielded by the heads of the departments, and the differing personalities and proclivities of the department heads and of the departments themselves from studio to studio. Can the individualities of art directors be exercised from within the dual system to which they are attached: the art department and the studio? How do art directors interact with movie directors, and what happens when art directors become movie directors? The issues raised by these questions affect the impact of decor on film narrative, some more directly than others. Publicity, a paratextual mode of storytelling, stimulates viewer interest in a film's stars, genre, and general subject matter but, as we will see, rarely its decor. The political structure of studios and art departments determines the power of design and style and the role they play in the film text. The success of the individual art director in imposing his or her vision on the interpretation of the script, in designing sets that control the mise-en-scène, can constitute an emphatic narrative intervention. Self-effacing craftsperson, expert technician, accomplished artist, the set designer moves variously through a system that generally demands only innocuous backgrounds but sometimes—and those are the instances that will interest us in later chapters—allows for decors of significant narrative power.

Art Direction and Publicity

Advance publicity features art direction for only a small percentage of films, those in which design is expressive of "spectacular" and "fantastic" financial and narrative investment. *Samson and Delilah* was presold to audiences who knew the temple would collapse at the climax; *Ben-Hur* (1959) turned around the track of its chariot race and the gigantic stadium in which it was staged; *2001: A Space Odyssey* required the creation of an elaborate world of the future; *Batman* and *Dick Tracy* reconstructed a comic-book style that surpassed the imaginings of readers already steeped in the iconography of the Bat Cave and Tracy's radio wristwatch. Except for these, and a handful of other films, there is little evidence to counter the general assessment that the industry and the public ignore art direction. It is therefore difficult to give much credence to William Cameron Menzies's 1927 statement that "the public is no longer satisfied with the settings, costumes, lightings, and groupings of last year, or yesterday. They [producers] have learned that pictures must be well composed, for a well composed picture is one at which the audience can look and see a lot with ease. The eye and the attention of the spectator is attracted to the right point and directed in accordance with the demands of the story."[1]

Menzies's assertion about audience sensitivity to the relationship between narrative and decor reflects, in all likelihood, the wishful thinking of an art director promoting his own profession. A decade later another designer, Bernard Herzbrun, shared Menzies's rosy assessment of audience interest in art direction: "Film patrons are definitely scenery-conscious when they see a picture. Hundreds of letters in our files testify to that fact. Some are requests for drawings of houses, cabins, interiors, and furniture; and some are curious to know how the Art Director approaches a picture when he starts upon its settings."[2]

Judging by the nearly total absence of reference to set design in posters and movie magazines, these "hundreds of letters" were dismissed by publicists, experts paid to know what kinds of films the public would pay to see.

The movie magazine was one of the Hollywood's most efficient publicity vehicles during the studio era. If its contents are an accurate indicator, the performer monopolized reader interest. In our survey of four popular monthly American movie magazines of the 1930s and 1940s we found but a single article that features significant allusion to art direction.[3] It concerns Bette Davis, who discovered herself on the same staircase and in the same room, redressed, in *Jezebel*, *Dark Victory*, *The Letter*, *The Old Maid*, and *The Great Lie*.[4]

The British *Picturegoer*, a publication in fact not exclusively devoted to movie stars, surprisingly has no coverage of art direction in the period 1945–1948 when British design was internationally recognized.[5] M-G-M's in-house publication, *The Lion's Roar*, contains a short piece about Garbo's interest in sets. The writer suggests that while most stars ask about their costumes, Greta Garbo is interested in the decor of her films: she did research for *Queen Christina* on a trip to Sweden and even paid duty on antiques and research material for the film project! This press-agentry ascribes the actress's motives to her early poverty, to the splendor she had witnessed in the Stockholm theatre, and to her need as an actress to draw the "mood from her surroundings." The article ends with a description of the fashionable ski lodge of *Two-Faced Woman*.[6]

Even for films with blatantly extravagant sets, art direction is rarely mentioned in explicit publicity materials. Of the dozens of press releases issued for the 1947 "top budget production" *Song of Sheherazade*, for example, only three focus on decor.[7] They refer to art director Eugene Lourié's experience in Europe, the size of the sets, and the authenticity of their period detail. An advertisement by Paramount for the quality of its films proclaims: "Splendor of staging! Luxury of dressing! Brilliancy of setting! You experienced fans have actually come to take these for granted in every Paramount Picture where the story requires them."[8] This claim, made relatively early in the life of the Hollywood studio system, validates the product by its expense and its relationship to story, equating cost with legitimacy in an effort to persuade the spectator that movies are worth the price of admission.

When the decor of a specific film merits publicity, it is only for high cost and size. Sets that flaunt expensive detail and great magnitude may, as we demonstrate in chapter 4, exert considerable narrative impact on the viewer. The numerous press releases for *A Night in Paradise* are tireless in detailing its extraordinary scope (fig. 1):

> Reminiscent of the lush, lavish days of *Intolerance*, *Ben Hur*, and other silent screen spectacles is the Lydian palace setting. . . . Largest indoor structure ever built for a Technicolor picture, the set was peopled by more than 500 players and working crew, numerous animals and birds, and unusual props. . . . The largest indoor Technicolor set ever built in Hollywood is now under construction at Universal. When completed, the huge set, representing King Croesus' palace grounds in 580 B.C. will completely cover one entire stage and part of another, 45,189 square foot area. . . . Sixteen vast pillars towering more than four stories high, covers one entire end of the stage. In the foreground there are two swimming pools, a huge Ionic pillared patio, a colonnade, two massive marble pylons, a garden and a statue of Aphrodite that towers three stories above one of the pools. . . . One scene requiring all the strength of permanent construction, that will

1. A *Night in Paradise*: the palace of King Croesus

be filmed on the big set, is the arrival of Delarai, beautiful Princess of Persia. . . . Seven barrels of lacquer were used to coat the white Grecian marble which predominates in most of the architecture. It will take 98,415 gallons of water to fill the pools. More than half a mile of scaffolding is in use. Forty-nine thousand feet of lumber will be used. A new ventilating system that will force fresh air in at floor level and exhaust the heat generated by 265 arc lamps, which will draw 25,000 amps and be manned by 93 electricians, has been installed. . . . In addition to the large regular crew of cameramen, grips, and others and the extra electricians, 94 additional technical men will be necessary when shooting starts.[9]

The releases for *A Night in Paradise* are suffused with a rhetoric common to all such publicity. Dimension and quantity are the primary standards. Similarly, the obligatory adjectives, "largest," "huge," "massive," "big," apply to the Capulet ball in a syndicated article that appeared in many newspapers on March 7, 1936, entitled "Balcony Scene Will Be Gorgeous in Film *Romeo and Juliet*." Although the author finds room to express amazement over the film's "mystic, fragile beauty," his piece is essentially concerned with

2. *Romeo and Juliet*: the Capulet ball

size and, by implication, cost: "The garden has amazing sweep and scope. Art Director Cedric Gibbons and his associate, Fred Hope, found the enormous stage none too large to accommodate their conception of the balcony scene. Every inch of the 52,200 square feet of available floor space has been used (fig. 2).[10] There is no hint that the "enormous stage" might in fact betray Shakespeare's intimate love scene. A squib on *The Shanghai Gesture* informs the reader that "this is one of the few picture sets which shows where the money went."[11] The souvenir programs that often accompany big-budget movies are inflected with the same hyperbolic prose. The occasional allusion to decor in ad copy also promotes extravagance. These relatively rare instances of press exposure for decor focus on the measurable, thus valuable, largesse of expense.

The movie poster generally attempts to convey some general features of the narrative—who stars in it, where it takes place—but is as chary in featuring decor as other publicity media. A random sampling of posters for a number of classic French films reveals purely locational graphic references: Venice in the background for *Volpone*, a schematic assembly line for *A Nous la liberté*, and the suggestion of a train for *La Bête humaine*. The exception, with its geometric and architectural shapes, is the poster design for *L'Inhumaine*, true to the film's subject, design itself. Those for the star vehicles *Pépé le Moko* and *Lola Montès* foreground the faces of their respective stars, Jean Gabin and Martine Carol. The most marketable elements of cinema, its recognizable star performers, are the

3. *Ben-Hur*: advertisement

most widely used figures in poster art. In 1988, the Academy of Motion Picture Arts and Sciences issued a poster (designed by Alexander Swart) commemorating the sixtieth anniversary of Oscar. On it are replicated publicity posters for the sixty films that won the Best Picture award. The vast majority of these posters feature the films' stars prominently. Several include, in subordinate position, indications of location and decor: the devastated church in *Mrs. Miniver*, a tiny Arch of Triumph and Eiffel Tower in *An American in Paris*. Of the four that show important elements of decor—the bridge of *The Bridge on the River Kwai*, the El staircase of *The French Connection*, the palace of *The Last Emperor*, and the gigantic statue of *Ben-Hur*'s chariot race—only the last gives priority to decor (fig. 3). *Les Belles affiches du cinéma* reproduces posters for seventy-five films made in the United States, France, Great Britain, Italy, and Japan between 1950 and 1980.[12] Even in those posters that publicize films whose titles designate buildings, *The House on Telegraph*

Hill and *The Alamo*, the structures are subordinate to other elements. Only *Orphée* emphasizes a decor—the ruined buildings of the underworld. In an exhibition catalogue devoted to a variety of publicity materials for Italian cinema from 1916 to 1942, of more than thirty posters only three emphasize elements of decor: the Roman boat of *Scipione l'africano*, the Alcazar fortress of *L'assedio dell'Alcazar*, the convent of *Un garibaldino al convento*.[13]

This rapid review of press media and publicity bears out the widespread contention that in Hollywood and elsewhere, scenery is not "box office." Though essential to the narrative film, art direction does not sell many tickets.

The Status of the Art Director

Art directors have spoken frequently and loudly about the recognition unfairly denied them. "One of the least publicized but most important strategically of the executives in any of the larger Hollywood studios is the art director. He gets little of the glamorous publicity accorded some of the others, but he is responsible for bringing into harmonious accord the various activities that go to make up the production of a motion picture."

The author (the article is subtitled "Little known to the public, they are, back stage, among the lords of the screen") goes on to describe the duties of this "executive" and the functions of the workers responsible to him, using as exemplars Cedric Gibbons and the M-G-M art department.[14] Another complains, "It's astonishing how little credit, in this land of all credits, goes to the creation of sets for motion pictures. . . . Do you realize that there is not a single shot made in a picture that is not laid out by this biped, the Art Director?"[15]

The publications of the Society of Motion Picture Art Directors, the *Monthly Bulletin* and its successor, *Production Design*, are meant to promote the industry's awareness of art direction. Daniel Cathcart, the editor of the *Monthly Bulletin* in the early 1950s, energetically states the case: "It's about time for the Art Director to consider his place in the Passing Parade. Shall it continue to be that of a critical viewer on the curbstone, or in the line of march somewhere near the lead?" The reason for this secondary place in "the Passing Parade" is "that most men 'above the line,' those who set studio policy, just do not know the scope of the Art Directors' knowledge of motion picture production."[16] Nearly forty years later, the March 14, 1989, issue of the *Hollywood Reporter* is devoted to art direction on the sixty-fifth anniversary of the Society of Motion Picture and Television Art Directors, IATSE Local 876.[17] The recurrent themes remain the art director's obscurity and the disregard of art direction by the film industry.

The Hollywood system of production is, as we have indicated, not alone in the neglect of the art director and art direction. In his description of the French film industry, Paul Bertrand states, "Often decorators fail to receive the rewards they deserve, for their work of modesty and collaboration is fused into a collective achievement, and is little to their advantage in a society in which discretion and naturalness are not materially recognised qualities."[18] Bertrand draws attention to the nearly anonymous art director in an enterprise that, more than any other, prizes the individuality demonstrated by fame. Lucien Aguettand reproaches the *Figaro* for failing to note the Exposition Internationale de Maquettes de Décors at the Cannes Festival.[19] Léon Barsacq puts the blame on film critics who have made the names of directors and even cinematographers known to the public but "keep silent" those of the art directors.[20] Giuseppe Sala, the director of the Centro Sperimentale di Cinematografia in Rome, protests that the art director is ignored in favor of the star and the director.[21] Ubaldo Cossa considers "the problem of [the neglect of] set design . . . among the most pressing in our cinema."[22] Cossa deems the degree of neglect in Italy greater than that in other countries. His contemporaries in the United States, England, and France might well argue this assessment with him. Vincent Korda suggests that the art director is often relegated to the role of artisan or technician: "The artistic value of innumerable productions would be greatly enhanced if only producers would take the art director into their confidence in the planning of a film."[23]

Alfred Junge feels compelled to defend the status of his billing on *A Matter of Life and Death*. In a letter to the film's publicist, he writes: "I should like my publicity to conform to the agreement as set out in my contract. I have already told you that some letters [referring to the production] have appeared with several names on them except mine."[24] Vexed over the misunderstanding that greets the work of the art director, Boris Leven clarifies his own contribution to *West Side Story* for the benefit of critic Arthur Knight. Knight actually acknowledged Leven's achievement as the film's production designer but went on to confuse the issue by linking him to Saul Bass, who designed the opening credits. After evoking his own long career, Leven states, "I respect and admire Mr. Bass's work in his field of graphic design, but Mr. Bass had absolutely nothing, and I repeat, nothing to do with either the conception, or the design, or the color or the ideas for lighting of any of the sets or backgrounds—or with anything that had to do with the visual aspect of the film."[25] Leven's indignation is undoubtedly lodged in the bitterness shared by so many art directors over the undeserved obscurity of their status.

Credit Lines

Who are the art directors? What titles have been conferred on these persons responsible in part or in whole for the sets? Informally they were sometimes called "builders of sets" and for the most part resented it, preferring, as did Preston Ames, "designers."[26] To make the point, the authors of a piece called simply "Set Builders" attempt to validate the profession's contribution to film production by harkening back to the heroic carpenters of old—from the prehistoric wielders of clubs, to Jesus himself, and finally to Abe Lincoln. Theirs is a paean to the uncelebrated, anonymous builders of Warner Bros. sets, a memorial to the faithful now dead, an honor roll of those who have labored long, all, like the writers themselves, "builders of sets."[27]

In the earliest days, the title was "technical director," the credit given William Buckland, for example, in *Intolerance* and *Birth of a Nation*. "Technical director" accurately described Buckland's role in D. W. Griffith's production team, especially with regard to lighting and special effects.[28] Some years later, the first Oscar in the design category was dubbed "interior decoration." In the 1930s, with the establishment of the set-shop hierarchy, the position that corresponded to the set or scenic designer on Broadway became the Hollywood "art director." Some, Cedric Gibbons among them, disapproved. "Art direction is not a proper name for the work we do," he insisted. "Architectural engineering describes its functions more nearly."[29] Here, as elsewhere, Gibbons emphasizes the technical side of the enterprise at the expense of the expressive integration of decor and narrative, a position that may reflect his own detachment from the actual design process. On the other hand, for Vincent Korda the "art" in art direction corresponds to the first syllable of "artisan," except when applied to his own work, where "art" is inextricable from "artist."[30]

The divided nature of the art director is reflected in Léon Barsacq's survey of the differing titles assigned to the set designer across national boundaries.[31] In France, in general, it is "architect-decorator;" in Germany, "architect"; in the Soviet Union, "painter-artist;" in Britain, in imitation of the United States, it is "art director." Edward Carrick, who engages in a similar comparison of terms, prefers "architect" or "decorator" since they more closely correspond to the activities of those of who "construct the backgrounds," which "are in the majority of cases architectural." In Carrick's view, "art director" is misleading since "he certainly never has control, as the American name suggests, over the 'art' of the film."[32] Here, Carrick echos Gibbons's reluctance to attach the cachet of art to the work of the set designer.

Regardless of nomenclature, the work is essentially the same, from country to country and through the decades. An architect alert to the three-dimensional volumes required for playing space and conversant with the history of architecture, an artist sensitive to the particularity of character or to the requirements of the dramatic situation, the great art director must have a dual allegiance. Many were indeed trained as architects. Art department heads Hans Dreier and Cedric Gibbons found a ready supply of talented architects in California in the 1930s, young men recently graduated from architecture school and unable to exercise their chosen profession during the dark days of the Great Depression. On the other hand, Lazare Meerson, Alexandre Trauner, Vincent Korda, and many others were trained as painters. None of the terms associated with art direction carried a particularly high status until 1939, when a special credit card was created for William Cameron Menzies's contribution to *Gone with the Wind*. "Production designer," asserted itself as the premier title of the film design hierarchy. As we will show below, it is, in fact, the production designer who organizes the narrative through design.

Hierarchy and Collaboration

In the table of organization, the head of the Hollywood studio art department (sometimes called the supervising art director) reported to the head of the studio or sometimes to the production chief, as did all department heads and producers. The head of the studio—a Louis B. Mayer, for example—had the final say over general studio policy and personnel: the kinds of films produced by the studio, the purchase and development of individual properties, and, most important, the casting of stars. Heads of production, on the other hand—Irving Thalberg, say, or Darryl Zanuck—also had direct creative input into the films, usually exercised in the phases of writing, editing, and reshooting. Yet Hal Wallis, the most powerful producer at Warner Bros. in the 1930s and early 1940s, "could rarely choose his cinematographer and film editor, and on *Casablanca* he was assigned a sound editor, Francis Scheid, whom he disliked."[33] The system had imperatives that superseded even those of a Hal Wallis.

The corporate structure of the art department mirrored that of the studio. Cedric Gibbons, the head of the art department at Metro-Goldwyn-Mayer from 1924 until his retirement in 1956, outlines how the art department was organized during the heyday of the studio system. "The studio art department today is a complex organization. At the head is the supervising art director. Then come the unit art directors, who are assigned, one to each production, to do the original sketches, and to 'follow through' until the picture is completed. . . . The department includes 'architectural renderers,' draftsmen."[34] After receiving an assignment from the supervising art director, the unit art director developed a design based on the script, sometimes in consultation with the film's director. This first step in the design process had, therefore, its origin in narrative. Many of the subsequent phases required the team of sketch artists, model builders, draftspersons, and illustrators.

Beginning in the late 1930s, the process of storyboarding the entire film became the practice for major productions. The storyboard is a breakdown of the film into continuity drawings of its shots. A representation of the film's narrative in something like a cartoon strip, the storyboard shows the placement of decor and actors and often indicates lighting effects as well as camera position. The sketch artists usually executed the storyboards. Jack Martin Smith describes the creation of continuity sketches:

> A set of continuity drawings means an artist sitting in his office all day long—he takes the script, scene for scene and breaks it down into different shots like that. And the art director makes little thumbnails like this. I probably made the thumbnails for all those things because I recall I did a lot of sketching. Just with pencil and yellow paper I'd break them down and give them to the sketch artist and he draws them up in a little better form. Then those are taken, and you'd discard one, and put this one, not quite the angle here but you have the plans—where the camera is, what the movement, what the movement of the vehicle is, how fast is it going to be going at that time.[35]

Other tasks were performed by illustrators. They fleshed out the ideas of the unit art director in highly finished pictorial and architectural renderings of the sets. The illustrations were often necessary to convey the visual scheme of the project to the director.

With minor variations, this corporate structure governed the work of art departments at all the major studios (see appendix A for a comparison of the staffs at Warner Bros., 20th Century–Fox, and M-G-M in 1944). The head of the department had titular responsibility for all the sets. He—no woman has ever headed a Hollywood studio art department—often received credit on every film produced, even when his role was limited to assigning the unit art director to the project and approving the final design.[36]

In our interviews with Robert Boyle, Harold Michelson, and Maurice Zuberano, we asked each the same set of questions regarding the workings of the studio art department; the substance of their answers varies very little. Boyle, who came up through the ranks of sketch artist and draftsman at Paramount in the 1930s before becoming assistant art director, and then art director at the major studios starting in the 1940s, speaks of the system with some affection:

> The producer would be the one to say, "I would like to have Ernst Fegté as art director. . . ." He would tell Dreier he requested Ernst Fegté. Now Dreier might say that Ernst isn't available, why don't you try so-and-so. . . . From then on, it sifted out to those of us who were the workers in the field. What I say is that the workers in the field did a lot more; all workers in the field feel that they do it all. We didn't do it all, but we always felt we did, because we were actually the hands-on people. We would draw the line. The fact is, though, an art director like Ernst—who could draw like an angel—would very often do several sketches on his own first, and they would probably set the tone. Bob Usher did his own sketches. Bill Menzies did his own sketches. These would set the tone of the look of the picture.[37]

Boyle characterizes the art department as a kind of atelier, with a free exchange of duties among the "workers in the field." These views are echoed by Maurice Zuberano, who started out as an illustrator in the mid-1930s: "In the very beginning, especially at Paramount, before the unions, we could cross over the lines easy, and that's how I came to design sets. Usually the art directors were the only ones to design sets. Because in those days you could draft and you could art direct and you could do anything you could do, before the unions."[38] Finally, Harold Michelson also evokes the spirit of enthusiastic collaboration and teamwork that prevailed until union regulations compartmentalized the work of the art department. For him, the pre-union period was the golden age of Hollywood design.[39]

The various subsections of the art department provided a ladder for advancement through the ranks, as Preston Ames's description of his own career at M-G-M illustrates:

> I worked on the board like everybody else did for four years or so. You were in the drafting room and you might be given something by sixteen different art directors: "You busy? Here, detail this for me and get it through, I want to shoot it tonight, O.K?" And then a little later, as they got to know your work better, you might be in a little office working like hell with just one art director, developing an idea and turning it over to the drafting room. Then finally they gave you a script for a little bit of a B-picture.[40]

The impersonal "they" to whom Ames refers is the management of the art department. In fact, Ames worked in the biggest art department in Hollywood, at the richest studio in Hollywood (see appendix A). According to Jack Martin Smith, "At Metro you could ask for the moon."[41] Ben Carré, whose career as painter and art director spanned sixty-four years, declares, "M-G-M had the best scenic shop I ever worked for. They had for forty years the best scenic work that can be had."[42] Some notion of the scope of the studio's resources is provided by Ames and Merrill Pye in their description of the permanent set used for auditorium and stage scenes. Filling two sound stages, it was built by the architects of New York's Radio City Music Hall and boasted an analogous system of hydraulic lifts and contour curtain. Four or five different styles of boxes and drapes could be used to vary the effect.[43]

Even art directors who have serious reservations about the practice of art direction in Hollywood are unstinting in their praise of the resources and work conditions made possible by the studio system. Boris Leven laments the disappearance of the "golden age" craftspersons who "made practically anything possible."[44] Maurice Zuberano finds it amazing "they get sets done as well as they do today with the absence of all the resources they used to have at the major studios."[45] And Robert Boyle decries the status of art direction in post-studio-era Hollywood; he places the blame on the producers:

> You see, now they don't even know what to ask for. . . . They don't find art
> direction necessary any more; they used to think it was part of the process,
> the filmmaking process. . . . People say, "We don't really need a production
> designer because we're not building anything; it's all location work." Well,
> my concept has always been that that's the most difficult, getting the right
> location. We're interpreting the script, not interpreting the set. If it says
> living room, what kind of living room is it? Whose living room is it?[46]

For all of its faults, according to Boyle, the studio system favored, in fact made possible, the work of art directors whose task it was to interpret the script through decor. Without the context of a stable art department and all the means at its command, such work can be at best only intermittent.

The hierarchical pattern differed to some degree at the major independents, where the head of the studio—a Samuel Goldwyn or a David O. Selznick—took responsibility for all aspects of production, albeit with differing degrees of creative participation.[47] Raymond Klune, production manager for Selznick, describes the interchange between Selznick and his art department regarding the basic design concept for *Rebecca*: "David always thought, and properly so that Manderley (the big home) was one of the important, if not the most important character in the story. We agreed with him." Selznick wanted to film *Rebecca* in England or on location elsewhere. The art department dissuaded him by raising two objections: the war in Europe had begun, and it was necessary to show the house both intact and in ruin. "So a concept that was totally shared by the art department and myself that the way to really effectively do Manderley was first to build probably the largest scale miniature that had ever been built, and second, a miniature half that scale and certain sections of it full scale. We had a terrible time with David on that. He didn't think we were right."[48] Particularly interesting is the fact that the art department prevailed over Selznick's preferences. As head of his own studio *and* his own producer, Selznick spared no expense to achieve the results he desired. In this case, these could be attained only through the creative use of models. In the end, the profligate producer gave in to the experience and pragmatism of the art department. The models of Manderley won the day.

Gene Allen describes the felicitous collaboration for *A Star Is Born* (1954), a film made by an independent production unit. Allen became assistant art director on that film when Malcolm Bert replaced the art director Lemuel Ayers, who had fallen ill. "Mal would do all the basics; he'd hear the ideas everyone had—Mr. [George] Cukor [the director], Sid Luft [the producer], Judy [Garland, the star]—about the kind of settings, interiors and exteriors, and see that it was done." Burt and Allen worked closely with the film's "special visual and color consultant, George Hoyningen-Huene." "He had very good taste, a background of art second to none—we neither of us had any real jobs, we interchanged and just talked and thought of things. He was terribly creative and helpful, and so we formed a sort of partnership. We were known as Cukor's art boys."[49] Eugene Lourié also found that independent production favored active participation: "I made many films for independent producers, where I had to work without the help of a well-established studio art department. As a result I had a deep, personal involvement in the making of many of the films I worked on."[50]

In Stanley Kramer's independent productions, Rudolph Sternad could claim significant leverage because his preproduction preparations were seen to advance budgetary objectives. His exhaustive planning was apparently unique in Hollywood for that time. "Consequently, Sternad occupies a singular position in the realm of production designers and art directors, the only member who sits on a picture from the day a subject is selected until it leaves the sound stages." Sternad contends that his methods could not be generally accepted by the major studios for fear that competing departments would resent the purview and power of art departments. "Not having ventured the experiment elsewhere, Sternad has not been forced to allay suspicions that he and his artists are conspirators in a gigantic scheme to take over the motion picture industry."[51]

A like spirit of cooperation did occasionally prevail at one or other of the major studios, of course. Merrill Pye describes the contributions of Arthur Freed, Nacio Herb Brown, and Roger Edens to the musical numbers of *Ziegfeld Girl*.[52] It is clear that both independent and studio productions thrived on cooperation. What distinguished the art departments of most of the major studios, however, was the rigidity of their hierarchical structures. There, it was the producer of the individual film who dealt directly with the heads of the departments, including, of course, the art department. Budget control was a major concern of studio management. Given the chain of command, the art department, if it stayed within its budget, exercised considerable autonomy. To cite a few examples: the great expense of a set for *Masquerade in Mexico* is justified because parts of it will be used for other films; Hal Wallis, executive producer at Warner Bros., instructs Henry Blanke, the producer of *The Life of Emile Zola*, just which sets can be modified or recycled in order to save four or five thousand dollars.[53] Jack Warner exhorts art directors to economize by eliminating detail.[54] So as not to raise the expectations of producers and directors, Sam Katz asks Cedric Gibbons to instruct his art directors to refrain from showing them sketches and models of sets that are not likely to appear in the films.[55]

The Supervising Art Director and the Attribution of Credit

Cedric Gibbons was the most famous, in fact the only famous, supervising art director of the studio era. If a moviegoer in the 1930s or 1940s knew the name of a single art director, it was surely his. Gibbons was credited with everything related to art direction at M-G-M for more than three decades. His photograph appeared in movie magazines. He was shown posing in the sleek, moderne living room of the house he designed for himself and his movie star wife, Dolores Del Rio. *Daily Variety* reports the Academy Award he received for *The Bad and the Beautiful* was his tenth: "Gibbons, who won his first Oscar for *The Bridge of San Luis Rey* in 1929, reveals that the recently-completed *Julius Caesar* was his 2,200th film for Metro, including features and shorts."[56] The writer of the article does not stop to wonder at the figure or at its implications: that Gibbons's output would have to have averaged more than seventy films per year![57] In fact, according to a stipulation of his contract, Gibbons was credited with the design for nearly *all* the films made at M-G-M while he was there. Not only could he not have designed twenty-two hundred films, but, according to all reports, he designed almost none—not even those for which he "won" the Oscar, which trophy, by the way, he was also credited with having designed. From these same reports, it is also clear that Gibbons had total control over design decisions, the personnel of the department, the assignment of tasks, and the attribution of credit.[58]

Judging from Jack Martin Smith's description of a typical M-G-M set meeting, Gibbons's power extended even further. "A preliminary set meeting always took place in Gibbons' office, with twenty leather chairs, and all the principal creators of films: director, producer, music director, etc. would sit in."[59] The place of this meeting and the twenty leather chairs suggest that the authority wielded by Gibbons at M-G-M extended much further than that of his counterparts at the other studios. He was at the studio's power center, a member of the "Executive Committee" that included Louis B. Mayer, Eddie Mannix, Benny Thau, Harry Rapf, and Al Lightman.[60] Writing about *Sea of Grass*, director Elia Kazan attributes more power to Gibbons than to the film's producer, Pandro Berman: "He was the most influential person on the lot except for the owners, Nick Schenck in New York City and Louis B. Mayer in Culver City."[61]

Imperious and formal, Gibbons did not mingle with his staff. Ben Carré states that when Gibbons visited the scene shop he "never came alone, always with some guest, so he did not have to talk to us!"[62] Robert Boyle describes the characteristic mise-en-scène of the interview between Gibbons and his art directors. The drawings would be "usually, as I understand it, put on the floor, so that the art director would have to be on his hands and knees with the drawing, and he would be standing there looking at it. It's a put-you-in-your-place sort of thing."[63] Directors, too, had their place, apparently as far as possible from where decisions on set design were made. Kazan alludes to this in his discussion of *Sea of Grass*: "It was Mr. Gibbons who'd made the decision, long before I was hired, to shoot my film before a rear projection screen, not out in the open country as I'd expected. He'd ordered the sets designed and built—I'd been walked through some of them, and they matched Katharine's [Hepburn] costumes."[64]

The authoritarian Gibbons was bound to clash with a headstrong director such as Vincente Minnelli. Minnelli had begun his career as a designer of Broadway revues. In a memo to Eddie Mannix of April 2, 1940, about Minnelli's arrival at M-G-M, Gibbons misspells Minnelli's name (Vincent Manelli) and then goes on to refer disparagingly to other designers "imported" from New York or London, before defining the protocols of the hierarchy he heads:

> I want to reiterate that I absolutely refuse to work under any conditions with any man designing settings unless he is brought in through me as a member of my department. The man may be the world's greatest genius. If he is, by all means give him my job. I find it tough enough as it is to work with the most sympathetic assistants I can secure. I do not feel that any of my men should take orders from anyone other than myself in the matter of set design, whether it be for musical numbers or the interiors of submarines.[65]

Gibbons's feud with Minnelli reached its peak during the production of *Meet Me in St. Louis* when the director insisted that the Smith house be a new design rather than an adaptation of an existing set. Having lost this battle with Minnelli, Gibbons refused from that day on to work with him.[66]

How was the ascribing of credit to himself on those twenty-two hundred films received by the members of Gibbons's staff? Some objected, of course, but most did not. Edward Carfagno, whose career was, in the main, spent at M-G-M, praises Gibbons as an administrator and accepts without bitterness the system of shared credit: "I didn't like it particularly, but I know it was the system. So what could you do about it?" Carfagno also captures the tenor of the relationship between the supervisor/administrator and the practicing art director: "You had to take all the drawings to him. He would look quickly and sign it. I don't think he could tell right off the bat if they were right or not. If there was something unusual you would explain that to him, and if he liked it, O.K."[67]

Preston Ames comes to the defense of Gibbons: "They always think that he never did anything and you did all the work. That's about the most erroneous statement in the world. There was a closeness there, there was a unity that you couldn't believe, because he wanted to know exactly what you were doing. Sometimes he influenced you. Sometimes he didn't."[68] But even a supporter such as Ames makes few claims for Gibbons's artistic contributions. And the head of special effects at M-G-M, Buddy Gillespie, seems to give an unintentionally ambiguous characterization to what Gibbons and his staff thought of each other: "Gibbons was so admired by the people on his staff, I don't think they ever felt any resentment that he would get the acclaim for a picture. I used to insist that certain of the men that worked for me had credit. He could never understand that, you know. He thought, 'Well Buddy, you're the guy who's in charge.'"[69] Gillespie is caught between his admiration of Gibbons and his own sense of fair play.

Gibbons was even reluctant to share the credit for projects that did not emanate from his department. George Jenkins designed *Little Women* for Selznick, to star Jennifer Jones. The sets were built, but Jones backed out, not wanting to compete with the 1933 version directed by George Cukor, starring Katharine Hepburn. The whole production was imported by M-G-M to be directed by Mervyn LeRoy, who had been slated to direct the Selznick production, and starred June Allyson in place of Jones. Jenkins affirms, "When I called Cedric Gibbons about it, he waffled; I guess he just didn't want my name on it."[70]

Van Nest Polglase ran the RKO art department in imitation of the Gibbons manner. According to Maurice Zuberano, Polglase "had a certain amount of taste but no time to exercise it, he was so busy being an executive." But whereas Gibbons is deemed responsible for the pervasive use of art deco at M-G-M, Zuberano asserts that Polglase did not create a "house" style at RKO: "We never saw him."[71] Orson Welles adamantly denies that Polglase was co–art director for *Citizen Kane*, the credit notwithstanding. "Van Nest Polglase for instance was very good as an executive and administrator, but if he ever designed anything himself, I never saw it. *Citizen Kane* was entirely the work of Perry Ferguson."[72]

The issue of attribution is taken up by many art directors. Hilyard Brown complains that "most of the major studios ran pretty much the same way" and that "the supervising art director . . . took credit for everything that was done in the department, which I objected to very much, and I still do." He contests Jack Martin Smith's credit as art director of *Cleopatra* (1962) since the work was done by John De Cuir. Smith "made no drawings. He didn't design anything. I object tremendously to that procedure."[73] Robert Boyle concurs: "We were all annoyed. Particularly when you did a picture in which you never saw the supervising art director except once in a while he would come by and ask you how it was going. But you had done all the work, had done all the conferences with the director. The supervising art director maybe hadn't even met the director. This happened. Usually they met him because of the political implications. But they would have very little do with it."[74]

While condemning the unjust recognition of the essentially absent supervisory art director, Boyle offers an admiring description of the method and style of Hans Dreier, the head of the Paramount art department. As a corrective to the many blanket statements about standard management methods at the major studios, Boyle and others praise Dreier's skill as a teacher and organizer and his genius as a working art director:

> I would say that in Hans's case, that his stamp was on everything. . . . Hans
> was running a very rigid, European school, and we were all students as far
> as he was concerned, and we were all kind of apprentices. Hans was a tre-
> mendous influence. Every day he made all the rounds, maybe two, three

times a day. He knew what everybody was doing, and he would give a critique of these things. He didn't always insist, but he would guide. He was marvelous at it, he would sort of guide the feeling."[75]

This is a portrait unlike the ones that emerge of the more aloof Gibbons and Polglase. Boris Leven, who also began his career at Paramount, contrasts Dreier's methods and operating procedures with those of Gibbons:

> [Dreier] was more than a good designer. Often his conceptions were brilliant. He was a great teacher and disciplinarian. I learned so much during the two years I was there. He knew in detail everything that concerned his dept. We were encouraged to go to various departments to "follow through" on the designs created by the "unit" art directors for whom we were working at that time. I remember, later on, I worked for a short period at M.G.M. No one was allowed to leave his drawing board.[76]

One outsider, John Koenig, a Broadway designer and teacher at the Pasadena Playhouse, discusses the burden the studio system placed on the artists caught up in it. "All the time I was out in California, I was surprised and hurt, as an artist, by the anonymity of the members who work there."[77] Koenig points out the pernicious effects of anonymity within a system whose greatest prize is renown. Without aspiring to the stardom of the actor, art directors have always felt they have the right to recognition for the work they have accomplished. And this recognition is, as we have seen, elided or shared.

Another outsider, Mordecai Gorelik, goes one step further. In an unusually vituperative attack, he contends that corporate management impinges on the quality of the art director's work. Gorelik denounces "the policy of glamorization" endemic to the movie industry as a whole and promoted by the supervisory art directors. "Let me say at once that this is not the fault of motion picture art directors, sketch artists or continuity artists." Gorelik is full of praise for his colleagues, most of whom "have integrity, sound taste and great technical experience, along with the ability to turn out excellent work under pressure. Some even have that touch of genuine dramatic imagination which marks the born scene designer." But he deplores the artificiality of Hollywood decor favored by studio heads and heads of art departments, executives who prefer safe, homogenized design to the truly dramatic set. "The studios accordingly do *not* choose their 'art' department executives from among their most dramatically gifted art directors or sketch artists. On the contrary, the nod usually goes to those who have a background of 'harmonious' Prix de Rome type of architecture or of interior decoration in a style of overblown rococo." He characterizes the supervisory art director as a budget-conscious pencil-pusher, interested only in money and power—not as the benevolent despot evoked by Gibbons's and Dreier's staffs.[78] Gorelik's animus is no doubt fueled by his aesthetic bias toward the realism that is reflected in the films he designed, *None but the Lonely Heart* and *Days of Glory*. His more important contribution is to the realism of topical dramas for Broadway: *Men in White, Golden Boy, All My Sons, A Hatful of Rain*. It is therefore not surprising that Gorelik negates the value of the quintessential Hollywood style. What he fails to recognize (and what we will demonstrate in chapter 5) is that "the policy of glamorization," with its hyperbolic unreality, may, in fact, serve a variety of narrative schemes.

Art Direction and the Movie Director

Even more damning than Gorelik's aesthetic argument is his statement about the relationship—the absence of relationship—between the art department and the movie director: "Any director who feels it necessary to discuss with care the why and wherefore of the settings that are handed to him is considered something of a crackpot."[79] Gorelik's sarcasm is aimed at the sharp division between the narrative carried by actors and dialogue and the narrative support provided by decor. Cedric Gibbons, for one, affirms that this division is part of the system: "I most vehemently and definitely agree with you that a set cannot be shown to a Director too soon. . . . If you remember, we built the street for specific and definite shots and I think [the director, Frank] Borzage will be much more able to understand the purpose of the layout if he is shown and stood upon the spot where the sketches were made from."[80] For his own good, really, Gibbons banishes Borzage, as he would all directors, from the planning of the film's design. Directors are, after all, incapable of visualizing. They have to see, actually see, stand on the sets. Boris Leven evokes, for instance, the indifference of director Lloyd Bacon: "Look, Boris, don't worry about it. Just give me a door here and a window there. It will be just fine. Don't worry about it."[81] Hilyard Brown generalizes this sentiment: "A lot of directors, they just kind of shrug it off and walk on the set and say, 'O.K. Where's the trap door. Where does he fall through the floor,' and you point to it, and you know, they're involved in other things."[82]

Brown makes a somewhat different point in distinguishing between the role of the director and that of the art director. After visiting a set that Brown had designed, a director remarked, "'It looks like you're directing the picture.' And I said, 'Well, Don, I am. You're directing the actors.' Which is, in essence, what an art director does. . . . Directors are essentially people directors, as they should be, and we're there to help them."[83] George Cukor practiced the division basic to Brown's formula: "Beginning with Hobe Erwin, Cukor's set designers were to function as much more than just that. It was they who would orchestrate the visual design—freeing Cukor to deal with the actors."[84] Cukor directed the actors; the art director directed the rest, as Harry Horner confirms: "Cukor is not really interested in camera setups. When I worked with him [on *Winged Victory*, *A Double Life*, and *Born Yesterday*], he would say, 'Harry, *you* set up the camera.'"[85]

Other directors were much more involved in the design process. Walter Tyler quotes Cecil B. De Mille during the production of *Unconquered*: "When you bring sketches over, I want to know what each person in the sketch is thinking."[86] Jack Martin

Smith finds Rouben Mamoulian very demanding.[87] Eugene Lourié writes admiringly of Jean Renoir's collaboration on *La Grande Illusion* and *This Land Is Mine*.[88] Paul Bertrand characterizes René Clément as a director who had "the gift of 'seeing in pictures' and that of being able to express it during the preparation, the result is a fruitful and gripping collaboration."[89] Robert Boyle confirms Hitchcock's role in the preparation of the visual scheme; Hitchcock was a director "who knows from the beginning what's going to be on the screen, and everything in his terms, was seen beforehand."[90] Boris Leven recalls Fritz Lang, who made a "structural breakdown of the script [*House by the River*] with every shot and every camera angle recorded on paper with colored pencils. I had to sit with him for days watching him doing this."[91] Julien Duvivier "was extremely aware of the 'look' of the film [*Tales of Manhattan*], and the decor meant a great deal to him."[92] With Robert Siodmak, Leven "discussed the settings, the locations and even the look and the style of the film [*Criss Cross*]."[93] The directors who took a passionate interest in art direction were, however, in the minority. Most others obtained excellent results from the art departments and thus saw little need for consultation. Mordecai Gorelik's observation concerning the general acceptance of strict compartmentalization corrects the notion that the collaborative art of moviemaking in Hollywood exemplified collaboration in the fullest sense of the word. Harry Horner often felt discouraged by the director's lack of interest in his contributions: "Sometimes it's heartbreaking, when you do not work with a sensitive director and you find that what you are doing not only is not appreciated but is not used. You know much more about the characters than an unprepared director who says, 'I'll just work on my improvisation.'"[94]

On the other hand, several art directors have seen dangers in the excessive reliance of the director on the art director, particularly if the director relies slavishly on the story-board. Horner himself notes: "There is a danger in having a production designer who plans every camera setup, as if to suggest that when they are put together they can become the film. You run the danger of limiting an impressionable director who can be intrigued by a visual effect rather than by the true development of the charcters."[95] Trauner, too, considers the storyboard a hindrance to the director during shooting, when the freedom of the eye may lead to effects far more interesting than those ordained by a series of prescriptive drawings. Trauner is particularly negative about "storyboards and little models. I think they throw off people's vision. . . . I prefer to show an illustration, a painted model that gives a completer image, truly visualized from a point of view, on which you can imitate the color and texture of the materials. Imagination works much better with a painted model rather than a constructed one."[96]

European Art Direction

Léon Barsacq concurs with Trauner's views on the tyrannical storyboard:

> American directors are now accustomed to this system of using an illustrated shooting script that they follow faithfully during shooting. There is

no doubt that it results in an appreciable saving in shooting time. However, it produces in the director a certain detachment regarding the purely visual part of his work, something like atrophy of his personal vision. Henri-Georges Clouzot, Claude Autant-Lara, and designer Max Douy have used a similar but far less rigid method in France.[97]

And Trauner applauds his mentor, Lazare Meerson, who was impatient with the standardization and functionality of even French studio production.[98] But it would be incorrect to judge the industrial methods of Hollywood by the run of the mill, just as it would be incorrect to assume that art direction in Europe is more "artistic" on the basis of the small number of major films produced annually by the various national cinemas.

During the "golden age" of the studio system, the fact that the art departments belonged to thriving corporate enterprises, with continuity from year to year—in fact, from decade to decade—meant that they had at their disposal resources that were the envy of many European colleagues. The grievances of Harry Horner or Mordecai Gorelik seem trivial when compared to those of art directors—including Barsacq and Trauner—working in Paris and Rome. The Europeans begin with strict limitations on time and space. Sets cannot be properly constructed if the sound stages are not available for sufficient periods of time, writes Barsacq.[99] Aguettand, Laurent, Pimenoff, Quinon, Trauner, and Brizzio join their voices to his in the report of French art directors made in Cannes in 1955.[100] And Trauner, who would have occasion to work in Hollywood, is able to see the strengths and weaknesses of both the European and Hollywood systems. The Americans may have too much money and be less flexible than the French, but Trauner appreciates the value of the great studio with its repertoire of methods and tools nonetheless: "In France, we have to re-create the tools from film to film because we have no place to store them. We have to reinvent all the special effects because there is no tradition."[101]

At the 1955 Cannes meeting, French art directors also complain about financial limitations. Their budgets, one-sixth to one-quarter of a film's total expenditures, are proportionally superior, however, to those allotted to major Hollywood productions such as *All Quiet on the Western Front* (16%), *Marie Antoinette* (4%), *Rosalie* (11%), *The Letter* (11%), *Meet Me in St. Louis* (11%), *Ziegfeld Follies* (10%), or *The Phantom of the Opera* (11%).[102] These percentages correspond to Leo Kuter's estimate that "the financial responsibility of the art director is roughly eight to ten per cent of the production cost of a picture, this figure representing the cost of settings, which, of course, varies with different types of production."[103] It is precisely the lack of a well-defined studio system on the Hollywood model that marks the difference in France and Italy during the first three decades of the sound era. The production facilities at Joinville, at Saint-Maurice, and at Cinecittà were utilized by many different production companies. Although some of these had long histories, they were subject to frequent changes of management and skimpy production lists. Between 1929 and 1960, the name "Gaumont" appears on only one hundred films.[104] In that period, Leo the lion roars on 1,189 M-G-M pictures; the lady holds up her torch on 1,430 Columbia pictures. Many European companies were fly-by-night, organized for a single film. The art departments in Paris and Rome did not lack talent. They lacked the stability of a studio policy that maximizes physical and human resources, the continuity that existed at Ufa in Germany, in the art departments of several British studios during the 1940s, and, of course, in Hollywood.

Other problems particular to France and Italy were the lack of coordination between the various departments and the lack of consideration given to art directors by the most powerful members of the production team.[105] Aguettand compares conditions in Berlin in the early 1930s where the art director is "a close collaborator with the director" to those in France, where he is "not highly considered."[106] Budget-conscious Italian producers insist on using cheap materials.[107] Commenting on postwar conditions, Virgilio Marchi accuses the producers of not allowing art directors the time necessary for proper preparation. But when it comes to paying the salary of the art director the producers feel they have all the time in the world. "We don't have the Americans' money."[108]

The Art Director on Location

One of the liveliest controversies surrounding art direction was triggered in postwar Europe by a confluence of material and aesthetic conditions that put into question both the status of art direction as part of the production system and the status of design itself. First in Italy, in the late 1940s, in response to the modest decorative requirements of neo-realism, and then with great insistence beginning in the late 1950s, during the first years of the New Wave in France, the debate rages between the advocates of constructed sets and the partisans of real streets and buildings.

Virgilio Marchi, whose work includes the florid, studio-based fantasy of *La corona di ferro* and the austerely neo-realistic *Umberto D*, finds fault with those critics who ignore the art direction of neo-realist films (fig. 4). According to Marchi, they notice only the spectacular and ignore the realistic representations of daily life essential to works such as *Umberto D*.[109] Marcel L'Herbier takes the other side. An adherent of an older tradition, and himself director of *L'Inhumaine*, renowned for its decors, L'Herbier reacts against the modalities that incorporate the real, as decor, into the fiction film. In his defense of constructed scenery, he claims that Max Douy's version of the Hall of Mirrors was truer than the Versailles original and goes on to wonder if neo-realism has not "in some way killed the idea of decor in the cinema."[110]

François Truffaut sounds one of the battle cries of the New Wave when he urges filmmakers to abandon sets constructed in the studio for the genuine article found in the real world: "You have to shoot in the streets, even in apartments."[111] Jean André condemns studio decor so "excellent" that it monopolizes resources and attention. He also fears that producers will want to exploit "excellent" decor at the expense of script and actors. In this cinema without constructed sets, André sees the art director as merely an adviser to the director on visual details, an artistic assistant.[112]

The defense of studio-based art direction is quick and emphatic. Max Douy and Jacques Lemare rail against the New Wave "amateurs who have the presumption to reinvent the cinema that they know nothing about."[113] Douy repeats his assertion that "for

4. *La corona di ferro*: the witch's tower

some time to come audiences will continue to prefer films made by normal staffs of qualified technicians, shot in beautiful exteriors or in well-made sets."[114] Lucien Aguettand
summons the ghost of the master illusionist Georges Méliès in his counterattack against
those who attack technique.[115]

The effects of the New Wave proved durable, however. More than a decade after
the first showings of *Breathless* and *The 400 Blows*, an article in *Le Monde* announces "the
death of the [French] studios," an event that "was predictible ever since the hard blows
struck against them by the 'New Wave' whose first aesthetic crest foreshadowed the last
gasp of papier-mâché." The author goes on to quote directors Agnès Varda and Claude
Lelouch, who spurn the falsity of the studio.[116] The response of eleven art directors to
this article serves as a manifesto in defense of studio art direction. They protest the notion
that the studios are obsolete and that the New Wave has done away with "papier-mâché"
scenery. Persuaded that, despite improvement in film stock, greater artistic control can be
achieved with artificial lighting, they cite the examples of distinguished directors who
prefer to make their films within the studio environment: Losey, Hitchcock, Welles,
Fellini.[117]

As it turned out, the ever-increasing recourse to location shooting following
World War II did not kill the art director. In 1954, Hollywood awarded the Oscar for Art
Direction to *On the Waterfront*, a film shot entirely on location. It was designed by the

veteran Richard Day, whose studio-bound decors had been admired since the late 1920s. This example supports Robert Boyle's contention: "The art director should be involved in location selection because that's as important and sometimes even more difficult than building. I mean, when you build something, you build it according to your own imagination, your own feelings. But when you have to go out and find it, it's difficult."[118] Conversely, film directors have not abandoned the sound stage. According to Ken Adam, even Truffaut would have liked "to return to the magical artificiality of the studio in the 1920s and 30s."[119] Martin Scorsese (*New York, New York*) and Francis Ford Coppola (*One from the Heart*) went to considerable lengths to achieve that "magical artificiality" that would later appeal to audiences of some of the most successful films of the 1970s, 1980s, and 1990s: the science-fiction epics of George Lucas and the comic-book spin-offs *Batman*, *Batman Returns*, and *Dick Tracy*. Thus, despite fundamental differences in modes of production from decade to decade and despite economic, technical, cultural, and aesthetic differences among national cinemas, art directors persist in the search for both the location that enhances realism and the design that translates the infinite possibilities of the imaginary.

Auteurs

In his review of *Ivy*, James Agee claims that "the real star is whoever was chiefly responsible for the dressing, setting, lighting, and shooting, and that, I infer from past performance, is the producer, William Cameron Menzies."[120] The "past performance" to which Agee refers includes Menzies's experience as art director starting in the early 1920s and occasionally as a director or co-director (*Things to Come, The Thief of Bagdad*) whose interests lean to decor and composition. But his renown as an authorial art director stems primarily from the time David O. Selznick dubbed him "production designer," a term that began to be used with some frequency only after the special credit Menzies earned for his contribution to *Gone with the Wind*. Selznick expected and apparently received from Menzies "a complete script in sketch form, showing actual camera setups, lighting, etc. . . . I plan to have the whole physical side of this picture . . . personally handled by . . . Menzies."[121]

What is the meaning of Selznick's mandate? It is well known that if anyone can be considered the author of *Gone with the Wind* it is Selznick himself. The extensive documentation on the making of the film identifies him as the guiding spirit, the constant influence, from preproduction to marketing, through casting, frequent changes in script, even changes in director. Given Selznick's sovereignty over all aspects of the film, one might argue that Menzies, the production designer, is merely one more corporate specialist, along with the director, cinematographer, and others, subservient to the will of the producer. One might also argue that the faces and bodies of Vivien Leigh, Clark Gable, and the other actors dominate the image track—not the decor. And Lyle Wheeler, who collaborated on that decor with Menzies, is, in fact, credited with the art direction of *Gone with the Wind*. Yet what Selznick calls "the whole physical side of this picture" is the domain of William Cameron Menzies. Through his continuity drawings, his imprint is indelible on the entire film.[122] If Menzies sets the precedent, then the production designer is responsible for the appearance and disposition of everything we see on the screen. So Agee perceives him in *Ivy* when he calls Menzies, the producer who functioned primarily as production designer, the film's real star (a point Joan Fontaine might argue), one short step away from calling him the film's real auteur.

In their exhibition devoted to the work of nine major art directors, *The Art of Hollywood*, John Hambley and Patrick Downing take that step quite explicitly on behalf of Menzies, Ben Carré, and Anton Grot, three of the eight directors they welcome into the canon.[123] Hambley and Downing establish a scale that rises from technical and administrative excellence, through increasing concern with narrative that translates as authorial intervention, to what they call the purely artistic. At the lower end are supervising art directors Gibbons and Polglase, who exemplify the architectural approach. "They were creators of places where action happened, never of action itself," and they provided "a consistency of style and mood and gloss." Charles D. Hall is credited with more sensitivity to "the script's original intention." Hans Dreier and Richard Day, though they lean further toward the artistic end of the scale, are "still essentially designers of sets and settings." Only Grot, Carré, and Menzies are treated as authors of narrative through decor. Menzies and Grot, in particular, "'wrote' films on their sketch pads and drawing boards long before the camera began turning."[124] Hambley and Downing's insistence on the equation between author and writing recalls Alexandre Astruc's "caméra-stylo," a governing code of the New Wave aesthetic. For Astruc and his contemporaries, the writer of the film text is the director, the person understood to control the image and sound tracks of the finished film. The storyboarding practiced by Menzies and Grot can, in similar ways, be understood as the written control of the image track. In any case, the assertion made by Hambley and Downing constitutes a strong claim for the art director as auteur.[125]

Another among the few critics to make this claim is Mario Verdone. His candidate is Hein Heckroth, particularly for his contribution to *The Tales of Hoffmann*. So interesting are Heckroth's designs, Verdone asserts with some abandon, that they overshadow the opera's libretto, the singing, even Offenbach's score. So rich is Heckroth's visual text that the film "resembles a 'film about art,' the art of Hein Heckroth."[126] Alberto Lattuada makes a more cautious case for Lazare Meerson's designs for the early talkies of René Clair: "Are not the images perhaps the first element that stimulates the imagination of the filmmaker? And was it not perhaps Meerson who created these images?"[127] And while denying auteur status to the art director, William K. Everson makes a convincing case for the view that Grot's expressionism so marked the films of Michael Curtiz that Curtiz has been given credit for Grot's style.[128]

Mary Corliss and Carlos Clarens were the curators for another exhibition, *Designed for Film: The Hollywood Art Director*, a 1978 show at New York's Museum of Modern Art. "Signature," in their lexicon, defines the influence of a single art director on more than one director. Corliss and Clarens contend, for example, that the visual scheme of *Rebecca* is more like Otto Preminger's *Laura* than it is like other Alfred Hitchcock films. "Could it be that the other signature common to both is that of Lyle Wheeler, the art director?" Although "signature" implies, of course, the imprint of a set designer's distinctive style, Corliss and Clarens remain adamant in not installing "the art director as this week's auteur, for the Hollywood film is the product of a corporate vision."[129]

In an effort to assimilate the notion of "signature" or individuality into the collaborative model, set designers have argued that the film text's visual auteur is, in fact, a combination of director and art director. Alexandre Trauner describes the collaboration between René Clair and Lazare Meerson as just such a creative, inextricable partnership, and Aldo Buzzi goes so far as to insist that "in *Le Million* everything bears Clair's signature, which means that we would not be in error to use those binomials found in music: Meerson-Clair, like Bach-Busoni."[130] Léon Barsacq devotes a chapter in a book on Jacques Feyder to the relationship between the Belgian director and Meerson, a merger of talents responsible for the universally admired *La Kermesse héroïque* and five other films.[131] Trauner, who with Marcel Carné and Jacques Prévert constituted the premier "poetic realist" team, proposes the collective author: "Who knows what an author is exactly. . . . It's a collective enterprise. Where is the hierarchy?"[132] While Trauner concedes that both hierarchy and pretensions to authorship are the rule in the movie business, to that rule he constrasts the exceptional circumstances and conditions that gave birth to *Quai des brumes*, *Le Jour se lève*, and *Les Enfants du paradis*, among others.[133]

But what of the art director who becomes the director? Lyle Wheeler says, "Generally, art directors don't make good directors. There have been only two good directors who came from the field: Alfred Hitchcock and Mitchell Leisen."[134] Do Hitchcock and Leisen remain art directors at heart? Do they capitalize on early experience as designers as they work on scripts, plan shots, stage scenes? Is that experience formative of their approach to narrative? The meticulous preplanning of Hitchcock and the decorative conceits of Leisen imply that some trace of the art director persists in the director. A predilection for *design* is obvious in *North by Northwest* and *Frenchman's Creek*, to name only the most striking examples. But this predilection is noticeable in the films of many other directors who never worked as art directors. Why, then, place Hitchcock and Leisen in a special category? Can more be asserted than that they belong to that category of directors for whom decor is not merely the necessary spotting of doors, windows, and stairs but a highly expressive element of the film text? Probably not.

Yet another art director became one of Hollywood's most successful directors—Vincente Minnelli.[135] Minnelli provides a useful example of the director with an abiding concern for decor. Preston Ames, art director for ten of Minnelli's films, credits him with the rare ability to "visualize the finished product long before it is even put on paper. . . . His whole photographic conception and his cutting and editing were there long before he started a picture."[136] Prior to production, Minnelli would work for weeks with research materials and with his own collection of photographs and drawings. He would then produce a "collage" that he used to convey his personal ideas to his collaborators, the art director and the costume designer.[137] A memo from John Houseman regarding the production of *Lust for Life* suggests the extent of Minnelli's investment in art direction and his determination with regard to the choice of art director: "I realize that enormous demands are made by Minnelli on an art director, but as regards the sets to be designed and built in Culver City, I think you must face the fact that Minnelli categorically refuses to work with Hans Peters and that if Peters remains on the picture we shall have catastrophic trouble. Minnelli's attitude is quite violent and unfortunately not to be changed."[138] Minnelli's interference in decisions usually reserved for the art department distinguish him from his fellow directors anywhere, but particularly at M-G-M. Earlier in his career, as we have noted, he defied the dictatorial Gibbons over the scenic plan for *Meet Me in St. Louis*, breaching studio protocol in order to bring his experience as art director to bear on the narrative.

Two other art directors turned directors deserve mention.[139] Edgar G. Ulmer worked as art director for F. W. Murnau, Max Reinhardt, G. W. Pabst (*Die freudlose Gasse*), and Fritz Lang (*Metropolis, Die Niebelungen, Spione*) in Germany, Mauritz Stiller in Sweden (*Gösta Berlings Saga*), and Erich von Stroheim (*The Merry-Go-Round*) and Ernst Lubitsch (*Lady Windermere's Fan, The Student Prince*) in the United States. For some of the German titles he was credited as *Bild Regisseur*, "the director for the picture itself who established the camera angles, camera movements, etc." Ulmer maintained that with Murnau (*Faust, Der Letzte Mann, Sunrise*, and others) he "invented a new role called 'production design,' which meant the designing of each and every angle."[140] Ulmer had a long career in Hollywood as director, primarily of B-films; critics credit him, in particular, with the Bauhaus look of *The Black Cat*.[141]

And finally, we return to William Cameron Menzies, who from 1931 to 1953 shuttled between the responsibilities of director/co-director and art director/production designer. Among the fourteen films for which he received directorial credit, the most celebrated is *Things to Come*. Yet even for *Things to Come* there is agreement over Menzies's indifference to what is generally the focus of the director's attention—the actor. The cast of *Things to Come*, "including Sir Ralph Richardson and Raymond Massey, found their director far too preoccupied with design, lighting, camera angles and spatial composition. It was a major flaw in all the films he directed."[142] Director Lewis Milestone goes even further: "The problem with Bill, when he directed, was that he detested actors. He said, you build a wonderful set, and then you put these Hamlets in it and they ruin it. As soon as they enter there is no more decor. Of course, that is true of any space. You have a splendid room and you give a party. When the guests arrive you don't see the room anymore."[143]

One glance at Menzies's storyboards confirms his commitment to narrative development. But the drawings of characters on storyboards are no more subtly executed than comic-book figures. The director's responsibility is to prevent actors from acting as if they were, in fact, cartoon characters, a role for which Menzies apparently had little affinity. Leisen, Hitchcock, and Minnelli, on the other hand, had no trouble bridging the gap between the drafting table and the sound stage; the elements of the film text are held in expressive balance with the decor, the actor unfailingy and classically at the center in, for example, the seedy border hotel that shelters the refugees of *Hold Back the Dawn*, on the sweeping staircase of a Nazi's mansion in *Notorious*, in the ballroom where Madame Bovary dances an ecstatic waltz.

The system of art direction was submerged beneath the Hollywood studio system and in the practice of feature filmmaking elsewhere. There is no doubt that production systems in general treated art directors and production designers as stepchildren, neglected along with writers and costume designers, perhaps more than cinematographers, in favor of stars and, sometimes, directors. But even as we reconfirm the hierarchies of the systems, we are reminded of their parts, factors in an equation that is less stable than immediately apparent. As practitioners of a subsystem, art directors, with greater or lesser imagination, sensitivity, and power, provide sets that have varying kinds and degrees of effect on films whose narratives they support and advance. The definition of these kinds and degrees engages us in the next five chapters.

Chapter 2

Set Theory and Set as Denotation

Not unexpectedly, given the general neglect of art direction, decor has received scant attention within the larger discussion of film theory. In fact, in the past half century, considerations on the aesthetics of set design have been advanced by just a handful of practitioners and by even fewer critics and scholars.[1]

Theorizing Decor

Only the Spanish critic Juan Antonio Ramirez, author of *La arquitectura en el cine: Hollywood, la edad de oro* [*Architecture in the Cinema: Hollywood, the Golden Age*], has ventured to isolate and define the properties of film decor.[2] Ramirez relies on the well-established comparison between decor and architecture to identify six properties of cinematic set design.

1. Film decor is fragmentary; only that which is necessary to the shooting is built or simulated through painting or miniature.
2. It alters size and proportion; depending on the illusion sought, it is either bigger or smaller than the scale demanded by architectural authenticity.
3. It is rarely orthogonal; it follows a logic that is not architectural. To the camera, the trapezoidal constructions, slopings, and angles necessary to the desired effect do not necessarily appear as deformations.
4. It is hyperbolic; it abolishes the insignificant and exaggerates either in the direction of simplicity or of complexity.
5. It is mobile, flexible, even elastic; it can be used and reused.
6. It is built rapidly and rapidly demolished; its cost, often as great as or greater than that of the architecture it emulates, has value only as photograph.

In marking the similarities and differences between the physiology of set and of architectural design and construction, Ramirez's taxonomy serves a fundamental comparison often drawn but rarely explicated. His classification disengages the set from its absorption into the film text, a first condition for the analysis of the narrative function of decor. Unfortunately, he devotes only very few pages of *La arquitectura en el cine* to that analysis.[3]

Two works by Italian Marxist critics and filmmakers offer full-length studies of the aesthetics of cinematic set design: the longer section of Baldo Bandini and Glauco Viazzi's *Ragionamenti sulla scenografia* [*Considerations on Set Design*] and Alessandro Cappabianca, Michele Mancini, and Umberto Silva's *La costruzione del labirinto* [*The Construction of the Labyrinth*].[4] *La costruzione del labirinto* is a semiotic study of cinematic decor for which the authors cite only two bibliographical sources, both flawed in their view by the absence of ideological grounding. The first, Léon Barsacq's *Caligari's Cabinet and Other Grand Illusions: A History of Film Design*, they consider too materialist, too firmly rooted in praxis; Bandini and Viazzi's theory/history, on the other hand, they judge too isolated from praxis, too idealist, too fully concentrated on the final product. Cappabianca and his colleagues summarize their argument on the theoretical status of film decor through the metaphor of a chain constituted by four rings. The first ring, representing nature (understood as the real untouched by human hands), is linked to the second, architecture, which in turn is linked to the third, the movie set, linked to the fourth, the film image. Architecture is meant to last a given period of time, at least a lifetime; it has a finite spatial structure and a definable function; it is part of history and obeys laws that are both structural and economic. Set design is essentially ephemeral; it lasts as long as the production of the film; it belongs to a poetic reality; its relationship is not with humans but with the film image. Because of its permanence and its connection to history, the nonmaterial film image is closer to architecture than it is to the essentially ephemeral movie set, therefore to the second ring than to the third. But, in its materiality, the movie set is closest to architecture.[5] The analogy advanced by Cappabianca and his co-authors positions decor in relation to architecture, the form to which it is most often compared. Their solution draws decor to architecture doubly by endowing decor with a double nature: ephemeral in its status as set, permanent in its status as image.[6]

In *Ragionamenti sulla scenografia*, Bandini and Viazzi posit their argument on the distinction between the "determining elements" and the "component elements" of film.[7] The determining elements are those that are essentially new to the medium and without which it does not exist: framing, choice of angle, editing, sets. The component elements, on the other hand, are variations on old forms: lighting, acting, sound. Bandini and Viazzi are primarily aestheticians. In fact, their principal contribution to the literature on art direction is a systematic and extensive definition of the relationship between cinematic set design and other arts and métiers, specifically theatrical set design, painting, architecture, music, and prose narrative. Bandini and Viazzi share this comparative method with most others who have theorized set design, as we have seen. Not surprisingly, the preferred point of departure, for critics, scholars, and practitioners who have considered this question, has been the contrast between cinematic set design and other older forms, those that share what Bandini and Viazzi call the "component elements of film" and whose poetics are securely established.

Bandini and Viazzi summarize these contrastive arguments, beginning with the parallel between film design and stage design. Set design in film is a determining element, according to Bandini and Viazzi; in theatre it is not. *Hamlet*, no matter the set and its inspiration, is always *Hamlet*, whereas designed by someone other than Trauner *Le Jour se lève* is an entirely different work.[8] A remake is not a revival; in film there can, in fact, be no new production.

The authors argue that as soon as the camera began to move, stage design was no longer suited to the film medium. Cinematic sets can, indeed must, conform to spatial and temporal rhythms; theatrical sets remain tied to the constraints of the stage.[9] Cinematic sets are in constant flux with respect to the narrative, while theatrical sets subsume the elements of the narrative, or that part of the narrative that they serve. Even where the cinematic set is one and unified—as in *Street Scene*, for example—it cannot be said to be single because it shifts with each movement of the camera, each distance and angle, each framing.[10]

Points similar to those advanced by Bandini and Viazzi have been made with reference to camera distance, specifically to the close-up, by Jean Epstein, Quenu, and Rudolph Arnheim. Epstein observes that in theatre the word creates decor, while in film, decor is created by gesture. Decor in film should be anatomical; the slightest movement of the eyelid in close-up is a moment of decor. Quenu argues that whereas stage decor can be only generally convincing, because of the close-up every detail in film decor must be altogether credible. Arnheim makes a similar point in contrasting the significance of details in film to their relative insignificance in theatrical decor.[11]

Cedric Gibbons, who, as we have seen, spoke and wrote extensively on many subjects surrounding set design, anticipated the point made by Bandini and Viazzi. Every stage designer, he claims, both theatrical and cinematic, knows the value of spotting doors, windows, and furniture correctly so that big scenes will play to their best advantage. In theatre, unlike film, however, rhythm is not directly related to design. Movie directors are responsible for the pace of the film. They cannot inject a swift tempo into the scene unless designers have been attentive to eliminating dead footage from the sets.

> The designer, for instance, may conceive of a grand staircase down which the star makes her entrance. The head of the stairway is seventy feet from the point she must reach to meet the characters assembled at the foot. But unless there is a valid dramatic reason for giving a lot of footage to her entrance, it takes too long to walk seventy feet. And there is no way in which the camera can speed up such a scene. A long shot, then a close-up, then another long shot, is stilted. The design, beautiful or not, is a bad photographic design. The whole entrance is dead footage. Nothing of dramatic value occurs, but the sequence must still be filmed. Good sets must be planned so that no unnecessary movements slowing up the action need ever be included.[12]

Bandini and Viazzi argue that the relationship between set design and camera set-up implies not only the practical necessity of relating the work of the set designer to the script, the director, and the cinematographer, as Gibbons suggests, but also the theoretical fusion of cinematic functions. Each time the camera frames any material at all, determines any angle or any distance, values of decor are defined; to the extent that framing implies decor, the presence of the director implies that of the set designer. So, if *Le Jour se lève* designed by Korda or Gibbons rather than Tranuer would be an entirely different film, so would *Le Jour se lève* designed by Trauner but directed by someone other than Carné.[13]

For Bandini and Viazzi, the correspondence of the film image to painting, like that of film to stage design, is governed not by the set designer alone but by those responsible for composition, for framing, angle, lighting, editing: the director and the cinematographer. Set design has the greatest congruence, according to these critics, to narrative and genre painting, to painting that accommodates psychology and anecdote, most specifically to the intimate and popular bourgeois art of the Dutch school of the seventeenth century and to a group of modern French painters that includes Seurat and Utrillo.[14] The analogy between cinematic set design and painting falters, however, both for Bandini and Viazzi and, twenty years earlier, for Quenu, with the introduction of considerations of color: painting implies color, and color is denied as even a virtual property of film, in spite of examples to the contrary—sporadic experiments at the time of Quenu, and occasional practice largely limited to Hollywood when Bandini and Viazzi were writing.[15] To illustrate their point, Bandini and Viazzi draw the distance between Auguste and Jean Renoir. For other theorists and critics—Jean Epstein, among many, in the polemic on *Das Kabinett des Dr. Caligari*, and Paul Rotha in his attack on *The Passion of Joan of Arc*—characters are not still-lives, sets are not paintings, and to conceive of cinema as a succession of painterly photographs of decor is to corrupt its very nature.[16]

Finally, Eric Newton synthesizes the comparisons between both film decor and theatrical decor and film decor and the plastic arts in the analogy of decor and sculpture.[17] Theatre decor is like sculpture in clay; it starts with emptiness and is filled with what the play requires. Film decor, like sculpture in marble or like quarrying, starts with fullness and selects what it desires. In Laurence Oliver's *Henry V*, the foreground, like sculpting in marble, is cinematic; the backgrounds, like sculpting in clay, are theatrical.

The efforts to locate the connections between set design and the visual arts, and to define that which is distinctive about art direction in cinema, reflect the larger ontological discourse that is as old as cinema itself: What is the relationship between cinema and theatre, cinema and the visual arts, cinema and music, cinema and literature? The historization and theorization of art direction is most valuable where it is most specific, where it signals the indebtedness of art direction to the other visual arts. It is at these intersections that we discover the eclectic nature of art direction, an enterprise most of whose practitioners began as architects and painters.

This review of the literature suggests that the aesthetics of set design, when treated at all, is understood comparatively, that is, in the opposition between film design and stage design, on one hand, and between film design and painting, sculpture, architecture, on the other.[18] Our own interest is in narrative and in the theorization of decor as an element of narrative, a line of inquiry that has been broached only sporadically and tangentially and by no more than a handful of practitioners and critics in the course of several decades.

Design Intensities

Only two of the elements of feature film are subject to being photographed: actors and decor. Actors have a narrative analog in character (Walter Huston, photographed, *is* Sam Dodsworth) just as decor has in fictional space (the set Richard Day designed becomes Sam Dodsworth's office). And of the two elements subject to photography, actor (or human figure) and decor (or place), it is the human figure that is privileged in film, particularly in the Hollywood sound film. The skill of the actor and the eloquence of the script focus the viewer's attention on what is said; the skill of the actor and the eloquence of the set, on what is seen.

As David Bordwell observes in *The Classical Hollywood Cinema*, character takes precedence over place.[19] So much is clear. But does it necessarily follow that immediately after even the most fleeting exposition of space, the characters take over the narrative?[20] And if they do, do they necessarily dominate the space to the same extent in all films? In other words, if character and space intersect at the point of the narrative, does character carry the entire burden of the story? If not, how can we understand (and, above all, analyze) the narrative function of that other photographed element, decor? It may be, as Bordwell points out, that "space will signify chiefly in relation to psychological causality."[21] But how else does it signify? Largely ignored by investigators of cinematic decor, these are the questions that guide the first part of our study.

There are, of course, exceptions to the general disregard of this subject. Considerations on the reading of decor—on when and how a viewer's heightened awareness of design is elicited by the narrative and, conversely, when a viewer's awareness of the narrative is heightened by design—have been advanced by William Cameron Menzies, Baldo Bandini and Glauco Viazzi, Anne Souriau, and most recently by Charles Shiro Tashiro. Menzies identifies four levels of interplay between "setting" and "effect," understood as narrative effect.[22] First, the setting may be negative, that is, it may constitute an irritating distraction. Second, the setting may be neutral, in which case it neither adds to nor detracts from the effect. Third, the setting may be designed with an eye to the intended effect and may, indeed, become a very important contributing factor to that effect. And last, the setting may become the hero of the picture, as Menzies speculates might occur in the filming of such a subject as *The Fall of the House of Usher*.

In their chapter on decor and poetics, Bandini and Viazzi consider films in which the last of Menzies's categories pertains. Among these are expressionist films—*Metropolis*, for example—whose pictorial elements are seen as overwhelming both character and narrative, and *La Kermesse héroïque*, where scenes in which the decor dominates alternate with scenes dominated by character.[23] Bandini and Viazzi make two points: (1) it is difficult to achieve a pictorial fusion between character and decor; (2) the dependency of decor and character is confirmed by the spectator's sense that an empty decor awaits the character's entrance in order to compose itself. They argue further that the decor either determines the psychology of the character, expresses the psychology of the character, or is subject to the actions of the character. Thus, with respect to character, decor is either in a position of dominance (*Pépé le Moko*, where the Casbah determines Pépé's very existence, serves as an example), of consonance (*Quai des Brumes* or *Wuthering Heights*, where the decor expresses the psychology of the character, acting as a mirror of their personalities), or of subordination (*White Nights* or *The Informer*, where decor is subject to the actions of the characters).

Souriau identifies three general functions of decor that affect the reading of the set: the decorative function, the localizing function, and the symbolic function. [24] In fulfilling its decorative function, film decor furnishes pleasing, even beautiful images, providing a spectacle replete with plastic values; through its localizing function, decor furnishes information to the spectator about the events of the film and where and when they take place; the power of decor's symbolic function permits it to express what either cannot be said or is best left unsaid, thereby investing the film with ideas and feelings, with signification. Souriau's essentially undetailed argument does not always stand up to scrutiny. After all, some sets are "decorative," some are not; most designs refuse the "symbolic" potential. Nevertheless, Souriau's propositions, along with those of Menzies and Bandini and Viazzi, introduce the question of the interdependence of decor and narrative and the effects of that interdependence on the viewer. And finally, Tashiro undertakes a reading of design in Joseph Losey's *The Go-Between* to ground his central proposition: that the logic of narrative needs to be disjoined from that of other functions, in this case art direction, so that their relationship can be more accurately understood not as the subordination of the latter to the former but as an exchange between the two. [25]

Our own argument begins like this: Very early in the production process, as we explained in chapter 1, art directors read the script. They are guided by this reading in designing a decor that subscribes to the script's narrative imperatives. In fact, the reading of the decor is intended to be inseparable from the reading of the narrative. The weight of the art direction on that reading will vary, however, primarily in accord with the degree of design intensity applied to the decor. A decor of conventional design intensity is likely to support a conventional reading of the narrative. A decor of high design intensity supports the production of an unconventional reading, a reading that may transcend generic categories by replacing the formulaic with the particular. An even higher degree of design intensity favors decor, privileging its role beyond that of simply supporting the narrative. In the main, set designers have limited the definition of their task to the first level. Our point is that the actual, as well as the virtual, status of set design can be best recovered through an analysis of all levels of design intensity.

Our argument goes one step further. In film, constructed set design functions with respect to narrative through its relative transparency or opacity. We have marked the stages of this passage as follows: from denotation, in which the set functions as a conventional signpost of genre, ambience, and character; to punctuation, where the set has a specifically emphatic narrative function; to embellishment, where the verisimilitudinous set calls attention to itself within the narrative; to artifice, where the set is a fantastic or theatrical image that commands the center of narrative attention. If we were to consider the passage from transparency to opacity by way of the categories we have defined in terms of, say, the American detective film, we might cite *The Maltese Falcon* as an example of the functional mystery in which the narrative weight is carried by essentially denotative sets, *Laura* as a film whose narrative is supported by punctuative sets, *The Big Clock* as a film that features embellishing sets, and *Blade Runner* as a film whose decors privilege their own artifice. We consider these titles in the pages that follow.

The same generic analysis is useful in shedding light on the following questions: What is the relationship between art direction and genre? How can we define the shaping effect of the big city street or the detective's office on the mystery? Of the dark cemetery or the even more sinister laboratory on the horror film? This generic inquiry is, of course, related to the further question of the connections between art direction and the reading of cultural codes. How, in classical Hollywood film, for example, does decor construct gender, race, class, and ethnicity? What is the function of place in films whose narratives center on the representation of culture? How does the intensity of the design of place alter the cultural expectations to which the standard code has accustomed us? If class as narrative is expressed through living and work spaces and through spaces of social inter-action, and recognized through repeated generic representations, the set coded for class/ culture cannot fail to become as familiar as the familiar narratives that play out in these spaces. Thus, we recognize the American myths of lower, middle, and upper classes in sets that constitute the living rooms of Stanley Kowalski, Judge Hardy, and George Minafer and the bedrooms of the three returning GI's in *The Best Years of Our Lives*. We recognize Bedford Falls, the small town that is the American dream of *It's a Wonderful Life*, and the perversion of that dream in the set of Pottersville that translates George Bailey's worst nightmare. Sets of all levels of design intensity are coded for genre and culture. It is the intensity of the design that allows the reading to move away from the formulaic to the subversion of the codes themselves.

Level One: Set as Denotation

In most films, decor carries a low level of narrative weight. It sets time, place, and mood and subscribes to the generally accepted depiction of the real. Time, place, and mood are often conveyed by the decor through conventional generic strategies and conventional depictions of cultural contexts. If, before viewing, a film is identified through its paratex-tual elements (title, cast, publicity) as a genre film, and if the generic designation demands no more than transparent decorative intervention, we consider it under level one. The detective film and the western, among the genres marked by realistic settings, most clearly belong to this level. Here, decor exploits "the reality effect" (discussed later in this chap-ter) both when it represents the everyday and when it represents the "real" of its genre.

In sum, the denotative set is low-budget, often stock, forgettable, rhetorically and stylistically undistinguished. It applies generic and cultural codes conventionally. It

participates in narratives that claim minimal description, narratives determined to depict·
the familiar through the verisimilitudinous.

Level Two: Set as Punctuation

Movie sets achieve a degree of opacity when they become specific and legible through
staging and photography. Released from their status as background, they acquire the
potential to punctuate the narrative and thus make claims on the attention of the viewer
during the course of the film. The result is a recognizable nexus of narrative and decor.
At such moments of emphasis, decor enters into a dynamic with narrative that establishes
not time, place, and mood alone but time, place, and mood as these center on the specificity of plot, theme and, above all, character, as well as on the related specificities of class,
gender, race, and ethnicity. In *Mildred Pierce*, the unusual design of a beach house serves
the narrative's liminal murder and its mixed generic imperatives (film noir, maternal
melodrama); the curve of a staircase is the shape of desire in *Letter from an Unknown
Woman*; a wall-crossing stile supports the theme of maturation in *Kings Row*.

Usually featured in A-budget films, the punctuative set aspires to be expressive. By
defamiliarizing the quotidian and the verisimilitudinous, it replaces conventional codes
of art direction with design strategies that advance the film's narrative propositions.
Genre and cultural distinctions are thus redefined, destabilized, or heightened to an evident, even memorable degree. At this level of design intensity, decor exploits the reality
effect as applied to the everyday (familiar, realistic) narrative and displays a correct measure of rhetoric and style.

Level Three: Set as Embellishment

Rather than simply locating the narrative in time and space and mood, decor sometimes
goes a step further than it does at the punctuative level in supporting and enhancing the
narrative. Often opaque, the sets of these films call upon decor for the powerful images
that serve either to organize the narrative or as analogies to aspects of the narrative. As a
consequence, art direction in these films displays an elevated level of rhetoric, of style;
here production stresses values that are highly determining, verisimilitudinous yet unfamiliar, and intentionally striking. Frequently, and at critical moments, the narrativized
decor is rendered specific and legible through self-consciously insistent figures. The exceptional features that accent set design at the punctuative level acquire at level three
significantly greater weight and duration. At the punctuative level the exceptional set can,
in a certain sense, continue to be perceived as essentially denotative by the viewer; at the
level of embellishment the viewer cannot fail to read the design as a specific necessity of
the narrative.

In fact, films that feature level-three sets exploit decor to support their decorative,
calligraphic ambitions in imitation of either art, here understood as painting (*Rembrandt,
La Kermesse héroïque, Fire over England*), or archeology (here we consider, among the

historical or period films, *Marie Antoinette*, *Conquest*, and M-G-M's *Romeo and Juliet* [1936] and, among the films set in modern times, *The Fountainhead*). They may propose immense, spectacular sets to keep faith with their own generic definition as colossal or spectacle films, genres named for decor (*Cabiria*, De Mille's two *The Ten Commandments*, the two *Ben-Hur* films, *Caesar and Cleopatra*, *Julius Caesar*, *The Fall of the Roman Empire*). Finally, they may lavish attention on elaborate constructions so as better to demolish them during extended scenes of disaster and de(con)struction (*Noah's Ark*, *Samson and Delilah*, *The Towering Inferno*, *The Poseidon Adventure*).

Level Four: Set as Artifice

To this level of design intensity belong sets that privilege their own artificiality. Prominently featured, consciously foregrounded, the set as artifice calls attention to itself as a consistently opaque object in pursuit of "the fiction effect." Design is rendered specific and legible through the invention of the patently unreal. The artificial set is predominantly descriptive, intent on defamiliarization. It displays a mannered degree of rhetoric, a style so high it is finally indistinguishable from stylization. The decor of artifice is, in fact, a primary focus of the narrative, challenging the force of plot and character. The viewer exits the theatre whistling the sets.

Here, decor has the privilege to create new realities, contexts apt for the monstrous and the uncanny, dream worlds conjured out of the fantastic, projective visions of the future—from the expressionism of *Das Kabinett des Dr. Caligari* to that of *Batman* via *Frankenstein*; from the Arabian Nights exoticism of *The Thief of Bagdad* to the fairytale magic of *La Belle et la bête*; from the utopia of *Things to Come* to the dystopia of *Blade Runner*. And then there are those films whose sets are in fact stages on which the narrative as performance unfolds, films in which the privilege of the artifice of decor is perhaps clearest: the giant staircase of *The Great Ziegfeld*, the glittering nightclub of *Swing Time*, the Globe Theatre of Olivier's *Henry V*, the movie queen's mansion of *Sunset Boulevard*.

Level Five: Set as Narrative

And finally, we consider those unusual films in which the field of reading is composed of a single locale. These are films whose decors we come to distinguish in the course of our viewing as essentially and surprisingly unitary. As denotation, punctuation, embellishment, or artifice, whether spatially simple or complex, strictly circumscribed or loosely contiguous, gimmicky or brilliant, the sets we study here confine the action to one place. In so doing, they challenge a fundamental expectation of our moviegoing experience: that through editing, the spectator will be transported from place to place—translated by the art department into set to set—across spaces that need be neither clarified nor charted. By virtue of their very ubiquity and independently of the degree of design intensity, the decors of these films establish and proclaim a privileged relationship to the narrative. They are, in fact, one with the narrative just as the narrative is one with them. Such texts may locate us in isolated spaces (the room in *Rope*, the office of *Counselor at Law*, the attic of *The Diary of Anne Frank*), spaces less constrained (the house in *Rebecca*, the castle in *Hamlet*, the hotel in *Grand Hotel*), or interiors and exteriors mediated by figures (the street of *How Green Was My Valley*, the courtyard of *Rear Window*).

The singularity of these sets can often be traced to their theatrical origins. They recall with deferential affection the restrictions of dramaturgy as well as those of stagecraft. But as André Bazin taught us through his reading of *Les Parents terribles*, these films—and these sets—are no less genuinely and resoundingly cinematic for having willingly submitted to superfluous constraints: those of the stage from which, through adaptation, film has so often alleged to have liberated the theatrical work.[26]

The Reality Effect

The first shot of Marcel Carné's *Hôtel du Nord*, following immediately upon the credits, captures not only the facade of the eponymous hotel but the canal, bridge, and street that will provide the space for the flimsiest of narratives, a pretext really for weaving together the daily lives of those who reside in the hotel (fig. 5). Designer Alexandre Trauner does not construct a poetic reality; he reconstructs a "real" reality in the studio, simulacra of the actual Canal Saint-Martin and the Hôtel du Nord.[27] These structures, drawn into a composition by the bridge and walkway, create an image that collects the film's narrative threads. It is, in fact, difficult even to recall the plot of *Hôtel du Nord* without summoning up that image. The re-creation of an actual Parisian site in the studio had enormous publicity value in and of itself. According to Trauner, even the film's producer conceded that "the publicity paid for the set. Many people came to see it. Picasso, for example. It was a kind of attraction."[28] What is uncontested is that thanks to its set, *Hôtel du Nord* has entered into French cinephilic mythology.[29] At one point, there was even an effort to have the hotel declared a historical monument. "In itself, it doesn't have much interest. It's a shabby, low-grade hotel. I believe it's the first time a building would have been designated only in memory of a film."[30]

Trauner's metro station set for *Les Portes de la nuit* achieved a different kind of celebrity. It was so widely publicized—and criticized—for the enormous expense incurred in its construction that few viewers could have been fooled into taking it for the real thing, this despite the meticulous effort to create a structure indistinguishable from the original.[31] Other reconstructions pass for authentic. Yet they submit to the fictions that contain them. So do many real deserts, forests, and cities, locations that have served movies since their very inception. Monument Valley, from John Ford to *Thelma and Louise*, may be the most illustrious example of a natural landscape whose configuration has entered the filmgoing imagination as a movie set. If Carné had utilized the actual Hôtel du Nord or the Barbès station he might have had to sacrifice a measure of control over their photographed image; their fictivity, however, would have remained intact. In narrative film, fiction appropriates locale.

5. *Hôtel du Nord*: bridge, canal, and street

Decor, whether constructed in the studio, reality modified to meet the needs of a shot, or reality unadulterated, creates the fiction effect. So do all the other realities in the film text. Artificial or appropriated from the real world, decor is a sign of movie life. Along with gesture, speech, and the presence of actors, it enters into the representation that defines the fictional status of narrative cinema. While we are here concerned with the artificial, the constructed, these remarks pertain also to the real. After all, Vittorio De Sica had no trouble turning Rome's central train station into a giant set for the romantic encounters of Jennifer Jones and Montgomery Clift (*Stazione termini* [*Indiscretion of an American Wife*]). To take other examples, consider the sets of *The Clock* and *Weekend at the Waldorf*, re-creations on M-G-M sound stages of the great hall of New York's Pennsylvania Station and the lobby of the celebrated hotel (fig. 6). Viewers, even travelers who knew these locales well, would have had no reason to doubt that the filmmakers had gone to New York and shot the scenes on location. This was indeed what the art directors intended.[32] In *The Clock* and in *Weekend at the Waldorf*, as in that vast majority of films that seek to produce a strong reality effect, which is to say the vast majority of feature films, the dominant narrative intention would have suffered drastically had the set, constructed or not, appeared other than true to life.

6. *Weekend at the Waldorf*: lobby

Display and Description

Decor's complicity in activating the reality effect is closely allied to the fact of its participation in film's capacity for description and display. Seymour Chatman argues that "it is
not that cinema cannot describe; on the contrary, it cannot *help* describing, though usually it does so only tacitly." In fact, writes Chatman, "the medium privileges tacit description," just as verbal narratives privilege explicit description. "Because narrative film keeps
characters and props persistently before our eyes and ears with virtually limitless sensory
particularity, there seems no *need* for films to describe; it is their nature to show—and to
show continuously—a cornucopia of visual details. But to say that such showing *excludes*
description implies a questionable definition of the term."[33] Characters and props, as
Chatman points out, certainly, but sets more persistently and more significantly.

It serves the purposes of our argument to understand "showing" as, on the one
hand, display, and, on the other, description. Shots of colossal sets or of elaborate stage
sets, such as those of the arena in *Ben-Hur* or the esplanade in *The Gay Divorcée*, as we
will have occasion to note in the chapters on set as embellishment and artifice, display.
These extraordinary sets are made available to us in one stupendous, encompassing visual
moment. We receive simultaneously the complexity of the whole and, if we have the
means or desire to discern them, the parts. The opening of *Rear Window*, on the other
hand, to cite Chatman's example, describes. As the camera travels through space in the

first four shots of the film, it undertakes the tacit articulation of a highly detailed description. No narrator offers a point of view for what we see; no overvoice provides a commentary.[34] Verbal articulation, if it occurs at all, is left to the spectator's inner voice. At the same time, however subtly, the camera engages in a hermeneutic project, slowing or quickening slightly here and there in its progress, investing parts of the description with greater or lesser emphasis, ascribing to them greater or lesser signification. In the exposition of *Rear Window*, story time is delayed until description has established the shape and content of the narrative's physical universe—as designed by the art director. The story is grounded in the topography of a set that, quite consciously unavailable in its totality for our immediate visual consumption, is scanned by the camera's eye in a series of shots relatively and variously long in distance and in duration that succeed in demonstrating the same close attention and sequentiality we recognize as the essential properties of literary description. In *Rear Window*'s opening, we are offered serial and wordless attention to contiguous parts of a set from which we are expected to reconstruct the whole. If we do not, at some point meaning may be obscured.

A Farewell to Arms (1932) and *How Green Was My Valley* provide two further examples of cinematic moments that privilege decor in exhibiting film's capacity to describe. In the first, visual description is heightened by the unusual narrative device of simultaneous and contradictory verbal description. The pregnant heroine (Helen Hayes), having taken refuge in Switzerland from the war raging in the north of Italy, writes to her beloved at the front (Gary Cooper) a letter describing the cozy, comfortable room she has taken in a Swiss town. As she rereads the completed letter aloud to herself, the camera pans to reveal a scene totally opposed to the one she describes. The room the camera surveys is, in fact, bleak, in dreary disrepair. The narrator's description is given the lie by the camera's independent descriptive eye. In the second, the exposition of *How Green Was My Valley*, visual and verbal description are contemporary and consonant, as is conventionally the case. The grownup Hew, his face unseen, describes first the lush, green valley of his youth, then the devastated landscape of the mining town of his maturity. In chapter 6 we discuss the effect of the extended verbal/visual description of the film's liminal and principal set.

The centrality of description to literature, particularly to realist fiction, is obvious—the physical description of characters, of course, but also, and perhaps predominantly, description of the material universe that contains them and their actions. Less obvious than the word's power to describe is the parallel property of the camera, and less current are systematic visual descriptions than systematic verbal ones. Far more current in cinema are the visual displays unavailable to literature. Both display and description are fundamental to the cinematic narrative, and both are dependent on the cinematic decor.

Set as Denotation

"The Good Set"

From Lazare Meerson to Gene Allen, from the middle 1920s to the present, across decades, national practices, and personal styles, again and again interviewers have asked set designers of all stripes and reputations to define "the good set." They have replied in unexpected and conspicuous unison that the good set is not the set we have defined as punctuation, embellishment, or artifice but the set that is essentially and modestly denotative. According to these practitioners, the good set is entirely subordinate to the narrative. More surprising and often contradictory is their insistence that by definition the good set (like the good nondiegetic musical track, for example) goes unnoticed, that the moment a set captures the attention of its viewers it can be said to have failed its charge—assertions challenged by the often impressive originality of their own designs.

As early as 1927, Meerson combined the two prescriptions. The real challenge, he wrote, is to design a set that is not only entirely integrated with the narrative but also passes before the eyes of the spectator unobserved.[35] Other designers put it somewhat differently. For Vincent Korda, decor must never intrude.[36] The audience must be unaware of the contributions of the art director. For David Rawnsley, the set must remain unobtrusive; any attempt to draw attention to it will only destroy the desired effect. In fact, "the greatest compliment that a viewer can pass is to say 'Sorry, old man—I didn't notice the settings.'"[37] In a similar formulation, O. F. Werndorff insists (1) that the best decors are those that go by undetected and (2) that the art director is most fully rewarded when the public, mistaking artifice for reality, remains unaware of the designer's efforts.[38] At the very most, decor is "a discreet, ever-present character, the director's most faithful accomplice," as Léon Barsacq, himself a model of discretion, put it.[39]

Peremptory, as usual, and less circumspect, Cedric Gibbons simply condemns design to oblivion, both during and after the cinematic event. The spectator is not to notice the sets while in the darkened theatre and not to remember them once the lights go on.

> If the average film-goer saw his favorite star on the screen last night, it is safe to wager that today he does not remember much about the settings in the picture. The story and the stars, he will tell you, were so interesting, he did not really notice anything else. Exactly. It was so interesting that he was not conscious of the background. Most people have the same experience, no matter how observant they may ordinarily be. However, this is no sign of failing powers of perception or old age. It is, instead, a compliment to the studio art department's efforts, for their ideal is not to build sets which will impress, but which will support and enhance the action and mood of the story. The audience should be aware of only one thing—that the settings harmonize with the atmosphere of the story and the type of character in it. The background must accentuate that person's role, and show him off to the best advantage. It is the guiding rule of the studio art director.[40]

Constructed or not, however distant from its theatrical origins, however cinematically evolved, not only is the set's place in the background, but, according to Gibbons, the set is the background. "Set," "setting," and "background" are, in fact, interchangeable.[41] What really counts, of course, is what occupies the foreground, therefore not the decor but those elements recognized as critical to the narrative: the writing (Harry Horner: "All great pictures and all great plays are in the writing, not in the designing, ever");

the story (Max Douy: "The designer should never forget that his first duty is *to express the film's subject*"); the characters (Léon Barsacq: "One should never forget that in film the sets are secondary—characters are primary"); and finally, the stars who impersonate them.[42]

Nonetheless, the gulf between what eminent designers have to say about the function and purposes of art direction and how spectators actually experience their designs can be vast. We need only recall the sets Meerson created for *La Kermesse héroïque*, Korda for *Rembrandt*, Werndorff for *The 39 Steps*, Barsacq for *Pattes blanches*, Horner for *The Heiress*, Max Douy for *Le Diable au corps*, Allen for *A Star Is Born*, and Cedric Gibbons's art department for so many extravaganzas of the 1930s and 1940s. These sets serve their narratives faithfully, in fact brilliantly. Yet they hardly pass unnoticed. For the less illustrious designers, the greater their accomplishment in creating the good set, the less great, paradoxically, the chances of securing the status they often claim is rightly theirs and has been unjustly withheld. The exercise of their métier according to the standard they so emphatically articulate is, necessarily, an exercise in self-effacement, in self-denial, in disappearance. If, as we demonstrate, set design and set designers receive little credit from their studio colleagues in more glamorous departments, little recognition from the public, little notice in the press, and relatively little scholarly attention, it is confirmation that they have succeeded in not "intruding," in not "calling attention," in "remaining unobtrusive," in being "the director's most faithful accomplice," in creating the good set.

The set that so many set designers define as ideal is a set that is essentially functional. For one thing, it blocks out the distances the actors need to travel. As Paul Bertrand points out: "The best set to represent a room is not that which is most luxurious and most tastefully furnished, but that in which the door is placed in relation to the window and the table where the director can in the smallest number of shots make his actors express what he had asked of them, without awkward transitions and in the most concentrated manner."[43] Describing his own method, Menzies maintained that the first thing he did when he started to sketch "is draw in circles for the faces of the actors. I figure out the set as a background to the group, even taking into consideration how many feet an actor will have to walk to get from center stage to exit at left center."[44] For another, it has the crucial though circumscribed charge of setting time, place, and mood. "It is . . . a question of finding for each film the setting best calculated to situate the action geographically, socially, and dramatically," writes Barsacq. "Certainly the effect of a love scene played by the same characters speaking the same words will vary according to whether it takes place in a gondola in Venice, on the sofa of a living room in a small town, or next to a kitchen sink."[45] "Sets should declare the moods of the story," states Joseph Urban. "And what is more, their arrangement and inclusiveness must be such that an audience will know without being told just what room a character is entering."[46] The set designer's role, according to Trauner, is to "support the mise-en-scène so that understanding can be immediate, sometimes striking, sometimes subtle, so that the viewer understands: a doctor is in his office, and it is clear whether this is a worldly physician or a poor one."[47] Successful sets, art directors tell us, are visual signs that direct a reading at once instantaneous and unambiguous.[48]

Setting Time, Place, Mood, and Culture

Sets whose function is essentially denotative carry a relatively small share of the narrative weight of the film for which they are designed—the weight of establishing time, place, and, in a general way, mood. The larger burden belongs by right, we are told, and certainly by industrial practice, to story, character, theme. Often, denotative film sets present images that subscribe to widely accepted depictions of the familiar, the everyday, the real as it corresponds to the spectator's direct experience of life. More often, they depict the unfamiliar everyday through conventional strategies consonant with our indirect and communal experience as spectators, an experience refracted through popular forms of representation including, perhaps first and foremost, cinema itself. Thus, as we have already indicated, the sets that interest us here exploit the reality effect both when it represents the real understood as the real of the everyday and the real understood as the real of its genre. We are more likely to locate them in the detective film and the western than in, say, the horror film, the fantasy film, science fiction, the spectacle film, the musical, or even in melodrama and in comedy, in those genres that demand minimal descriptive intervention rather than those that warrant significant decorative mediation.[49]

7. *The Maltese Falcon*: Brigid's rented apartment, Brigid (Mary Astor) and Sam (Humphrey Bogart)

Let us take the examples of *The Maltese Falcon* and *Winchester '73*. The first a detective film, the second a western, they have in common the denotative status of their sets; they share further the peculiarity that a prop is the coveted and elusive trophy that drives the narrative. In *The Maltese Falcon* (1941), the eponymous character is the black (naturally) bird itself, first seen behind the credits, a worthless replica, we discover at the end, of a priceless centuries-old bejeweled statuette.[50] Eponymous also is the Winchester rifle, model 1873, seen in the first shot of the film, a perfect example of its kind, "one in a thousand."

The Maltese Falcon has the following principal sets: (1) the office of Sam Spade (Humphrey Bogart); (2) Spade's apartment; (3) the rented apartment of Brigid (Mary Astor); (4) the hotel room of Gutman (Sydney Greenstreet); and (5) the office of the district attorney (fig. 7, fig. 8). These are, of course, coded as appropriate spaces for the introduction and development of mystery characters and for the unfolding of the generic mystery plot. They set time (the present), place (downtown San Francisco, though it could be any large port city), and mood (calculating, grim, menacing). We have seen these sets or other barely distinguishable locations many times before; we recognize them at once and expect to see them again. We need not, therefore, take further notice. In fact, we are encouraged to take as little notice as possible. Our attention is attracted by noth-

8. *The Maltese Falcon*: Gutman's hotel room, Wilmer (Elisha Cook, Jr.), Joel Cairo (Peter Lorre), Gutman (Sydney Greenstreet), and Sam on the floor

ing, or virtually nothing, that transcends denotation as defined by the requirements of the genre and the logic of the particular fiction.

The film's design takes the point further. The decors, it turns out, resemble not only countless other detective film sets but also, somewhat more suprisingly, each other. No distinguishing coding separates Brigid's modest drawing room from Guttman's more sophisticated and larger living quarters. They are effectively neutral and virtually interchangeable. Both have fireplaces around which crucial conversations take place; both have windows in the background. It would make equal—and hardly different—narrative sense if Brigid occupied Gutman's suite and Gutman Brigid's. After all, a hotel room in a detective film need denote nothing more than a hotel room. If Spade's office is typical of the place of business of the paradigmatic private eye (resembling therefore, among others, the locations of his own previous cinematic incarnations)—that is, small, cramped by its worn desk and leather chair, telephone, and file cabinet—it has the further distinction of resembling Sam's apartment, itself typical of the private-eye residence. The apartment and the office have in common not only the "look" but the tools of the detective's trade: desk, chair, telephone, files. At home or at work Spade's quarters reflect Spade: coherent, reliable, relentlessly understated to protect the purity of his professional/personal statement—and, above all, masculine. Why would the office and the home be coded differently? It's all the same to the hero. The most arresting design feature of the film is the writing on the glass door and window panes of the office: "Spade and Archer" and, after Archer's death, "Samuel Spade." Legible either forwards or backwards, from within or without, the glass inscribed with the name of the hero tells the spectator that Sam Spade is to be read without filter, without decorative interference, transparently, over and over again, one way or the other, as Sam Spade. The Maltese falcon is only a pretext for that repeated reading.

Clearly, the sets of *The Maltese Falcon* exploit the reality effect as it represents the real of the genre; they also suggest the real of the everyday. In *Winchester '73*, the reality effect is lodged in the historic, cultural, and exotic real of the genre alone.[51] Some viewers may be familiar with the ageless landscape of the American West, of course; none is personally familiar with the specifically postbellum West ostensibly replicated in this film. Despite the absence of direct spectator knowledge of the decor and the far greater variety of sets in *Winchester '73* than in *The Maltese Falcon*, the essentially denotative art direction of this western carries a burden of narrative weight not much greater than does the studied minimalism of the detective film.

The story begins on July 4, 1876. The Centennial Rifle Shootout is about to take place in Dodge City, Kansas, where Wyatt Earp is U.S. Marshal and no man is allowed to wear a gun. Dodge City is an established junction with a number of streets, at least one large several-story structure, and a two-story saloon, porticos projecting from each story. It has a corral, of course, a land office, a stagecoach stop, a Wells Fargo office, and a railroad depot. The relatively elaborate decor is coded as we would expect, each element a familiar sign not only of time and place but of the kind of narrative that is about to unfold. Yet, with the exception perhaps of the shootout at the house on the homestead, none of the sets is narrativized, neither the main street of Dodge City, nor the shack

9. *Winchester '73*: the Tascosa street (Stephen McNally)

where the Indian trader plays solitaire while waiting for Chief Little Bull, nor the besieged cavalry encampment, nor the outlaws' hideaway in the hills, nor Tascosa, the one-horse frontier settlement with its dusty street and primitive saloon (fig. 9). These decors contain the narrative; they do not advance it. Still, all the structures of *Winchester '73*, in and between Dodge City and Tascosa, are culturally coded as masculine and white. They serve and reflect the powerful men, good and bad, who are invested in conquering the territory—all except the farmhouse, domestic thus feminized, ordered and light, walls lined with wallpaper, wallpaper hung with cameos, kitchen shining and comfortable, and the adjacent barn. Thus, predictably, masculine is opposed to feminine in the contrast of sets: dark and light, bare and full, rough and polished.

     Once out of town, the landscape itself becomes the decor, as familiar to the spectator as any of the film's interiors. In fact, the rocks where the final duel is played out seem no less constructed than the back-lot Dodge City or Tascosa. And the Winchester is quite obviously as much an excuse for the cowboy's latest breakneck ride across the western landscape as the black bird is for the careening across town of the contemporary urban detective.

     This is not to say that all mysteries and westerns have exclusively denotative sets nor that simple denotation cannot be the function of decors typical of other genres—the comedy, for example, or the melodrama. In fact, punctuative sets mark *The Big Sleep*, to take another instance of a Bogart private-eye film.[52] *Duel in the Sun*, which we discuss in some detail in the next chapter, is an example of a western with significant punctuative sets. John Ford's obsessive return to Monument Valley has established that landscape as an ultimately recognizable and emphatically decorative set. In the chapter on decor as artifice, we consider the archly designed musical western *Red Garters*. Nonetheless, unlike the fantasy film or the horror film, for example, the detective film and the western do not actually require that their decors be anything other than denotative. To gauge the distance between denotation and subsequent levels of decoration, we need only compare the bare and practically indiscernible ravine that serves as the place of Archer's murder in *The Maltese Falcon* with the house by the sea that is the site of murder in *Mildred Pierce*, a film whose punctuative decor is the point of departure for our next chapter.

Chapter 3

Set
as
Punctuation

If set as denotation, at the essentially functional level, includes classificatory information about its own generic status as discourse and about the identity of the protagonists and the locus of the action, at the level that engages us in this chapter it makes obviously punctuative, expressive connections among genre, character, and place. In films whose sets are denotative, expression is carried primarily through dialogue and action. Decor becomes manifestly expressive when its representations of the real convey not only the generic, the identificatory, and the locational but the specific coherences of a given narrative. Such decor punctuates, structures, inflects the narrative with marks of emphasis. It exhibits these defining properties:

1. It is verisimilitudinous.
2. It enhances the familiar by foregrounding the design through staging and photography.
3. Its level of rhetoric is "middle," "correct."
4. Intermittently opaque, it invites reading and can be perceived as an image with manifest pictorial and compositional elements rather than a representation of the real, everyday world.
5. Its specificity exceeds standard generic and cultural codes.

"Mildred's"

At the time *Mildred Pierce* was in production, Jack Warner circulated a memorandum warning cinematographers and art directors to use their "ingenuity and devise new means of cutting corners without losing any of the quality." Warner was concerned that the art directors were including "too much detail" and that the cinematographers were indulging in "low camera angles and ceiling shots, which take time to light and slow us up."[1] It is tempting to speculate that Warner was reacting to the rushes of *Mildred Pierce*, a production whose values afforded the cinematographer Ernest Haller the opportunity to indulge in elaborate, time-consuming camera angles and virtuosic lighting. Anton Grot provided the ceilings, the walls, and the staircases that invited Haller's invention. More important to our argument is Grot's invitation that we read decor as a complex and dynamic presence within the text. The properties of *Mildred Pierce* are exemplary of the punctuative level, as we have defined it. An A-film whose budget undoubtedly irked the frugal Jack Warner, *Mildred Pierce* flaunts the production values of its elaborate mise-en-scène in its first minutes and then insists on a variety of highly particularized locales to tell its intricate story.

Although the text carries almost no evidence of the United States at war, *Mildred Pierce* is meant to be perceived as contemporary to its audience. The costumes and the decor place it squarely in the mid-1940s.[2] Although the action unfolds in California, the middle-class neighborhood depicted is something like home to moviegoers throughout the United States. If Mildred's first restaurant seems a trifle more posh than the usual roadside stop, it would be recognizable to the readers of the popular magazines whose glossy photos often featured spreads of the latest in commercial and home design. The same is true of Monte's moderne beach house and the Beragon mansion. These sets are located in the "middle," "correct" diction we associate with realist fiction. They punctuate and highlight the narrative at moments in which the mise-en-scène and lighting exploit their specificity.[3] It is then that decor challenges conventional generic and cultural codes.

Mildred Pierce retells the American dream: by dint of hard work, enterprise, and vision, each of us can climb to the top of the economic ladder.[4] Mildred (Joan Crawford) begins by baking pies in her kitchen and eventually heads a chain of restaurants that bear her name—Mildred's. Through her courage, entrepreneurial gifts, and imagination, she transcends her lower-middle-class origin. Her fortune allows her to marry the impoverished scion of an "old family" (at one point she actually hands him a check and says, "Sold. One Beragon.") and thereby acquire the patina of American aristocracy.

Mildred's progress from her modest house in Glendale to the Beragon mansion in Pasadena fits the generic patterns of melodrama. The highly charged confrontations between Mildred and her daughter Veda (Ann Blyth), and the death scene of the younger daughter Kay, root much of the film in the family melodrama; the opening sequences of *Mildred Pierce* exhibit the stylistics of film noir. This bifurcated generic allegiance is conveyed by decors that also serve the fiction's cultural and social myths. The sets help to weave genres and myths into a pattern that, in exploiting both, succeeds in surpassing them as well. A film centered on the representation of American classes as a function of place, *Mildred Pierce* is finally about the fragility of the American dream, first realized, then lost. And it is the fragility and loss of the dream that draw on the conventions of the maternal melodrama and film noir for their inflection, in performance, in mise-en-scène, in decor.[5]

Narrative priority is given to a murder, an event absent from the James Cain novel upon which *Mildred Pierce* is based. This murder, the film's opening sequence, is staged in a decor that draws attention to itself, provisionally indicates the film noir genre, and creates a climate of unease for the reading of the narrative. Here, the identification of class—two exterior shots of a beach house, then brief shots of its interior—is, of course, not yet part of the "American dream" scenario. We see a "beautiful" house in a "beautiful" place, then a dying man falling to the floor, uttering the name Mildred. The pan/tilt, from the corpse on the floor to a mirror cracked by bullets and a door, intensifies the sense of dislocation. The audience is denied the expected reverse shot showing the murderer. In fact, the identity of the murderer will not be revealed until the final moments of the film.

The next scene shows an unidentified woman walking onto a sordid pier.[6] The viewer cannot fail to link the name Mildred to the woman (and to the actress, Joan Crawford, for whom *Mildred Pierce* is a star vehicle) and to assume that she is the person who shot the man in the previous scene. This impression, which the narrative will ultimately disprove, is sustained by the forbidding and foreboding set of the pier. Indeed, Mildred is on the verge of committing suicide. Only the arrival of a policeman stops her from jumping into the ocean (fig. 10). While the pier is shown very briefly, the strategy of its early placement and the nature of the action for which it serves as a stage ensure its narrative/visual charge. After all, a suicide site always demands attention. The pier and the pierside dive that Mildred enters at the end of this scene are related to noir conventions:

10. *Mildred Pierce*: pier, Mildred's (Joan Crawford) suicide attempt

the seedy nightscape, the seedier night spot, the apparent social dislocation of a woman wearing an expensive fur coat and hat.[7] None of this decor, however, seems to announce a maternal melodrama, a genre with which Joan Crawford was not, in any case, previously associated.

The dive belongs to Wally (Jack Carson), Mildred's partner, who has just conspired to sell her out. She invites him back to the beach house. That decor, rapidly glimpsed in the murder scene, now articulates the film's most elaborately staged action. As we explore the dwelling, we become increasingly disoriented. The more we see, the less we understand. The very conventions of domestic architecture are made to serve the specific noir narrative of *Mildred Pierce*. This is not merely a house of the affluent; it is a house whose unusual layout puts into question standard notions of the placement of doors, of stairs. Mildred and Wally pass from the living room/entrance level (without seeing the corpse), down a spiral staircase (where Mildred must reach for an unconventionally placed light switch), to the den/bar area. Mildred succeeds in leaving Wally alone in the house so as to pin the murder on him. He panics, runs through the rooms, tries to open all the doors on both levels. The house turns into a cage as he moves past the various textures of its walls—panel, paint, glass. After discovering the body on the floor, Wally finally breaks through a glass door (fig. 11). A moment later, on the beach, he is arrested.

Grot explained his formula for designing mysteries in a discussion of *Doctor X*. Despite the important differences between the more flamboyant and weighty decor of *Doctor X* and the distinctly moderne look of the *Mildred Pierce* beach house, Grot's

11. *Mildred Pierce*: Wally (Jack Carson) escaping from the Malibu house

remarks have pertinence to the later film: "The primary purpose of set designing is to establish the mood of the story. In *Doctor X*, that mood of the story is mystery, of course, but we have tried to build menace into the sets. . . . We design a set that imitates as closely as possible a bird of prey about to swoop down upon its victim, trying to incorporate in the whole thing a sense of impending calamity, of overwhelming danger."[8] In fact, much of the *Mildred Pierce* beach house episode is shot in low-angle that, together with high-key lighting, emphasizes shadows and bizarre spatial relationships. Conventional in film noir, low-angle/high-key stylistics give a surprising edge to a movie that turns out also to be about class and maternity, subjects that normally require the viewer to grasp fully the relationships between characters. Yet this crazy house of a dwelling, with its unfamiliar proportions, unpredictable planes, deep shadows, and locked doors, keeps the viewer in a state of uncertainty from the film's very first images. The emphatic inscription of the Malibu beach house makes us particularly attentive to the other decors. While none is as unusual in design, several exert significant weight on the narrative just the same.

The deeply shadowed police headquarters, for example, is both disorienting and threatening. Neutral in terms of class coding, it is an apt point of departure for the film's flashback, an itinerary of class mobility whose starting point is an ordinary house in Glendale. Only when Mildred begins to tell her story, nearly twenty minutes into the film (about one-fifth of its total duration), do we begin to glimpse, along with daylight, a clearly shaped narrative. Far removed from the startling dislocations and noir stylistics of Malibu, we are plunged squarely into (1) the family/maternal melodrama—the spoiling of children and the breakup of a marriage and (2) the class narrative—the ambitious wife, the husband who loses his job, the daughter eager to own beautiful clothes and to live in a beautiful home. We see a street in a middle-class neighborhood in which, Mildred's overvoice tells us, "all the houses looked alike." As we observe Mildred bustling through the apparently unremarkable decor, we hear her say that she has been in the "kitchen all my life," a statement whose incongruence, given Joan Crawford's glamorous clothes-horse image familiar in 1945, is increased by the viewer's memory of the stylish furs she wears before the flashback.

The house may look like all the others on the block, but its layout is exposed with the exceptional care that distinguishes punctuation from denotation. The characters enter through its exterior doors; they pass from zone to zone, from the first to the second floor. Mildred's daughters, Veda and Kay, find Mildred in the kitchen/dinette. From the kitchen we can see Veda at the piano in the living room.[9] Veda runs up the clearly visible stairs to her bedroom to try on and contemptuously reject the dress Mildred bought with her hard-won savings. The living room is the scene of the final argument between Mildred and her husband Bert (Bruce Bennett) and of their surprisingly undramatic, understated decision to separate (fig. 12).

Because the articulations and spatial relationships of the Glendale house are fully exercised at the outset by the mise-en-scène, its living spaces, intended to appear average, representative of many similar ones, participate in the opacity shared by all the film's decors. But that opacity, by the nature of punctuation, is intermittent. Once the punctuative decor's layout is firmly established in the viewer's eye and mind, and once that

12. *Mildred Pierce*: set still of the Glendale house

layout has established the narrative situation of the characters, the Glendale house recedes into its denotative normalcy until called upon to emphasize yet another narrative event. Its status is transparent in the next sequence, during which Mildred tries to assess the effect of the separation on her financial situation, and Wally pays a visit that ends in a failed attempt at seduction. The characters traverse the now familiar living room, dining room, and kitchen. At this point, the articulation of the rooms follows the narrative's logic somewhat passively, that is, without punctuation.

When we return to Malibu, bright sunlight minimizes the eccentricity of the beach house and erases the noir events of the film's opening—the murder and entrapment. At this point, its modernity reflects Mildred's energy and confidence (fig. 13). The beach house is the place in which she satisfies her desire to better her family's condition by becoming an entrepreneurial, independent woman: she persuades its owner, Monte Beragon (Zachary Scott), to lease her a property where she will establish a restaurant. A palpable image of the life to which Mildred aspires, the comfortable beach house suits Monte's seduction of Mildred (fig. 14). She returns to her own lower-middle-class home in Glendale only to learn, in the conventional transgression/retribution scheme of melodrama, that her daughter Kay is dying of pneumonia. Thus, obliquely but unmistakably, the film noir beach house of the first sequences, transformed by sunlight and then by a

13. *Mildred Pierce*: Monte (Zachary Scott), Wally, and Mildred first meet at the Malibu house

14. *Mildred Pierce*: the mirror reflection of Monte and Mildred embracing at the Malibu house

fireside night of love into the locus of Mildred's leap up the social ladder, is related to the maternal melodrama.[10]

Mildred's progress in the world of work is charted by her contrasting workplaces. She begins as a waitress in a nondescript, poorly run eatery where she learns something about the restaurant business; she herself designs her first establishment, the up-to-date Glen Oaks Boulevard restaurant. Monte and the film's viewers share Mildred's guided tour through its linked yet sharply defined areas: entrance, bar, table area, kitchen, office, parking lot. The highest mark of her success is the fancy Beverly Hills restaurant, where a large office and private patio blur the distinction between workplace and domicile.[11] As in the modest Glendale house and the Malibu beach house, the restaurant sets favor a flow of movement and show different playing areas simultaneously.

It is, in fact, the contiguous zones of the Glendale house that provide one of the most strongly narrativized uses of decor in *Mildred Pierce*. The wrought-iron banisters of the staircase appear throughout; sharply defined borders to a very narrow, very short staircase, they also define one of the film's most shocking confrontations. Announcing that she is pregnant, Veda has succeeded in winning a large settlement from her husband's rich mother. When she and Mildred return home, the truth emerges: the pregnancy was a fraud, a ploy to extort money. Horrified at her daughter's deceit, Mildred is further shocked to learn that Veda will use the money to leave her and the lower-middle-class values she represents. Veda wants "to get away from every rotten, stinking thing that even reminds me of this place—or you." She calls Mildred a "common frump" and runs for the stairs. Mildred stops her in the curve of the banister, its most radical articulation. She grabs the check and tears it up. Veda slaps her; Mildred falls, then orders Veda out "before I kill you." The essential element of the maternal melodrama, the fury of mother-daughter emotions, is condensed into physical conflict enacted on the spine of the home that represents the class tensions of their relationship. The Glendale house, with its sense of confinement centered on the mini-staircase, expresses what Veda despises: Mildred's lower-middle-class status.

Mildred will lure Veda back to her with a grand house and a grand staircase—one that happens to have belonged to Monte, Mildred's lover/husband, Veda's lover, her ticket to the upper classes and the agent of her revenge against Mother. In successive scenes, the old Beragon mansion in Pasadena first appears as a Victorian "white elephant," then renovated, a page out of *House Beautiful*. Its contiguous entrance, foyer, grand staircase, and living room belong to those multiroomed configurations that invite the complex mise-en-scène accommodated by many punctuative decors.

The flashback ends, of course, where the film began. In the Malibu house, the murder now makes sense and the generic schemes now redefine each other. Film noir, the maternal melodrama, and the myth of social mobility finally intersect. Mildred's narration has reached a point just prior to the murder of Monte. She discovers Monte and Veda embracing against the bar. Veda, the ambitious, heartless daughter, has gotten where she wants to be: into Monte's house and presumably into his bed, the house and bed of the sophisticated blueblood her mother has married. The murder, the noir event about to take place in the house that has reacquired its initial noir aspect, now derives its sense from both the maternal melodrama and the American myth of social mobility. It draws its power from the mother-daughter and class tensions that have animated the entire flashback. Mildred has sacrificed herself to a daughter who wishes only to humiliate her, to extort luxuries that will ruin her, to undermine her business by plotting behind her back, to steal her husband, and finally to abandon her. Family and class are denatured in a noir confrontation where the rival women happen to be mother and daughter. A few moments later, when Monte rejects Veda, she shoots him. She prevents Mildred from calling the police with the line "It's your fault I'm the way I am."

Although the Malibu beach house never truly harbors a family, it is nonetheless the proper locus for dialogue that defines Veda, the materialistic daughter and murderess, and Mildred, the ambitious, self-sacrificing mother. The scene for this conflation of murder and maternity is a dwelling whose planes, unable to settle into patterns of conventional living space, give shape to the heroine's class aspirations, a business transaction, two assignations, and finally a murder, a decor that connects the film's multiple generic needs and its mythic aspirations.

Following Veda's arrest for the murder of Monte, *Mildred Pierce* concludes with yet another punctuative decor, the portico of police headquarters through which Mildred and Bert, her first husband, exit together, with the suggestion that their future is as full of hope as the dawn that greets them. Others have commented on the scrubwomen seen in the preceding shot, reminders that a woman's place is on her hands and knees, cautionary figures for women like Mildred who take on a man's work in a patriarchal society.[12] Yet, whatever intentional or accidental subversion of the "happy" ending is served by these scrubwomen, the final shot excludes them. It is dominated by the monumental portico, a frame for the studio-created cityscape toward which Mildred and Bert walk. In the patent foregrounding of its status as artifact, decor here signals the fiction effect. The unnatural dawn ends not only the long night at police headquarters but the long night of Mildred's narrative. Following her telling of the story, the enlightened, transformed survivors emerge into the light of day. As Mildred and Bert "walk away" from the lurid details of greed and murder, the portico, this outsized articulation between the interior and the exterior, punctuates the boundary between the end of the action and The End of the film.

Repertoire of Decorative Punctuation in *Mildred Pierce*

Through the foregrounding of the exceptional set and the manipulation and variation of more ordinary ones, *Mildred Pierce* exhibits an inventory of the punctuative functions of decor. These functions fall into the broad narrative categories of structure, genre, character, and theme. The sets of *Mildred Pierce* demonstrate, in some cases, more than one function:

Structure

1. Opening and closing. The Malibu beach house is a liminal set, which is to say that it opens the film and establishes a complexity of narrative expectations. The portico

of police headquarters is a conclusive set; it closes the film and signals the exhaustion of narrative possibilities, of narrative itself.

2. Narrative crisis. The pier situates a life and death decision; the staircase in the Glendale house provides the focus for the mother-daughter conflict; the Malibu beach house—love nest, murder scene, site of class representation—sums up the narrative's complex itineraries in its final appearance.

Genre

1. Film noir. The liminal Malibu beach house is progressively amplified as a noir locus, from Monte's murder, through the entrance of Wally and Mildred, to Wally's entrapment. It reacquires its initial noir aspect while fulfilling the generic needs of the maternal melodrama during the final confrontation of mother, daughter, and lover. The pier and Wally's pierside dive support the initial noir decor.

2. Maternal melodrama. The decorative characteristics of this genre are less insistent than those of film noir. Here, the purportedly undistinguished Glendale house furnishes the apt decor, exceeding denotation in the detail of its layout, in the opportunities it provides for fluid mise-en-scène, and in the focalized staging of the staircase encounter.

Character

1. As Mildred explores the various sections of her first restaurant with Monte, she demonstrates her ability to succeed.

2. The pier and pierside dive show Mildred, in fur coat and hat, to be "out of place."

3. In bright sunlight and then cozy firelight, the noir characteristics of the Malibu beach house are effaced. The house becomes the scene of entrepreneurial and sexual satisfaction.

Theme

1. The highly inflected set of the Glendale house illuminates Mildred's activity as a homemaker but also as a woman with ambitions beyond those accorded her place in class and economic hierarchies.

2. Contrasting sets reflect the differences between characters and mark the stages in a single character's life. Mildred's progress up the social ladder is charted by the move from one restaurant to another more prosperous, from lower-middle-class Glendale to aristocratic Pasadena. The transformation of the Pasadena house from white elephant to showcase is keyed to Mildred's determination to win Veda back by catering to her daughter's insatiable desire.

Demonstrations of Punctuative Decor

In the remainder of this chapter we will exhibit these several functions of punctuative decor through a range of texts. As they do in *Mildred Pierce*, many of the sets we consider serve more than a single function; we will treat each according to the function that dominates. The liminal sets of *Captain Blood*, for instance, are examples of decor that surpasses generic requirements. That of *Dodsworth* is intended to express the spirit of the character who lends his name to the film's title.[13] For the purposes of our argument, we will illustrate each function with just a few examples. Our choice of films is by no means exhaustive, nor can it be. Punctuative sets are pervasive in cinema.

Structure

Opening and Closing

Le Jour se lève has a liminal set, the tall, slender working-class building in which the protagonist, François (Jean Gabin), lives, where he murders his nemesis, Valentin (Jules Berry), where he relives the events that brought him to murder, and where he finally puts a bullet into his own heart. In the film's first image the camera follows two carthorses into the square, emphasizing thereby entry into the narrative space, dominated by the six-storied building (fig. 15).[14] Although the building's architectural materials and details were certainly familiar to French audiences, its isolated position on the square, along with the privilege of its placement within the narrative, makes it a memorable image. Here,

15. *Le Jour se lève*: the street and François's building

through the melding of the everyday and the exceptional, *Le Jour se lève* manifests an exemplary decorative aspect of poetic realism. François's room was originally supposed to be on the third floor; the producer wanted to economize by cutting two or three stories. But designer Alexandre Trauner persisted in his resolve to construct a tall building because it fit the narrative's logic (François needed to be isolated from the crowd) and because it "corresponded to the character." In fact, Trauner ascribes the failure of the U.S. remake, *The Long Night*, to the placement of the protagonist's room on a lower floor.[15]

This tall structure is indeed the proper site for the anguish of François, a man of the people who, in surrendering to passion, moves beyond class. In one of the film's most spectacular scenes, he refuses the urging of his comrades, massed below in the square, to give himself up to the police. Further accentuating the building's height, its interior is narrativized just moments after the opening. As a blind man climbs the stairs, we hear the angry voices of François and Valentin. Following the sound of a shot, Valentin emerges from the room and tumbles down two flights to come to rest at the feet of the blind man, whose perplexity reflects that of the viewer. What has brought François and Valentin to this moment? The proportions and isolation of the building provide part of the answer. Its height is underscored when, from above, we see the depth of the entire stairwell lined with the curious faces of its inhabitants.

The use of liminal sets is frequent in the Carné-Trauner-Prévert collaboration. It is from the prompt establishment of expressive physical reality that derive the tone, atmosphere, and sense of tragic destiny so characteristic of their films. Theirs are not particularly well-stiched plots. Many instances of narrative causality are elided, sacrificed to allow places, objects, and faces to speak, to allow the viewer to learn and recognize the distinctive voices of Arletty, Louis Jouvet, Jules Berry, and so many others. In *Le Jour se lève*, the relationship between Valentin and Françoise that incites François to murder is suggested but never made explicit. What exactly are the dirty dealings between Zabel (Michel Simon) and Lucien (Pierre Brasseur) in *Quai des brumes* into which Jean (Jean Gabin) stumbles? And what has transpired between Zabel and his so-called ward Nelly (Michèle Morgan)? We are never quite sure. Such unresolved questions should leave viewers unsatisfied, and indeed would if the films did not proffer the other, abundant satisfaction of mastering the rich links between the characters and the worlds they inhabit.

Trauner's quayside *Hôtel du Nord*, the Boulevard of Crime in *Les Enfants du paradis*, and the Barbès metro station in *Les Portes de la nuit* are liminal sets for fictions in which the city impinges heavily on the characters. This is also true of the enormous replica of New York's Pennsylvania Station constructed by M-G-M's art department for *The Clock* (fig. 16). The specifics of its size, configuration, and components are integral to the characters' initial encounter; it roots their relationship in a highly charged urban context, a place of comings and goings that are favored by the set's expansive dimensions; that relationship will subsequently be tested by the stresses of city life; the implicit timetables of the station serve as correlatives to the eponymous clock and the press of time that defines the whirlwind courtship and marriage of the protagonists. A context for the immediately recognizable Robert Walker and Judy Garland—stars singled out in the crowd, characters who "meet cute" on an escalator, who seek and find each other there again

16. *The Clock*: set still for Pennsylvania Station

after another city crowd separates them—M-G-M's Penn Station exemplifies the reso-
nant set that recurs during the course of the film it introduces.

Penn Station is also the conclusive set in *The Clock*. The soldier and his new wife
say good-bye to each other; the camera pulls back, and their story and their characters
recede into the crowd from which they initially emerged. This enormous set allows then
for what Stephen Harvey calls "a God-like View" and a final image that "is strange, disquieting. With his accent on the uncertainties of life and love in war, and the alienating
crush of the metropolis at any time, Minnelli fashioned a happy-ending romance that feels
like tragedy." [16] Even if one does not share Harvey's sense of the tragic, there is no denying the unsettling sense of incomplete narrative closure created when characters to whom
viewers have become attached through a film's duration are lost in a vast public space.

A country cottage befits the private conclusion of *Random Harvest* (fig. 17). The
quaint design of the cottage and its idyllic setting near a stone bridge contribute to its
far-fetched coincidences and romantic conceits. The fortunes of war (the hero is an am-
nesia victim) and peace (the celebration of the armistice) bring together two individuals,
Charles (Ronald Colman) and Paula (Greer Garson), who should have been divided by
class; they marry and live in the picturesque cottage that signifies their isolation from the
realities of past and present. They are separated when an accident restores Charles's long-

17. *Random Harvest*: Charles (Ronald Colman) and Paula (Greer Garson) at the cottage, on their wedding day

term memory but destroys recollection of his life with Paula. Bearing different identities, they meet again and enter into a marriage of convenience. It is only when Charles rediscovers the edenic cottage that he finds in himself the man who loved Paula. It is, in fact, the key to the front door of the cottage that also unlocks Charles's memory and effects satisfactory narrative closure, with love triumphant. A similar closure, the return of memory, is located in another English cottage, albeit a menacing one, in *Love Letters*.[17] And the decorative power of this kind of rustic dwelling is fully exercised in the aptly entitled *The Enchanted Cottage* where the house, on view through much of the film, offers the final proof of its power, along with that of love, at the fade-out.

Narrative Crisis

Mildred Pierce and her daughter Veda play out their melodrama of power and submission on a confining staircase. The structure of a staircase is conventionally used to indicate relationships of domination and subordination; it may also provide a narrowing, energizing, concentrating frame. Design, lighting, and camera angle abet the dramatic focus provided by the doorways, windows, and furniture of horizontal playing spaces. But with its delimiting railings, its articulated steps, curves, and landings, the staircase comes equipped for focus. It invites a dynamic of passage for characters who may also be displayed in attitudes of presentation, usually suspended above or below the plane of the lens. We will examine the staircase decor as a frequently exercised site of narrative crisis in this section, and we will pursue it in the succeeding chapters.

The Strange Love of Martha Ivers demonstrates the value of a repeatedly narrativized staircase. Freestanding and widely curving, thus flaunting its articulation, this staircase provides movement and disposition both lateral and vertical; it accommodates punctuative instances of character relationship and action. Soon after the film's opening, the adolescent Martha is about to make yet another attempt to run away from her despised aunt (Judith Anderson). The sequence is visible during intermittent flashes of lighting (there is a convenient power failure) that increase the impact of the appearance of the staircase and the characters who climb and descend it. Martha's young accomplice Sam, in search of Martha's cat, slides down the long banister; shots of Mrs. Ivers mounting the stairs to investigate the noise are intercut with shots of the cat. Halfway up, Mrs. Ivers begins to beat the cat with her cane. Martha then descends, snatches the cane, and crashes it down on her aunt's head; the woman falls down the stairs. Martha and her other young friend, Walter, stand over the body while Martha tells Walter's father that a large man killed Mrs. Ivers. The murder and its cover-up will haunt Martha and Walter through the rest of the film as surely as the image of the staircase returns to remind the viewers of the circumstances of the crime.

The staircase is next seen years later. Sam (Van Heflin) has returned to town, and Martha (Barbara Stanwyck) shows him the house, redecorated and modernized. Martha has now replaced her imperious aunt. She is in command of the house, of Iversville, and of her husband, Walter (Kirk Douglas), who has become district attorney. A complicated tracking shot follows Martha and Sam as they mount the staircase, the center of Martha's dominion as it was the scene of the crime. In a later sequence, near the end of the film, Walter, drunk, falls at the bottom of the stairs in the same spot where Mrs. Ivers fell (fig. 18). Martha incites Sam to murder the unconscious Walter and believes, for a moment, that he will comply. In a shot that shows the sweep of the staircase and all three figures, Sam descends and Martha stands where she struck her aunt years before, thinking that at last she is about to gain what she wants: liberation from Walter, and the love of Sam. Then, in close-up, her expression changes from satisfaction to disappointment as she watches Sam minister to Walter, not murder him. The staircase, defined as the place of evil by Mrs. Ivers (striking the cat), Martha (striking Mrs. Ivers), and the complicitous Walter and his also complicitous father, now demonstrates Sam's good. It participates in and punctuates the dramatic and moral turning points of the film.

The staircase occupies a like place in Alfred Hitchcock's mise-en-scène: "The staircase pervades his films—as a household location, a site of ordeal, and a model for moral change."[18] Conveying ordeal and moral change, the staircase punctuates crucial narrative elements: the playboy Johnny (Cary Grant) carrying an ominous glass of milk up to his rich wife Lina (Joan Fontaine) in *Suspicion*; the double nature of Uncle Charlie in *Shadow of a Doubt*; Alicia (Ingrid Bergman) slowly climbing when she realizes she has

18. *The Strange Love of Martha Ivers*: Sam (Van Heflin), Martha (Barbara Stanwyck), and Walter (Kirk Douglas) on the staircase

been poisoned in *Notorious*; the spectacular identity games in the bell tower at the conclusion of *Vertigo*; the death of Arbogast (Martin Balsam), falling backwards, in *Psycho*; the camera tracking down and backwards during one of the murders in *Frenzy*.

Hitchcock also calls upon other forms of elevation to sustain moments of narrative crisis. Robert Boyle designed a cantilevered house for one of the final sequences of *North by Northwest* (1959):

> Once you say that it's going to have to cantilever because he's [Cary Grant] going to be in a precarious situation, he has to be in a situation in which he can see into the living room, up onto the balcony, and that she [Eva Marie Saint] crosses the balcony into the bedroom and he can see her in the bedroom. So it had to be designed like that. If it's just an ordinary porch, or something, it couldn't be. So he has to be in a position where if he's dislodged, he will fall to his death. There has to be some suspense there. And then, cantilevered meant modern, so it just fell into place. I didn't superimpose it, the script superimposed it on me.[19]

Hanging over a chasm, this house, a veritable jungle gym for Cary Grant, who climbs on its outside beams and creeps stealthily through its exposed interior, not only accommodates yet another spectacular peril for the hero but coheres with other perilous heights present in the film: the UN building that looms over him, his uncontrolled automobile descent down a mountain road, the attack of the crop-dusting plane. It is also a fitting warm-up for the vertiginous drops awaiting the Grant and Saint characters on the faces of the presidents sculpted into Mount Rushmore.

Elevations and staircases also function as markers of narrative crisis in contexts less sensational than Hitchcock films. In *Letter from an Unknown Woman*, the adolescent longings and grown-up desires of Lisa (Joan Fontaine) are exercised on the winding staircase of a modest apartment building in turn-of-the-century Vienna. Seen at many instances during the film, the staircase marks Lisa's crushing disappointment when, after her long vigil, the unsuspecting object of her infatuation, Stefan Brand (Louis Jourdan), mounts it with another woman; Lisa then dejectedly descends. Later, from the point of view Lisa had occupied during the vigil episode, we see her ecstatically climb the staircase beside Stefan. And yet another register of tension is apt for light-hearted romantic comedy. *It Started with Eve* places the soon-to-be-united couple (Deanna Durbin and Robert Cummings) on opposite sides of an absurdly ornate double staircase (fig. 19).

19. *It Started with Eve*: Anne (Deanna Durbin) and Jonathon (Robert Cummings), temporarily at odds

We do not mean to suggest that art directors are limited to radical elevations, sweeping staircases, and cantilevered houses for narrative accent. A single example of an emphatically horizontal set, the hallway of an upper-middle-class apartment in *The Best Years of Our Lives*, indicates how unprepossessing decor may be used to mark narrative crisis. Here, images of deep spaces prepare for the homecoming of Al Stephenson (Fredric March), returning after his war service. Al passes through a downstairs lobby, enters an elevator, emerges from it on his floor, proceeds down a corridor, and then rings the bell at his own front door. The hallway inside is the site of reunion with his wife Milly (Myrna Loy). This space, shown from the nearly head-on perspective that emphasizes its depth, is sharply defined by the most common elements of domestic architecture: a window and door on one side, doors on the opposite side, another door as background. Al and Milly embrace at approximately the midpoint of this hallway. It is the core of their home, where the relationships that link husband and wife, parents and children, are articulated in the close proximity of doors, certainly the best place to enact the highly emotional return of this devoted husband and father. The moment is exploited by the depth-of-field staging of director William Wyler, by the deep-focus cinematography of Gregg Toland, and in the deceptively deep and deceptively normal hallway designed by George Jenkins.[20]

Genre

Walled Caribbean towns and Spanish galleons are commonplaces of pirate movies. The viewer expects the strong pictorial values of such locales in "swashbuckler" films and is certainly not disappointed by the sets of *Captain Blood*.[21] But several of Anton Grot's designs for this film exceed even those high expectations. Reminiscent of his work for *Svengali* (a film we discuss in chapter 5), the first scenes have a sketched, storybook look, with sharply skewed diagonals, patently false skies, and deep shadows. At the very outset, the tale of adventure suggests not only a pirate movie but a work of literary fiction, a book with illustrations. If this style had been sustained, the film's decor would qualify for inclusion in our chapter on sets as artifice. Here, in the narrative's privileged opening position, the palpable fictivity of the decor is congruent with the genre demands of the historical adventure film. In his design for a gigantic waterwheel, however, Grot transcends the conventions of genre (fig. 20). With its outsized wooden gears and dominant superstructure, this decor does more than indicate mood, place, and the dire straits of Blood and his fellow plantation slaves. The brief appearance of the waterwheel, minimally related to the necessities of plot (other sites might have been chosen for the forced labor of slaves), distinguishes *Captain Blood* from more conventional examples of genre and exacts from the viewer a keener level of attention. The purpose of that attention is, for a moment, to release *Captain Blood* from the familiar codes we associate with its genre. But if genre is surpassed, it is not forgotten. In fact, the extraordinary decor provides the viewer with a reinvigorated access to overly familiar elements of the genre. The function of the waterwheel is analogous to Erich Korngold's celebrated score for *Captain Blood*, music so striking that it will subsequently define the genre it surpasses.

20. *Captain Blood*: Captain Blood (Errol Flynn) turning the waterwheel

An Edwardian melodrama, *Ivy* satisfies the decorative demands of its genre with finely appointed interiors and detailed plaster moldings that root the narrative firmly to its period. In his unspecific but positive assessment of producer William Cameron Menzies's contribution to the film, James Agee must have been responding to the overall quality of detail; he also must have been struck by the pertinence of the decor to the narrative's demands. [22] Redolent of the clandestine is the steep alley staircase descending to the love nest of Ivy (Joan Fontaine) and her adoring Roger (Patric Knowles). Setting is also crucial to the film's climax when the murderous Ivy runs frantically around her flat in search of an incriminating handbag, then back to an elevator shaft where she falls to her death. This attention to decor expresses the dynamics of conflict in domestic space that is so often the center of melodrama (*The Suspect*, *Gaslight*, etc.), Edwardian and not. But *Ivy* stakes its claim for distinction in a spectacular indoor-outdoor ballroom set, where the spectacle is ultimately the revelation of Ivy's duplicitous nature (fig. 21). Attending the ball with her husband Jarvis (Richard Ney), she is clearing the path toward her new lover, the wealthy Rushworth (Herbert Marshall), by brushing off her last, Roger. She stages her flirtation with Rushworth in a little stone pavilion on an artificial lagoon. The jealous Roger interrupts, and Rushworth retires. It is here that Ivy tells Roger that their affair is over and tries to resist his embrace. The other guests go onto the terrace to watch the fireworks display, which, it turns out, provides a background for the

21. *Ivy*: the ball, Roger (Patric Knowles) in foreground

quarreling silhouettes of Ivy and Roger. The on-screen observers (with the exception of Rushworth) have no way of knowing precisely what is transpiring between Ivy and Roger. For us, the decor turns their meeting into a spectacle of transgression.

The art direction of an Edwardian melodrama surpasses its conventions through the opulence and complexity of its decorative conceits. The western is a genre, as we demonstrated in the preceding chapter, that is primarily denotational and whose severely limited repertoire of sets would seem to tolerate neither opulence nor complexity. For *Duel in the Sun*, it is in the introduction of Pearl Chavez (Jennifer Jones) that art direction challenges the modest dimensions of interior space conventionally dictated by nineteenth-century western locales and accommodates producer David Selznick's penchant for the hyperbolic.[23] This departure is, of course, related to the film's most striking generic infraction: the foregrounding of the love story and of Jones, the female star. First we see a patently artificial matte shot showing Squaw's Head Rock, the place where the "duel in the sun" will be staged. Accompanying this monumental image is a voiceover narration, intoned by the familiar and portentous voice of Orson Welles, that relates character (Pearl) to place (Squaw's Head Rock) to myth (the flower growing where Pearl died). As if this were not sufficient to establish the measure of the protagonist, immediately following the prologue there is a sequence (added long after the film had been

22. *Duel in the Sun*: Pearl's mother (Tilly Losch) dancing in the Presidio

written and gone into production) designed to explain Pearl's conduct, her sexual nature and allure. We see young Pearl dancing for an audience of children in front of the Presidio, a drinking and gambling establishment whose large interior far exceeds the proportions of the frontier saloons to which most moviegoers are accustomed. An even more striking design element is the shape of the bar, eccentric to the straight-line norm (fig. 22). Pearl's mother (Tillie Losch) dances on a platform in the middle of a rectangle. We see parts of the big hall, including an alcove in which Pearl's card-playing father, Scott (Herbert Marshall), submits to humiliating comments on his wife's provocative dancing. The entirety of the set is on view for less than twenty seconds before the camera follows the dancer around the perimeter of the rectangular bar. In the course of the dance, she leans down and falls into a man's arms for a kiss. They leave precipitously. A few moments later, Chavez kills his faithless wife and her erstwhile lover.

The action that takes place inside the Presidio lasts barely two minutes. The set will not be seen again. It has served its punctuative purposes—opposing genre expectations and providing an image upon which to construct the character of Pearl Chavez. It will, from this point forward, be impossible to think of *Duel in the Sun* as a "mere" western. Pearl's little dance in front of the Presidio is an innocent version of the maternal spectacle of a woman's sexual (read sinful) nature. (The idea of Pearl as sinner takes material shape in a later sequence when, enticingly draped in a blanket, she is presumably made pure by the ministrations of a "sin killer" [Walter Huston].) *Duel in the Sun* is inflected by Pearl's two-sided nature, the good and the bad, the chaste and the wanton.

These sides correspond to the two brothers she encounters, the virtuous, idealistic Jesse (Joseph Cotton) and the unprincipled, hedonistic Lewt (Gregory Peck). During the dance in the Presidio, the woman is the site of sexual spectacle; the spectacle is dramatized in the tensions between Pearl, Jesse, and Lewt. From the initial breach of genre in the Presidio, *Duel in the Sun* proceeds to call upon the hyperbolic in the love story and in more familiar configurations of the western: the conflict between the cattlemen and the railroad, the shootout in a saloon. The final confrontation in the particularly striking and anthropomorphized landscape of Squaw's Head Rock suits the unmistakably biblical scope of a narrative in which the brothers Lewt and Jesse are under the sign of Cain and Abel.

Character

As for the Presidio of *Duel in the Sun*, so for many of the sets we discuss in this chapter: whatever its structural or generic function, decor inflects the viewer's understanding of character. When we speak of Mildred's Glendale house, François's room, the staircase in

23. *Dodsworth*: Sam Dodsworth (Walter Huston) in his office

the Ivers mansion, or the hall in Al Stephenson's apartment, we are not designating ownership and occupancy alone. We expect the spaces of fiction to be expressive of the people who inhabit them. Punctuative design sometimes provides that expression.

Celebrated for its modernism, the liminal set of *Dodsworth*, Sam Dodsworth's (Walter Huston) office with its picture window and backcloth rendition of his factory, is one of the sets most frequently cited in books and articles on art direction.[24] Somewhat surprisingly, then, this set is on screen for only twenty seconds (fig. 23). Its narrative purpose is clear. Dodsworth has just sold his interest in the factory that bears his name, visible in the shot. Standing at the window of an office that exhibits his wealth, his power, and his commitment to progress, surveying the extent of what he has created, Dodsworth is about to embark on retirement and we on a narrative journey during which he comes to terms with his identity. At the film's climax, he becomes once again the kind of man whose vision and energy are conveyed by this liminal set.

A quite different sort of man is characterized in the opening sequence of *Laura*. A tracking shot through a richly decorated apartment brings into view a large Chinese statue, various objects in display cases, a fancy grandfather clock (a duplicate figures prominently in the film's denouement), and finally an enormous marble bathroom filled with furnishings that most people would place in the living room (fig. 24). This shot accompanies the voiceover narration of the man (Clifton Webb) sitting in the bathtub:

24. *Laura*: Waldo Lydecker (Clifton Webb) in his bathtub, Mark McPherson (Dana Andrews) on right

"I shall never forget the weekend Laura died. A silver sun burned through the sky like a huge magnifying glass. . . . I, Waldo Lydecker, was the only one who really knew her." The decor emphatically establishes Lydecker's taste for the recherché, the extravagant. As he says condescendingly to the detective, Mark McPherson (Dana Andrews), "It's lavish, but I call it home." The position of the bathtub, its length perpendicular to the wall so that three of its sides are exposed, would have suited the ablutions of Gloria Swanson in one of De Mille's sex comedies. With a shelf and typewriter traversing its width, the bathtub is the "study" of a columnist. No Marat awaiting the knife of Charlotte Corday, Lydecker, it will turn out, is the film's murderer. But at this point in *Laura*, he is a sarcastic, condescending snob in love with Laura's memory.

In one of the film's many ironies, the tub of the liminal scene displays both Lydecker's nakedness and repressed sexuality. He despises the muscular, athletic bodies of the men who would steal Laura from him; he opposes his spiritual relationship with her to what he disparagingly calls "earthy." It is, of course, Lydecker's desire that is most earthily exposed in the entire course of the film. Lydecker in tub with typewriter is observed by an "earthy," taciturn, "meat and potatoes" man, Detective McPherson. But McPherson is not all "meat and potatoes." During his investigation—interviews with those who remember and adored her, the examination of her apartment—McPherson falls in love with the portrait of the presumably dead Laura. He comes to share her values, which are also those of the effete Lydecker. Art direction becomes integrated into the core of the narrative as it objectifies, through furniture, living spaces, and a portrait, McPherson's extraordinary infatuation with a dead woman he never met.

Theme

A great Victorian house, rising from the prairie in nearly comic solitude, serves as the primary anchor for George Stevens's *Giant* (fig. 25). In a sprawling narrative whose duration spans three generations of a Texas family and the profound local changes that accompany the transition from a cattle-baron to an oil-baron economy, the house expresses continuity in its immutable silhouette and the disposition of its rooms; the passage of time is clear in the transformation of interior furnishings and decorations. The house locates the clash between domestic gentility and the rough-and-ready manners spawned by the boundless land conveyed in the film's title. Oversized outside and in, as much of a giant as the state itself, the house remains a graspable point of reference that inflects the thematics of the narrative.[25]

When environment is assigned to express social issues, particularly those of class conflict and mobility, decor becomes the marker of the narrative's itinerary. The despair of the everyman hero of *The Crowd* is caught in the passage between the tiny flat he shares with his long-suffering wife and the enormous office that engulfs him in a sea of desks (fig. 26, fig. 27). At home the kitchen is in a closet; the door to the bathroom is always flying open. The Murphy bed and a cupboard door that swings back and forth make palpable the frustrations of the marriage. The depersonalizing office exposes the disharmony between character and place on a grander scale. More than three decades later, Alexandre Trauner designs a similar office to convey alienation in the workplace for *The*

25. *Giant*: the house on the prairie

26. *The Crowd*: John (James Murray) and Mary (Eleanor Boardman), the unhappy couple, in their flat

27. *The Crowd*: the office

28. *The Apartment*: the office, C. C. Baxter (Jack Lemmon), the compliant worker

Apartment (fig. 28). A low ceiling, its overhead lights seemingly stretching to infinity, emphasizes crushing demoralization.[26]

With the exception of one set, the decor of *Kings Row* owes its claim to the punctuative category through the wealth of detail enhanced by lighting, cinematography, and staging. Selective illumination and deep shadows invest the components of the image with an aura of signification; depth-of-field staging puts actors in a dense physical context that foregrounds and highlights objects, furniture, and architectural features. The punctuation here is discreet, far less underscored than in *Mildred Pierce*, for example, or in *The Strange Love of Martha Ivers*. The makers of *Kings Row* far exceed the turn-of-the-century denotational requirements of the fiction without dwelling on either the picturesque or the outlandish.[27]

The sets of *Kings Row* provide a useful example of the depiction of class difference and the impact of class on character. Both *Kings Row* and *Our Town* (two of the seven collaborations between William Cameron Menzies and director Sam Wood) thematize the communities whose titles they bear. But where Thornton Wilder's "town" celebrates homogeneity in an idealized vision of loving connections among people, Henry Bellamann's Kings Row is a small city stratified by class distinctions, by fears and rivalries, by sexual desire and repression that surface in scenes of sadism and madness. The limited scope of Kings Row prohibits anonymity, promotes gossip, forces different social classes into contiguity. The result is the clash of opposing values. This topography charts the film's basic narrative premise. Following the opening credits we see a placard that reads

Kings Row 1890
A Good Town
A Good Clean Town
A Good Town to Live In
and a good town to
Raise Your Children.

These assertions stand in ironic opposition to much of the subsequent narrative.

The sharpest class conflicts are between (1) the upper middle class, represented by Dr. Gordon (Charles Coburn), his wife (Judith Anderson), and their daughter Louise (Nancy Coleman), and (2) Randy Monaghan (Ann Sheridan) and her working-class family. Their houses are, respectively, spacious and cramped, rounded gingerbread Victorian and linear functional (fig. 29, fig. 30). One has a grand, curving staircase, the other a short, straight, narrow one. The Gordons live on the good side of town, the Monaghans on the wrong side of the tracks, opposite the depot. The link between these two families and houses is Drake (Ronald Reagan), born to the upper middle class, a good-natured wastrel first in love with Louise, then with Randy.

The simple Monaghan kitchen is revealed well into the film, at a point of narrative crisis. Randy and Drake have argued, partly over class differences. Up to this point, Drake has not been allowed into the Monaghan house. He now bursts in to proclaim to Mr. Monaghan his intention to continue courting his daughter. Through Drake, the positive affect and honest working-class values of Randy's family, exemplified by their

29. *Kings Row*: the Gordon house, Drake (Ronald Reagan), Louise (Nancy Coleman), and Parris (Robert Cummings)

humble, utilitarian dwelling, are dramatically opposed to those of Dr. and Mrs. Gordon, vicious snobs who keep their daughter, Louise, a prisoner in their mansion. Drake wills his own imprisonment in an upstairs bedroom at the Monaghans' after the sadistic Dr. Gordon needlessly amputates his legs to punish him for his "wild" ways and attentions to Louise.

Kings Row is, in fact, the story of five houses, five sets, five sets of values. The decorative differentiation among the four prosperous ones is slight, but sufficient to allow the viewer to make sense of a heavily plotted best-seller squeezed into a 127-minute-long film. Of the four middle- to upper-class houses, the ostentatious Gordon's is the site of arrogance and bigotry. Drake's, the least sharply differentiated, furnishes a point of contrast between his initial bourgeois comfort and the world of the Monaghans into which he moves after losing his money and his legs.

Related more directly to Parris Mitchell (Robert Cummings), the film's principal protagonist, the two remaining houses are more highly narrativized. One is a place of madness and learning that leads to Parris's vocation as a psychiatrist. Here reside Cassie (Betty Field), her father Dr. Towers (Claude Rains), and her insane mother. Little Parris is one of the few guests at Cassie's birthday party; the gossipy, close-minded townspeople

30. *Kings Row*: the Monaghan house, Drake, Mr. Monaghan (Ernest Cossart), and Randy (Ann Sheridan)

have prevented their children from attending. Paris sees Mrs. Towers at the upstairs window. He enters the house to say good-bye to her, as he has been instructed by his beloved grandmother, and he is stopped by Dr. Towers. Parris's upbringing and good nature, later cultivated by his mentor, Dr. Towers, are connected to the dark, enclosed world of mental illness in this shot of a boy partway up the prohibited staircase. The house of Parris's grandmother, Madame Van Eln (Maria Ouspenskaya), is a place of love and high culture. Early in the film, when the boy Parris (Scotty Beckett) returns from school, he pauses in each window of the parlor to greet his grandmother and tell her how much he loves her— in French. In a later scene, Madame Van Eln speaks of her imminent death to her lawyer, Colonel Skeffington (Henry Davenport), and Dr. Gordon. The doors to the hall are opened, emphatically revealing the straight staircase that the old lady laboriously mounts with the help of her faithful maid. Colonel Skeffington says, "When she passes, how much passes with her. A whole way of life." That whole way of life is subsumed in the character and in the house whose articulations have been made to reflect both her and her values, values shared by the young woman, Elise (Kaaren Verne), who comes to live in the house later in the film.

In *Kings Row*, the theme of class distinction is corollary to the theme of maturation, literally depicted as we see Drake, Parris, Randy, and Cassie first as children, then as young adults. In order for complete maturity to be achieved (and class distinctions transcended, as for Randy and Drake), the narrative must be liberated from houses that, in this "good clean town," harbor insanity and a sadistic surgeon, houses whose inhabitants are prompt to condemn any infraction of the rigid code of behavior: Drake's flirtatiousness, Randy's free and easy ways. And Drake must be liberated from the trauma of losing his legs. Just before the conclusion, Parris quotes his grandmother to Drake: "Some people grow up and some just grow older."

The image of maturation is not a house but a means of passage, a stile. Invested with the most specific narrative purpose in the film, this structure bridges the wall between the road and the Van Eln nursery. We first see it near the beginning of the film, just after Parris and Cassie, as children, have gone swimming and have spoken of their affection for each other. Later, following the unhappy birthday party, at the stile Cassie tells Parris she will no longer be permitted to attend school. The daughter of an insane woman, menaced herself by "inherited" insanity, she will be tutored at home by her father. After she runs off in tears, Parris crosses the stile and we hear Erich Wolfgang Korngold's "Kings Row" theme, first muted, then stirringly repeated in the next shot, in which, at a slightly different angle, we see the feet and legs of the grown-up Parris crossing back over the stile.

Just before the end of the film, Parris cures Drake of his depression with the truth about Dr. Gordon's vindictive mutilation and a morale-boosting recitation of "Invictus." He runs down the slender stairs in the Monaghan house, through the railroad yard, then over the stile. An unseen chorus sings the Korngold theme to the words of the poem, and we see Parris racing toward Elise, toward the grandmother's house, in long shot. It is at the conclusion of *Kings Row* that the shape of this house, Parris's affective center, is fully disclosed.

In support of its thematic burdens, there are thus two orders of punctuative sets in *Kings Row*. The first comprises the houses. They indicate class and the degree to which class impinges on the narrative. The stile belongs to the second, pitched at a more aggressive degree of punctuation. Invented for the movies (there is a stile in the novel, but it bears no narrative weight), an element of decor that is specific to this film (everyone lives in a dwelling related to his/her economic situation, but not everyone crosses a stile), a structure of passage, it locates unforgettably, with considerable help from Korngold's fanfare, the coming of age of Parris Mitchell, in this fiction about coming of age.

At the level of denotation, the houses and paths of *Kings Row* show us a boy in a midwestern community in 1890; the public square of *Le Jour se lève* connects a French worker to his neighbors after the era of the Popular Front; the kitchen and living room of *Mildred Pierce* place a Los Angeles housewife in 1945. But when they function punctuatively, the sets for these films convey much more than where, when, and how their characters live. Their images give shape to the dramatic context that produces and explains the sensitivity of the future psychiatrist, Parris Mitchell, the confusion and despair of François, the ambitious mother love of Mildred. The Ivers mansion and its staircase not only mark Martha's social caste in two distinct temporal epochs; they configure her murderous rage. An oversized saloon announces Pearl Chavez's sexuality in *Duel in the Sun*; a marble bathroom expresses a specific brand of sexuality for Waldo Lydecker in *Laura*. A simple hallway becomes the site for a nation's celebration of homecoming in *The Best Years of Our Lives*. In these films, as in so much narrative cinema, we must read the punctuative sets as we do the emphatic articulations of any text.

Chapter 4

Set
as
Embellishment

"It's very important, when you do a job, even if it's a reasonably modest job, basically commercial, as they say, to find something at some point that makes it interesting, to perform an act of daring and skill. I can't work any other way."[1] The necessary and captivating *something* that Alexandre Trauner insists must occur *sometime* in the course of even the most routine assignment is read by the spectator as a moment of striking visual intervention. In fact, in those sequences of *Le Jour se lève*, *Hôtel du Nord*, and *Les Portes de la nuit*, discussed in the preceding chapter, in which Trauner displays the set designer's prowess (and power), decor goes a perceptibly aggressive step further in punctuating the narrative than it does where its function is simply, and from Trauner's point of view unsatisfactorily, denotative.

Trauner's celebrity as an art director hangs on this expressed determination: to push the terms of the designer's assignment as far as they need to go in order to meet and enhance the terms of the narrative. The sets of *Love in the Afternoon*, *The Nun's Story*, *The Apartment*, and *Irma la douce* are, according to our definition, like those of *Le Jour se lève*, *Hôtel du Nord*, and *Les Portes de la nuit*, essentially punctuative. For *Drôle de drame*, *Juliette ou la clé des songes*, *Land of the Pharoahs*, *Les Visiteurs du soir*, and *Les Enfants du paradis*, narratives in which history and fantasy distance the viewer from contemporary reality, Trauner's decors press further. Unwilling to serve the narrative as instrument of punctuation alone, they advance it through the sustained presence of embellishment.

Decor at the embellishing level of design intensity claims neither the transparency of the denotative level nor the translucence of the punctuative level. At this level, decor begins to take on the opacity that defines the final stages of our taxonomy. It calls upon powerful images that serve to organize the narrative; it exhibits an elevated level of rhetoric. Verisimilitudinous yet unfamiliar and intentionally arresting, embellishing sets insist on values that are highly determining; they oblige the spectator to read design as a specific

31. Les Visiteurs du soir: the walls of the castle

necessity of the narrative. Thus, to take one example, the opening sequence of *Les Visiteurs du soir* features an extended preparation for the liminal decor, the fortress in which the plot actually unfolds. We see the "Devil's Envoys" (the film's U.S. title) on horseback, traveling a considerable distance through a natural landscape before arriving at the "medieval" castle, astonishing not only for the elevation of its walls but for their luminosity (fig. 31). This bastion is, quite obviously, newly erected, at a long remove therefore from the viewer's own experience of ancient buildings observed directly or in photographic reproduction half a millennium and more after their construction. Through the artifice of resolute authenticity, the castle's shining ramparts emphasize the magic of cinema within the context of this specific narrative—replete, as the viewer will discover by and by, with tricks and transformations of all kinds. For *Les Enfants du paradis*, to take another example, Trauner designed what was then the most expensive French movie set ever built, the Boulevard of Crime, a theatre-lined avenue we observe teeming with activity at the opening and closing of the film (fig. 32).[2] In its magnitude and its accommodation of both public and theatrical space, the Boulevard of Crime captures the scope of a two-part, three-hour-and-fifteen-minute-long film in which actors who play on and off the stages that lie behind the facades are never far from their audiences, the citizens of Paris who circulate on this thoroughfare.

32. *Les Enfants du paradis*: the Boulevard of Crime

The medieval castle of *Les Visiteurs du soir* and the nineteenth-century urban boulevard of *Les Enfants du paradis* are emblematic of the calligraphic decor, one of two subsets of embellishment as we have defined it. *Land of the Pharaohs* serves as an example of the other, the colossal set. In *Land of the Pharaohs*, Trauner has the rare opportunity to perform the art director's "act of daring and skill" both on a grand scale and before the viewers' very eyes: he participates directly in the narrative by affecting to replicate the stages of the building of the pharaoh's tomb, from conception to completion, through the actual construction of the colossal set—in the fits and starts, the fragments and parts, dictated both by the standard exigencies of set assembly and by the eccentricities of this particular plot. And he has in the sympathetic character of Vashtar (James Robertson Justice), the master architect, an analog to himself, Trauner, the master art director. The narrative strategy that allows Trauner to show off his talent is further accentuated by the off-screen voice, an overlay limited to the scenes of construction, that offers the spectator a didactic commentary on the genius of architectural ingenuity the ancient Egyptians commissioned and bequeathed to future civilizations as one of the wonders of the world.

The calligraphic and the colossal will engage us in particular in this chapter. That the intensity of their design—the embellishment of their sets—is at the heart of the cinematic project is disclosed most immediately by their very designations: these are, in fact, genres that derive their names from their decor.

The Calligraphic Decor

We owe the introduction of the term *calligrafismo* into the cinematic lexicon to Giuseppe De Santis, the neo-realist film critic and director. De Santis aimed his elegant slur at that formalist tendency of Italian film production during late Fascism that favored highly decorated versions of history and myth and adaptations of late nineteenth- and early twentieth-century fiction. Among the best-remembered examples of this style are *Ettore fieramosca*, *La corona di ferro*, and *Un colpo di pistola* (fig. 33, fig. 34, fig. 35).[3] Similar denunciations were hurled at directors and art directors by the *Cahiers du Cinéma* critics and New Wave directors fifteen or so years later as they challenged a certain tendency of the French cinema, the "cinéma de qualité," known disparagingly as the "cinéma de papa."[4] For De Santis, the calligraphic film was generally historical in subject and designed in the knowledge and imitation of the history of art. We borrow *calligraphic*—rid of its pejorative connotation—to describe films belonging not only to Italian production in the late 1930s and early 1940s but to the American and European studio product that shares with De Santis's Italian illustration the triple inheritance of history, fiction, and the plastic arts. We choose for our examples a group of European and American period films of the 1930s: *Rembrandt*, *Fire over England*, *Conquest*, *Marie Antoinette*, and *La Kermesse héroïque*. The protagonists and many of the other characters that inhabit the first

33. *Ettore Fieramosca*: tomb

34. *La corona di ferro*: the bedchamber of the princess

35. *Un colpo di pistola*: interior

four fictions are historical figures. The narrativization of the putative events of their lives requires the reconstruction of an environment whose authenticity is not validated through the filmgoer's direct observation but refracted through his or her experience of art and architecture. The last, *La Kermesse héroïque*, has no biographical pretensions, yet no less essential to its narrative logic is the depiction of a Flanders familiar through its allegiance to the well-loved iconography of seventeenth-century painting.

Imitation of Art

Art directors have been clear in acknowledging their debt to painting, drawing, and print-making. The decors for *The Lower Depths*, Jean Renoir's film based on the play by Alexander Gorky, were, according to Eugene Lourié, inspired by Gustave Doré's etchings of mid-nineteenth-century London. Lourié's decision to base the film's design on Doré's model implied, of course, the decision to omit "ethnically Russian details." [5] In effect, the set designer rejected a faithful translation of his source's literary realism in favor of the affinity and resonance for his own subject he recognized in the illustrations of a fellow Frenchman and visual artist—however far removed Doré's images of London might be from the Volga town of the drama's actual setting. [6] *Porgy and Bess* provides another, more extreme example. For "Catfish Row," Oliver Smith sought inspiration in the seventeenth-century Flemish painters De Hooch and Vermeer and in the eighteenth-century Venetians Canaletto and Guardi, all of whose works are obviously at a significant temporal, spatial, and cultural distance from the film's own location: an African-American urban neighborhood in the South in the early twentieth century. "I tried to imagine how they would have painted Charleston if they had been there at the time Porgy roamed the streets in his goat cart," writes Smith of his European models. [7]

In the films that interest us here, *Rembrandt* and *La Kermesse héroïque*, set designers Vincent Korda and Lazare Meerson choose as their models paintings that serve not only as inspiration, as do Lourié and Smith, but as authentic sources of documentation; they cross the line that separates homage from quotation. Art imitates art in the highly embellishing sets of these period films. What better visual source for the recreation of the past than the representations of the masters who applied their talent to portraying their world and those that inhabited it, warts and all? And what better example than an artist whose work is not only recognized as undisputedly canonical by art historians but has immediate recognition value among a very wide public? Rembrandt van Rijn is the subject of the biographical film produced and directed by Alexander Korda in 1937.

In setting the story of Rembrandt's maturity and declining fortunes, Korda's decors imitate the paintings of the artist and of other Flemish contemporaries. The episode that triggers the peripeties of the plot is the unveiling of a work immediately identifiable as *The Night Watch*, a group portrait commissioned by the militia company of Captain Frans Banning Cocq. (fig. 36). The moment of disclosure provokes not the expression of admiration expected of the subjects, assembled friends, and relatives but their mounting laughter. Rembrandt is denounced by his furious patrons. Most, in fact, refuse to pay. After all, the painter had not kept his part of the bargain. He failed to execute a flattering

36. *Rembrandt*: the unveiling of *The Night Watch*

resemblance. The mirror the militia confronts at the portrait's unveiling reflects the artist's sense of the real; the members of the guard are prepared to recognize themselves only in the ideal.

It is precisely the pursuit and realization of this ideal that attracts us to Korda's sets in imitation of Rembrandt. The translation of time, of place, of mores, and the translation of medium, erase the warts intolerable to Cocq's city guard. The geometry of the chamber floor, its soaring dimensions, the diagonals that divide and deepen the frame: these represent to us the distant, secure, and comfortable world the Flemish painters have taught us to see—in perfect contrast of light and darkness, perfectly proportioned spaces, perfect compositions, perfectly decorated, calligraphically perfect.[8]

Two years earlier, in 1935, Lazare Meerson, who began his career as a painter, had designed Jacques Feyder's *La Kermesse héroïque*, the film that served Korda, no doubt, as a cinematic model for *Rembrandt*.[9] At moments (one thinks especially of the "typical" street scene that appears in both films, complete with canal and little bridge), the similarity of the decors is such that a casual viewer might conclude that the sets of *La Kermesse héroïque* had been reused for *Rembrandt* (fig. 37). A closer viewing makes clear that while Korda submits to Meerson's influence, plagiarizing a perspective here or a detail there, the sway that he allows Meerson to exert over his own style is, in fact, limited.[10] Unlike

37. *Rembrandt*: street and canal

Meerson, Korda does not appear to be particularly interested in breaking with the theatrical past. Nor is he interested in adopting new materials—iron, glass, cement, oil paint—that create a sense of true construction, promote the possibility of a multiplicity of textures, and support the illusion of surfaces and, above all, of spaces no longer new but well used, even worn.[11] Korda's Flanders, smooth, cool, pristine, imitates the compositions of the great masters; Meerson's Flanders, sometimes rough, often frayed, has the originality of a faithful translation.

Almost immediately *La Kermesse héroïque* became one of the canonical texts of set design, its decors among the few to attract critical attention. In Barsacq's copious allusions to the work of Meerson, he makes several points that have become commonplace in discussions of this film: (1) Meerson achieves a synthesis of the Flemish town on the restricted space of a studio sound stage; (2) thanks to the ingenious positioning of the camera, the angles of the shots are both interesting and varied; (3) the scaled height of the architectural elements of the model enhances the sense of perspective; and (4) the size of the houses is reduced with respect to life scale to facilitate framing.[12]

The episodes of *La Kermesse héroïque* unfold in essentially contiguous decors; they oscillate with predictable regularity between exteriors and interiors.[13] An occasional Dutch landscape and numerous crowded townscapes alternate with the domestic tableaux of genre painting: a child's bath, a woman polishing the silver. And among the interiors there is, of course, the ineluctable sitting for a young and talented painter, this time Jan Breughel at work on a group portrait of the city fathers—the burgomaster at the center of the council table and the standard bearer in the foreground. The conduct of the narrative corresponds to this oscillation: during the interior scenes, the characters dominate and the plot is advanced; during the exteriors, the decor dominates and transitions are effected. The stairs and balconies that lead to or overlook the streets are the interior/exterior stages upon which the crucial moments of the farce are played out: the exhortation of the townswomen to feminine arms by the burgomaster's wife (Françoise Rosay); the affectionate gaze of the more worldly older couple (Rosay and Jean Murat) on the young couple in love; the unmerited acclamation of the cowardly burgomaster (André Alerme) by the crowd gathered to celebrate the departure of the Spaniards, and the town's salvation—all barely one day after the terrifying announcement of the enemy's imminent arrival. If Meerson's facades are smaller than life, the rooms they hide are not only far bigger than these same facades can possibly accommodate but disproportionately large by seventeenth-century Dutch standards as we know them through painting. These are rooms that allow the characters to come to life and play out the narratives for which genre scenes are coded; they are also fitting platforms for the extraordinary actors accustomed to the stages of neo-classical French comedy, it too a glorious expression of the seventeenth century, to which Charles Spaak's diction, Feyder's direction, and the acting of Françoise Rosay and Louis Jouvet pay affectionate homage.[14]

In 1937, the year of Vincent and Alexander Korda's *Rembrandt*, Meerson was assigned another Korda production designed to exploit the narrative premises of history. *Fire over England* tells the story of the defeat of the Spanish Armada—and Spanish tyranny—by England's genius for liberty and justice and her queen's ingenious application of courage and ruse. The proud Philip II is represented by his somber, austere study. The film's major sets are those of the castle of the contrastingly humane Elizabeth I. Here, the past is rendered in decors that imitate not painting but book illustration. The textures of the palace walls, their tapestries, embossed columns, cavernous spaces molded by long shafts of light and often, as in *Rembrandt*, divided vertically in two, one side much deeper than the other: these recall the plates of an oversized history of the reign of Queen Elizabeth (fig. 38).[15] Both sets and narrative celebrate England's past glory on the eve of yet another European war.

Imitation of Archeology

The designs of *Rembrandt*, *La Kermesse héroïque*, and *Fire over England*, modeled on painting, drawing, and printmaking, are exceptions to the more common method of suggesting the historical past through the imitation of architecture and the decorative arts. The heads of the Hollywood art departments and major art directors had, like Meerson, seen for themselves the predominantly European originals they were imitating. Gibbons, for example, had toured extensively and is reported to have developed his taste for art deco in 1925 during a visit to the Paris Exposition Intérnationale des Arts Décoratifs et

38. *Fire over England*: castle interior, Queen Elizabeth (Flora Robson) and the young hero, Michael Ingolby (Laurence Olivier)

Industriels Modernes; Paramount's Hans Dreier was German; Warners' Anton Grot was Polish. Above all, the studio art departments had at their disposal the lavish resources of the research departments, the photographs provided by traveling research teams, and the illustrated texts available in the voluminous libraries of M-G-M, Warner Bros., and Paramount.[16]

The pursuit of archeological accuracy did not, however, triumph at every turn nor at any cost. The ultimate purpose of pleasing the audience—and selling tickets—was bound to prevail where it needed to. So, for example, in *Conquest*, a 1938 M-G-M production and the most expensive film made that year, the ambition to achieve the faithful reproduction of early nineteenth-century interiors fell, at a crucial moment in the narrative, to the irresistible appeal of the "big white set." The opening sequence; the entrance of the galloping cossacks into the salon of the Polish nobleman's palace; the set of the Castle of Finkenstein in East Prussia, of the Parisian *hôtel particulier* in the rue du Houssaye, of the Schönbrunn Palace in Vienna: all accede to historical restraint. But for the ultimately romantic moment of the presentation of the young and ardent Maria Waleska (Greta Garbo) to the conquering Napoleon (Charles Boyer), history gives way to narrative and spectacle. According to Hambley and Downing, this scene represents the best example of "the dichotomy between Gibbons' insistence on both the authentic and the

glossily antiseptic. . . . The film is full of perfect details and convincing sets for the Na-
poleonic court, with the exception of one great ballroom which is wonderfully but anach-
ronistically executed all in sparkling white. Thalberg was right. The audiences loved it."[17]

The importance of research to art direction finds its extreme example in the massive documentation that supported the design of *Marie Antoinette*, the second most expensive film of that year. M-G-M's publicity department claimed that eleven thousand
photographs had been sent from Versailles to Hollywood. These were adjunct to a collection of twenty-five hundred books, drawings, and other visual materials assembled specifically to assist the designers and craftspeople in conceiving the film's ninety-eight sets.
However swollen these numbers may have been by publicity department exaggeration,
the research effort was clearly impressive. In addition, M-G-M purchased numerous
eighteenth-century furnishings in a three-month French buying spree that "resulted in
the largest consignment of antiques ever received in Los Angeles."[18] What could not be
bought was duplicated in the studio shops.[19] Whole rooms from Versailles were re-
created, often with considerable and quite conscious license: the double grand staircase
(known as the Ambassador's Staircase) that appears in the film had been demolished in
1752; the ballroom, which never existed at Versailles, is an attempt to evoke the Hall of
Mirrors; and the chapel recalls Fontainebleau, not Versailles.[20] Preston Ames's retelling
of Gibbon's explanation for the redesign of Versailles reconciles the claims of authenticity
with those of dramatic license:

> A great many architects came to Metro to see our sets and congratulated
> Cedric Gibbons on his authentic reproduction of French Renaissance
> architecture, with particular emphasis on what he did with Versailles.
> Mr. Gibbons looked at these gentlemen and said, "If you will study very
> carefully what we did, you'll see we did everything except copy the archi-
> tecture of Versailles, because if we had, photographically it would have
> been absolutely nothing. The molding and design are so delicate, so sen-
> sitive, they would never come across on the screen. So consequently, we
> had to redesign the entire thing so it would photograph properly!"[21]

In the end, the *Hollywood Spectator* displayed the following headline: "Marie Antoinette
Too Long; Cedric Gibbons Its Hero."[22]

In fact, Cedric Gibbons and his art department are not the heroes of *Marie Antoinette*, a conventional narrative that succeeds in its primary purpose: to serve as a star
vehicle for Norma Shearer and to engage viewers in the fate of the doomed queen she
plays. The calligraphic embellishments may provide a spectacular context for *Marie Antoinette*, but they contribute little to its specific articulations.[23] Clearly, the portrayal of
the palace of Versailles is suited to the heroine's station; it displays the extravagance that
brought an oppressed people to revolt. Nonetheless, its elements function at a low narrative level. The decor inflects character, plot, or mood only occasionally: a mirror reflects
a bed that the royal couple fails to occupy on Marie's wedding night; an exceptionally
wide staircase is available to her as she makes a rapturous diagonal descent toward the
lover (Tyrone Power) waiting in the garden. But these are relatively insignificant touches

in a visual scheme whose main purpose is to persuade viewers, in the most general way, that they are beholding an adequate representation of late eighteenth-century court life in France. In fact, the oversized gowns and wigs of *Marie Antoinette* make the case for opulence at least as forcefully as do its numerous richly decorated sets.[24] Intended to strike the spectator with awe, ostentation in the guise of authenticity is a major calligraphic charge of Hollywood decor and costumes. At M-G-M, it was applied liberally.[25]

Imitation of Modern Architecture

The films we discuss above are narratives about times and places distant from the experience of the spectator. That distance—temporal, spatial, or more often both—generates an opacity that is translated by the viewer as high style. High style, however, does not necessarily depend on the temporal or spatial remove of the narrative; it can just as well accompany a setting that is both local and contemporary. In these cases, it is distance of class that most often produces the desired rhetorical effect. High style, after all, is the habit and taste of high society—no less calligraphic for its modernity and almost as remote from the quotidian of the spectator as a Renaissance throne room or a Louis XVI salon. Breeding or position paired with wealth find themselves as comfortably at home in the elegance of a modernist apartment as they do in the splendor of ancient palaces.[26]

Two settings most often the object of the calligraphic moderne are the apartment of the kept or otherwise spoiled woman and the office of the corporate magnate. *Susan Lenox (Her Fall and Rise)* provides an example of the first. At the moment of her social and financial apogee (whose moral equivalent is, of course, the depth of her "fall"), the heroine (Greta Garbo) is framed in an urban residence of sensational modernist design.[27] *The Big Clock* provides an example of the second. Capitalism is represented here by the headquarters of Jannoth Publications, whose New York office recalls Rockefeller Center's RCA Building, complete with statue of Atlas in the lobby. The big clock itself, the elevator, the boardroom, the office of the firm's chief executive (Charles Laughton): these form a modernist maze wonderfully suited to the unusual white-collar chase that precedes the denouement. But the paradigmatic example of the calligraphic moderne is, of course, *The Fountainhead*. It features among its several defining sets the apartment of the world-weary woman and the office of the powerful entrepreneur.

The Fountainhead is, in fact, a narrative about the politics of modernism in architecture. In the transposition from novel to film, art direction becomes a primary function of the narrative. Embellished by their imitation and defense of the high style and the inspiration they draw from the works of Frank Lloyd Wright, the film's decors are the calligraphic sites and symbols around which that narrative is organized.[28] The terms of the architectural debate, articulated early on by Howard Roark (Gary Cooper), the film's hero, are lodged immediately and firmly in the antitheses that define the larger ideological controversy: genius vs. mediocrity, creator vs. parasite, the individual vs. the collective, freedom vs. slavery, and, ultimately, good vs. evil. In representing the positions that define competing discourses on architecture, in pitting the inspired expression of truth and beauty understood only by the happy few against the vulgar standard pleasing to the crowd, the film's decor, comprising both miniatures and constructed sets, conveys powerful and conflicting political and social messages. It also aspires to the civic education of the masses, the moviegoing public, through the cultivation of public taste for the avant-garde.

As they illustrate the discourse on architecture, the miniatures, in fact architectural models, serve as crucibles for the development of character and plot. All the players of *The Fountainhead*—heroes, heroines, and villains—are defined in relation to the debate surrounding architecture. The relationships between and among them, including the passion that binds Roark and Dominique Francon (Patricia Neal), hang on their association with that debate and the miniatures that represent it. The characters live, work, love, argue, die. Architecture, manifest as model, is, in *The Fountainhead*, a matter of life or death. It is, therefore, not surprising that the narrative premises of the film are often implausible: a crusade against the purely modernist lines of the Enright House launched by a daily newspaper (the *New York Banner*, "The Newspaper for the People") is responsible for the phenomenal increase in the paper's sales; the reversal of the *Banner*'s editorial position on the absolute right of the artist to the integrity of his work accounts for the sudden decline of its publisher's fortunes; a fascistic architectural critic, Ellsworth M. Toohey (Robert Douglas), posing as a populist, plots the destruction of the American way and prepares his own ascent to power through the manipulation of the dispute that opposes modernism to tradition; and, above all, the uncompromising vision of a single artist figures as a determining force in the political and social life of a modern metropolis.

But norms of narrative probability are not at issue when applied either to the principal plot (the progress of Roark's career) or to the subplot (the love affair between Roark and Dominque). At issue are the film's sets as representations of the idea that determines both the career and the love affair. The Enright House, Roark's first major commission, the Cortlandt Houses that provoke the narrative crisis, the Wynand Building that provides both the work narrative and the love narrative with a triumphant climax: these projects and images punctuate and define the plot. The development of the narrative follows their development as projects. Each begins as an architectural drawing; the rendering becomes an architectural model; this same model, or cinematic miniature, finally poses as the completed structure itself. The narrative serves as a gloss to the evolution, from concept to construction, of what finally photographs as a building. So do the lengthy speeches and verbal confrontations on architecture, in particular, and the individual and society, in general, that mark the film's dialogue. The decor renders the architectural debate visible; the debate determines the course of the plot. The visual and verbal opposition of innovation and tradition, radicalism and conservativism, purity and corruption, ends with a defense of the rights of modern architecture to exist (like the individual) for its own sake.

The plaster miniatures are the most direct representation of the terms of the debate, as the addition of a classical pediment to Roark's model for the Security Bank of Manhattan demonstrates most clearly. The sets of offices and residences constitute a more indirect representation of the controversy: Wynand's office and home, Dominique's apartment, her father's country house, Roark's apartment and later his office, to name

39. *The Fountainhead*: Roark (Gary Cooper) shows his plans and model of the Security Bank

only a few. The sets are no less defining than the miniatures. For one thing, the offices are defined through their position on high floors of very tall buildings; their enormous windows look down on the skyscrapers that, for the most part, Roark detests, those that play at being Greek temples or Gothic cathedrals. Sets and miniatures become interchangeable during the presentation of Roark's plans for the headquarters of the Security Bank. As the scene opens, we see a skyscraper of extreme simplicity, taller than the buildings behind it, framed by two other even taller buildings. The camera tracks back as Roark enters the frame, and we are made aware that the skyscraper at the center is actually a model placed on a table in front of a large window (fig. 39). The two framing skyscrapers are then understood as the buildings outside, even though we know, of course, that they are models as well. We have, for a moment, taken the architectural model for the set, which, model or not, the conventions of cinema demand that we accept as real.

How conscious the film's director was of the importance of the decor to the narrative is reflected in King Vidor's shooting script for *The Fountainhead*. The script includes that rare annotation "Notes about the Set," followed by the subheading "Roark's Psychology, and Suggestions."

It is *extremely important* that Roark's room be kept completely in character with him. He is quite poor at this time. He knows that whatever money he got for the Enright House will have to last him for a long time, and he is not the type of man who would waste money on personal luxuries. Also, he is too great an artist ever to want any second-rate junk around him. Therefore, his room must be extremely, startlingly simple. It is not the simplicity of squalid poverty, but the simplicity of deliberate intention. The room must be large, with a feeling of space and with an absolute minimum of furniture. He would want his home to be as functional as his buildings. He would have only the things he needs and nothing else. He would never make attempts at homey comfort or prettifying. *Above all*, there must not be any pictures on the walls. The walls must be bare. There must be one large window, a couch, a drafting table, a few chairs, a dresser, a wooden filing cabinet for his drawings—and that is all. No curtains, no rugs, no boudoir pillows, no *books*, no fancy lamps or ash trays and, for the love of God, no vases of knick-knacks. The furniture must be modern and very simple—the kind of good, but inexpensive modern that one finds sometimes in New York. An impression of beauty can be achieved by the proportions and the relations of the objects in the room. The effect of the room must be the same as the effect of Roark's character: direct, stark, purposeful, austere. Since the love scene is to be played in evening clothes, its effect—against the simplicity of a room that looks ascetic like a monk's cell—will be most startling.[29]

The room we see corresponds closely to the notes, although far less of it is made in the seeing than in the telling (fig. 40). Roark's apartment is displayed with no particular insistence. The walls are not bare as the notes prescribe; they are hung with architectural drawings, among them, prominently displayed, a rendering of the Enright House. The love scene is photographed mostly in two-shot against a portentous view of skyscrapers that recalls, so that we do not miss the point, the film's numerous office sets. The principles that apply to work apply to sex. The two strands of the narrative, work and love, and the two genres of decor, architectural model and set, converge once again.

Colossal

Carthage and Babylon

Gigantic sets, the sweep of history, grandiose if not grandiloquent diction and gestures, all in one film on one immense screen—that was *Intolerance*. But before there was *Intolerance* there was *Cabiria*, the most famous of the Italian silent epics, the acknowledged ancestor of the colossal set and, more generally, of the constructed decor. *Cabiria* was conceived, produced, and directed by Giuseppe Pastrone. With *Cabiria*, the constructed set emerged completely developed and demanding to be imitated.[30] By 1913, art direction had broken free of the traditions of easel painting and the theatrical drop, in fact of all two-dimensional forms. The illusion of the third dimension was conquered and here to stay.

40. *The Fountainhead*: Roark's apartment, Dominique (Patricia Neal) and Roark

The set that assured *Cabiria*'s commercial success and, to a large extent, its en-
during reputation is the prodigious Temple of Moloch and particularly its monstrous
exterior (fig. 41). A monumental image of the fearsome divinity itself, the facade of the
temple is terrifyingly anthropomorphic: an immense sculpted head warns of the horrors
that are staged within. Out of one of Moloch's three eyes and down the fingers of his
clenched fist runs the gentle giant Maciste carrying little Cabiria, saved from the fires that
burn in the deity's belly, flames fed by the perpetual sacrifice of little children. Within the
temple, crowds of extras fill a deep and complex space as they adore the ravenous, vora-
cious, and pitiless god. It is the third century B.C., and we are in North Africa; the Punic
Wars rage.

Pastrone was determined that the studio-built walls of Cirta, the palace of Queen
Sophonisba, and, above all, the Temple of Moloch contend effortlessly with the effect of
the natural real he would entrust only to nature herself: the waters of the Mediterranean,
the sands of Tunis, the Alpine snows. Thus, no papier-mâché structures, no wrinkled
backdrops, no trompe-l'oeil painted decor would do. The temple's facade, the city's
walls, the palace's rooms would be replicas constructed in materials designed to withstand
the play of the narrative. The facade would be the site of the pursuit of Maciste by the
faithful of the sacred temple he had defiled; the walls would be scaled by the enlightened

41. *Cabiria*: the temple of Moloch

forces of sweet Roman reason and charity; the Alps would be crossed by the diagonal march of the armies of Hannibal, complete with elephants, visible both in the foreground and in the distance across a screen large enough to accommodate Pastrone's panoramic vision. The cost would be made up in the box-office receipts—and it was.

The pull to imitate commercial success aside, how can we explain the influence of Italian cinema on other European production and, especially, on American set design and construction? *Cabiria* was not the first spectacular film to prosper in the international market. In fact, the thriving pre–World War I Italian film industry (in 1914, Italy had approximately fifty production companies, twelve in Turin alone) specialized in historical extravangazas. Barsacq suggests that we look for an answer to (1) the contributions of architects, "who replaced stage designers and scene painters," and (2) "the large-scale use of decorative sculpture and staff techniques, both specialties of the talented Italian craftsmen."[31] We know that with the outbreak of the war in Europe, many of these crafts-persons made their way to the United States and some eventually to Hollywood.[32] How can we take the measure of the direct contribution of immigrant cinema workers to the Hollywood studio art departments? Our answer is offered not by scholarship but by the intuition of informed and sympathetic narrative invention.

Good Morning, Babylon is the affectionate homage paid by Paolo and Vittorio Taviani (themselves heirs to both the Italian historical and realist traditions) to the odyssey of transplanted Italian artists and artisans and to their contributions to American silent cinema. Behind the credits of *Good Morning, Babylon* we see a pastel wall, then the facade of a Romanesque cathedral as the tarp that had covered it during repair is removed. Two workmen are seen crouching in one of the squares of the facade. Nicola and Andrea are the youngest of the seven sons of Bonanno Bonanni, master restorer of Tuscan churches and descendant of the stonemasons who had built them originally. They are putting the last touches on a relief of a standing elephant. Until several minutes into the film we are unsure whether we are looking at a set or at the facade of an actual cathedral.

Soon after, Nicola and Andrea emigrate to America. In the course of a horrifying journey across the continent, they meet up with a train that carries Italian artisans, builders, and laborers to San Francisco to work on the construction of the Italian Pavilion at the Panama-Pacific Exposition. Enter D. W. Griffith to attend a showing of *Cabiria*. He watches the film twice, the second time alone in the theatre, then dictates a congratulatory telegram to Pastrone—which he decides not to send. His response, he resolves, will be *Intolerance*, a film even more ambitious than that of his Italian rival. To a reporter's question about what he had found most impressive about *Cabiria*, the celebrated director replies: the black elephant. No wonder, then, that the Bonannos are commissioned to draw the sketches for Griffith's elephants, a double tier, the first on pedestals, the second on columns, destined to frame the titanic court of Belshazzar.

But despite Griffith's direct order, Nicola and Andrea, caught in the web of Hollywood envy, are thwarted in their efforts by the head of the art department. In a desperate ploy to attract attention, they build an oversized replica of the standing elephant that filled the niche of their beloved cathedral. When the model is set on fire by jealous studio arsonists, set design itself becomes the focus of the action. The sculpture is the point on which the narrative turns, the motif of the American success story, the emblem of a classic rags-to-riches narrative about immigrants in the great land of opportunity. At the premiere of *Intolerance*, Bonanno's sons, stonecutters and set builders, participate in the happy ending by doing what no set designer has ever been permitted to do: share the spotlight with the director and actors (fig. 42).

What influence *Cabiria* had on Griffith is a matter of debate.[33] Griffith did not see the film at the San Francisco exposition, alas. However, according to Joseph Henabery, actor and assistant director on *Intolerance*, he knew of the skillful manipulation of plaster of Paris by the Italian craftspersons who had worked on the exposition's replica of the Doge's Palace and had even lured two of them to the studio to develop what was unknown until then: a plaster workshop, which produced, among other statuary, the lions and elephants of *Intolerance*.[34] Griffith may well have seen *Cabiria* in a theatre in New York or in Chicago; it ran for months on end during the course of 1914. The story that he secured a print of the film and screened it again and again in secret is in all likelihood apocryphal. And suggestions that Griffith borrowed from *Cabiria* innovations such as the close-up, the traveling shot, the pan, or intercutting are belied by the evidence of these techniques in the work of other Griffith precursors and in Griffith's own early work.[35] Griffith's debt to Pastrone may finally be limited to a shared attitude toward the role of colossal decor within the narrative. The most compelling connection between the two masters of spectacle may be a common understanding of the function of the embel-

42. *Good Morning, Babylon*: the set for Belshazzar's court in *Intolerance*

lishing set. In fact, it is through the embellishment of the massive architectonic space of Belshazzar's court that the parable on pre-Christian intolerance establishes its affinity with *Cabiria*—even if, in the end, through the towering crane shots that repeatedly embrace the whole of the gigantic set, Carthage is dwarfed by Babylon (fig. 43).[36] The affinity remains nonetheless and is most persuasively, if most poetically, established in the Taviani representation. After all, does it really matter that none of the several elephants in *Cabiria*, live or plaster, is black?[37]

The Gate, the Arena, and the Forum

Mammoth doors serve as entrances and exits to Babylon's immense fortifications. One of these is the gate left open for Cyrus by the villainous priests of an unfashionable and vengeful idol. Through their treachery, the Persian armies penetrate the ramparts of Babylon, and Bel defeats Ishtar, the popular goddess of love. Early on, the silent screen had produced the biggest and best set of its kind; the gates of *Intolerance* would not easily be outdone.

Seven years later, in 1923, Cecil B. De Mille tried his hand at gigantic ancient bastions in the color prologue to *The Ten Commandments*. This time, through the doors of the city of Ramses II, the tribes of Israel, set free at last, pour forth in a great and dusty multitude of men, women, children, and animals preparing to be led by Moses across the wilderness to the promised land. The gate is lined by an avenue of twenty-four sphinxes and four colossi of the pharaoh, a processional space whose size takes the measure of the

43. *Intolerance*: Belshazzar's court

hordes that form the Exodus. That same gate and avenue provide the frame for the departure of Ramses and his equestrian army in pursuit of the Israelites to the Red Sea.
Thirty-three years later, as De Mille prepared his second *The Ten Commandments*, he
replicated the set of the 1923 version, in both scale and composition (fig. 44). That
De Mille maintained the design of the gate and avenue bears intertextual witness to a
movie pioneer's pride. So great was the original achievement that the advantage of three
decades of technological progress could not top it; the formidable constructed set of the
early 1920s is as extravagant as any to which a mid-1950s extravaganza could aspire. Most
elements of cinema—sound, color, lighting, special effects, and, in this case, certainly
plot—were refined if not transformed in the decades that separate the first from the second of De Mille's *The Ten Commandments*. But the colossal set can do no better, we are
to understand, than pay boastful homage to the past by repeating it.[38]

For the Circus Maximus of the 1959 *Ben-Hur*, the art directors of M-G-M are
similarly indebted to the example created by their 1925 predecessors (fig. 45, fig. 46).
Both sets dwarf horses and drivers with gigantic statues of crouching figures in the center
of the arena. In the first, four tall columns draw overpowering vertical lines; suited to the
wide-screen ratio of the second, the context of surrounding hills stresses the horizontal
plane. *Ben-Hur*'s arena focuses the narrative conflict between Judah and Messala in a

44. *The Ten Commandments* (1956): the gates of Ramses' city, the Exodus

45. *Ben-Hur* (1925): the Circus Maximus

46. *Ben-Hur* (1959): the Circus Maximus

chariot race to the death before the assembled populace. The decor lends its prodigious dimensions to the opposition of a Roman and a Jew; their enmity, born near the start of the films and nourished through their considerable durations, fills the huge decor. The most significant measure of these spectacles is, of course, sheer size. The audience in the movie theatre is thrilled to be included in the far larger audience that witnesses the event.[39]

The stakes are higher in other "arena" films, *Fabiola* and *Quo Vadis?*, for example, where no less than Christianity and the Roman Empire are pitted against each other. *Fabiola*, a post–World War II Italian superproduction dedicated to "the offended, the persecuted, the victims of all violence," ends when, after martyred Christians suffer horrible torture, the gladiators, refusing to fight, throw down their swords, and the spectators joyously celebrate the triumph of the new faith by climbing the barricades erected in the middle of the arena (fig. 47).[40] The initial narrative premise of *Quo Vadis?* is the historical one: that the people of Rome require spectacle. The capricious Nero (Peter Ustinov) is alternately exhibitionistic and loath to appear before the rabble. During the triumphant return of the Roman legions, the city, its people, and its emperor are on display in a huge public space in front of the palace (fig. 48). Here, Nero on a balcony is the object of spectatorial gaze before the audience that is all of Rome. At the conclusion of *Quo Vadis?*, the Colosseum collects the film's narrative threads in the confines of its arena and on the tiers and terraces that accommodate the populace and its mad emperor (fig. 49). The private and the public intersect: Poppaea's (Patricia Laffan) desire for revenge against Marcus (Robert Taylor), the man who spurned her; Marcus's anguish over the plight of Lygia (Deborah Kerr), the Christian he loves; the celebration of Christ's power through the pronouncement of Peter (Finlay Currie) and the martyrs' song-filled acceptance of death; the centurions' revolt against Nero. Here, as decor locates the nexus of private concerns during public events, it participates in the creation of narrative intensity.

47. *Fabiola*: the arena

48. *Quo Vadis?*: the public square in front of Nero's palace

49. *Quo Vadis?*: Nero (Peter Ustinov) in the Colosseum

In *The Fall of the Roman Empire*, the fate of Rome itself is decided, appropriately enough, at its urban center, the forum. After long sequences played in a rough fortress on the snow-covered German frontier, the immense agora appears in a burst of sunlight and architectural detail. The size and complexity of the decor mark not only the end of an emperor's reign but the field for the chaos and confusion that, as the narrator tells us, signal the beginning of the fall of the Roman Empire (fig. 50). In this place of civic display, we see a funeral pyre intended for the sacrifice of Emperor Comodus's sister, Lucilla (Sophia Loren), and his rival, Livius (Stephen Boyd), and the eventual burning of a host of barbarians. In thrall to his own power, Comodus (Christopher Plummer) emerges from the sculpture of a gigantic hand. The forum and the arena intersect when Comodus and Livius fight to the death in a ring delimited by upraised shields; the victorious Livius walks off with Lucilla, and the corrupt senators begin to bargain over the now vacant throne. As the camera pulls back to disclose the expanse of the forum, the trajectories of personal and political histories are, once again, collected in a vast public space. Here, as in colossal film in general, the viewer's response to the embellishing set is shaped by the cachet of antiquity. The movies have the power to raise the ruins, columns, statues, and stadiums not only to astound us but to authorize and validate fictions about peoples, the despots who oppress them, and the prophets they look to for salvation.[41]

Finally, the decor of *Caesar and Cleopatra* is exemplary of both subsets of embellishment—the calligraphic and the colossal. This film version of George Bernard Shaw's

50. *The Fall of the Roman Empire*: the forum

play was conceived as a hefty calling card for the British film industry within the international market. Producers J. Arthur Rank and Gabriel Pascal were, in fact, criticized for embarking on so costly a project during parlous times. As one reviewer saw it, "The wasteful extravagance attending its making is a byword in film circles. . . . In these austerity days, such prodigal and largely needless spending is hard to excuse."[42] Shooting began six days after D-Day and continued through frequent bombardments; materials were extremely scarce.[43] Yet the art direction gives no evidence of these constraints. The largest interior set, the ancient palace of Memphis, with columns nineteen feet in diameter weighing two tons each, wound up occupying more than twenty-eight thousand square feet of floor space (fig. 51).[44] Its grandeur is indeed apt for the scene in which Caesar teaches the timorous Cleopatra a lesson in power. Shaw's subject is, after all, her political education. The colossal is implicit in the very names of the protagonists; the narrative that links their epic destinies demands decors built to scale.

But what of the playwright's film text? His scenario and dialogue adhere closely to the text of his drama. As in Shaw generally, the dialogue is the medium charged, above others, with conveying the author's intentions. Theatrical image and action serve words meant to be savored. In De Mille's *Cleopatra*, on the other hand, it is the visual (in

51. *Caesar and Cleopatra*: Caesar (Claude Rains) and Cleopatra (Vivien Leigh) in the palace of Memphis

particular, the barge at Tarsus), not the verbal, that we relish, Claudette Colbert's expert delivery notwithstanding. And if, unlike the screenplay Waldemar Young and Vincent Lawrence wrote for De Mille, much of Joseph Mankiewicz's script for his *Cleopatra* aspires to be Shavian, its most memorable conceit is Elizabeth Taylor's wink, the centerpiece of a colossal Roman procession. Of course, all three Cleopatra films boast monumental palaces and public spaces and, to varying degrees, other aspects of embellishment proper to the re-creation of antiquity—decorative and architectural flourishes that generate the pleasure of the calligraphic. But in Shaw's *Caesar and Cleopatra*, decor has the distinction of complementing witty dialogue with the wit of calligraphy. The mixture of Roman, Greek, and Egyptian visual motifs is a playful comment on the narrative's cultural matrix, redolent of the tensions between the Roman Caesar and the Greek-Egyptian Cleopatra, as evident, for example, in the shooting script's description of Cleopatra's Alexandria music room: "The walls are covered with delicate murals. Slender pillars round the walls, Greek with Pompeian detail in the Capitals. There is a decorative pool in the centre." The "cozy" sphinx where Cleopatra first meets Caesar ("a dear little kitten of the [Giant] Sphinx"); the enormous palace of Memphis where the Roman general tests her mettle; the Alexandrian palace, a hybrid of Mediterranean cultures, whose roof garden is by turns luxurious and threatening; the quayside where she bids farewell to Caesar, a colossal public space meant to vaunt the puissance of rulers: these are the decors that chart Cleopatra's progress from impressionable girl to flirtatious, imperious, and dangerous queen.

Catastrophe

We have contended that the set embellishes the narrative both through the intertextual system of reference we have defined as calligraphic and through its power to intervene as a figure for the colossal. This intervention is nowhere more conspicuous than in the diegetic destruction of the colossal set. Although destruction is nearly always the narrative crux of the disaster film, not all disaster films exhibit highly narrativized sets. The more widespread the catastrophe, the less likely it is to be associated with a single memorable structure or even a cluster of structures. So many fissures open the pavements of *San Francisco*, so much rubble falls, that one set cannot possibly convey the total impression of the earthquake. The same is true of the conflagration that concludes *In Old Chicago*. On the other hand, a sure way to foreground the narrative function of the set is to destroy it. This is the destiny of colossal decor in those films in which an identifiable structure contains, wounds, and kills a sufficient number of victims to proclaim its generic status as a site of catastrophe.

Taking their cue from Cecil B. De Mille, who specialized in relating spectacularly violent cautionary tales from the distant past to melodramatic scenes of twentieth-century sin and redemption, Warner Bros. produced *Noah's Ark*.[45] Here, the great flood was an end-of-the-world warning inserted into a World War I narrative. The filmmakers could safely assume audience familiarity with the ark and the animals, as well as spectator curiosity about Hollywood's representation of traditional illustrated Bible stories. Freely transforming one of Noah's sons, Japtheth (George Bancroft), into a hero blinded and chained to a mill wheel, the script focuses the tempest and flood on his miraculous rescue of the beloved Miriam (Dolores Costello) from drowning in the temple of the false god, Jaghuth (fig. 52). Prior to its collapse, the temple as decor is exploited as the site of Miriam's near sacrifice. The cataclysm that engulfs city and populace is concentrated within the temple (and thus within the narrative); the power of the flood can be measured by its destruction of tall pillars and the god's gigantic statue.[46]

De Mille took the Bible as his source for another fiction of a blind hero who topples a temple. Publicity for *Samson and Delilah* conspired with widespread knowledge of the sacred text to prime the audience for both the structure and the feat. The image of an idol—Dagon, the god of the Philistines—appears on the screen even before the film's credits. Soon after, we see the Earth revolving in swirling clouds and struck by lightning, more pagan devil gods, and the reappearance of Dagon at the end. Accompanying this cosmographical/anthropological sequence is producer-director De Mille's own voice-of-God, a sound well known to those many members of the movie audience who heard it every Monday night as he introduced the Lux Radio Theatre. As is his custom, De Mille authorizes this spectacle by calling upon the big issues: the devil god signals the oppression of one people over another; Samson personifies the desire for freedom that burns in the human heart.

Although *Samson and Delilah* is definitely a spectacle film, prior to the final sequence its decor is not particularly spectacular. Colorful fabrics rather than extraordinary structures accent the sets. During these scenes, expectation of the culminating disaster is

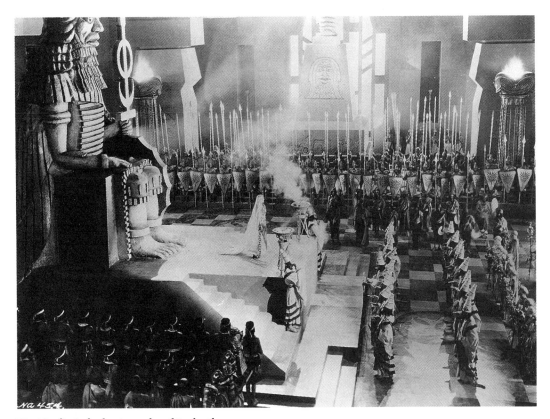

52. *Noah's Ark*: the temple of Jaghuth

meant to sustain interest. Yes, the audience is treated to images that exploit the famous bodies of the film's stars (Victor Mature and Hedy Lamarr), as well as several moments of violent action (Samson slaughtering lions with his bare hands and Philistine soldiers with the jawbone of an ass). Along the way, however, there is not much narrative tension. The film's conclusion, sixteen and a half minutes long, brings together the oppressing Philistines and the oppressed hero, a Jew whose deity finally restores his strength that he may smash the false Dagon (fig. 53). Samson's agony and faith, the jeering Philistines, and Delilah's love (an improvement on the Book of Judges?) are all on view in the temple, and all resolved by its destruction. But this noisy and visually arresting finale is a triumph not of narrative closure but of production values. The true heroes are the art and special effects departments who provide sensational renderings of the temple, the mammoth statue of Dagon, and the catastrophic end.[47] Here decor, embellishing not only through its exotic design but especially through its protracted collapse, is the principal actor.

The Bible, it turns out, has no monopoly on colossal catastrophe. *The Poseidon Adventure* and *The Towering Inferno*, to take two examples, are fictions set in the twentieth century. And distinct from biblical films, where disaster is punctual and conclusive, the sinking of the ocean liner and the conflagration of the skyscraper nearly fill the durations of their respective narratives. We see the exterior of the *Poseidon* only briefly before it is capsized by a tidal wave, first beneath the credits and several times again during the

53. *Samson and Delilah*: the temple of Dagon

opening sequences. More important than the integral shape of the ship are its cabins, decks, and public rooms, since it is they that acquire narrative value—principally by being turned upside down (fig. 54). This extraordinary defamiliarization is manifest especially in the first-class dining saloon, festooned for a New Year's Eve party and filled with passengers.[48] The set slowly rotates onto its back: people hang from tables and fall *down* into the glass-paneled ceiling; a priest (Gene Hackman) exhorts the others to climb *up* to the bottom of the ship; an explosion inundates the room with water, drowning all but the few who heed his urging. This scene propels the rest of the narrative: the passage of a small band of people, some of whom perish, through topsy-turvy, perilous decors, through obstacles that include stairs reversed, jammed doors, and flooded corridors. The overturned luxury liner is a colossally disorienting and threatening maze.

To the grand-scale disaster of *The Poseidon Adventure*, *The Towering Inferno* adds a number of calligraphic visual gestures.[49] The fiction is subsumed by a skyscraper, the last word in design. The scenic helicopter ride that opens the film has the sole purpose of providing views of the new building that dominates San Francisco's skyline. This is a calligraphic event: the presentation of architecture as an object of visual pleasure. People on the street below look up and gape at its height; its ruin, its de(con)struction, constitutes catastrophe on a colossal scale.

54. *The Poseidon Adventure*: the overturned dining saloon

Although much of *The Towering Inferno* takes place in the building's rooms, hall-ways, and staircases, the camera repeatedly cuts to its distinctive profile, with various areas ablaze on its surface, and to the explosions that shatter its windows.[50] The dynamic exchanges between the interior and the exterior become more frequent and varied as the fire inexorably climbs the skyscraper to consume the city's elite, trapped in the roof-garden restaurant (fig. 55). The rescue efforts further narrativize the tower's shape and height: controlled by a gravity brake, a small, glass-walled elevator slowly creeps down its side, is dislodged from its track by a blast (one of its passengers falls to her death), and is finally lifted away from the building by a helicopter's crane; a breeches buoy that links the restaurant and a nearby building allows for the transport of women over the abyss until several hysterical men wrest control of it and fall to their death. Throughout these peripeties, we rarely lose sight of the "towering inferno." The last-minute reprieve of the men who remain trapped in the restaurant occasions an even more striking view: water released from rooftop tanks pours out of the shattered windows, quenching the fire from top to bottom.

55. *The Towering Inferno*: the
        skyscraper

The Towering Inferno is enacted by a galaxy of current movie stars (Paul Newman, Steve McQueen, William Holden, Faye Dunaway), returning movie stars (Fred Astaire, Jennifer Jones), and other famous actors. Still, its embellishing decor comes as close as that of any movie to achieving narrative primacy. Near the film's beginning, just before the dedication ceremony, as mounting banks of floors are progressively illuminated from within, the tower becomes an architectural spectacle and a breathtaking light show that wins the applause of the in-film onlookers, surrogates for those in the movie audience. As in many films with embellishing sets, the disclosure of the narrative object is an emphatic moment of display, meant to elicit the wonder of all spectators. Cinema revels in its capacity to capture, in a single overwhelming image, the temple of Moloch, Belshazzar's court, the Circus Maximus, the statue of Dagon, the tallest skyscraper in the world.

Chapter 5

Set
as
Artifice

"It took a great deal of mind searching to arrive at the design of the gambling casino. Von Sternberg rejected one conception after another until one day I came to him with an idea of a circular interior in which the circular tiers receded downward and the lowest level represented 'hell' where the gambling stakes were beyond reason. He was intrigued" (fig. 56).[1] Boris Leven's set for *The Shanghai Gesture*, conceived and readily perceived as a visual metaphor, is designed to preclude reception as the literal representation of its referent, a gambling house. It is not conspicuous metaphoricity alone but outlandish size, shape, and complexity of decorative detail that identifies the set of the casino as artifice. No viewer could have ever frequented such an establishment.

Metaphor is not necessarily reserved for the degree of design intensity we have called artifice. Nor does artifice require a specifically metaphoric intention on the part of the designer. The basic functions of establishing time, place, and mood apply to the set as artifice as they do to the denotative, punctuative, and embellishing sets. Conversely, we sometimes read these sets as metaphors: Leven's house in *Giant* is a sign of solitude; Trauner's office in *The Apartment* signifies anonymity; Menzies and Carl Weyl's fence-crossing stile in *Kings Row* signals the passage into maturity. Other decors are nearly comic in the flagrancy of their emblems: the phallic skyscraper dominated by the standing figure of the architect/lover at the climax of *The Fountainhead*; the big clock that hyperbolizes the obsessive punctuality of the publisher/murderer in *The Big Clock*. But these sets, however metaphorically, symbolically, or even allegorically they may impinge on their respective narratives, never cease to serve the reality effect. They continue therefore to be read as representations of true-to-life locales.

What distinguishes the gambling casino in *The Shanghai Gesture* is that its call to legibility is predicated on the fiction effect. Viewers are not meant to see it as a verisimilitudinous construction of a gambling den, however exotic. We are invited to read it as an unreal, imagined place—an allegory for Hell. We cannot fail to take account of its design as highly stylized architecture proposed quite plainly as the site of fiction. Sometimes

56. *The Shanghai Gesture*: Boris Leven's sketch for the gambling casino

punctuative, frequently embellishing, the set as artifice commands attention to its status as decor for film. All constructed movie sets are artificial, of course. In this chapter, we reserve "artifice" and "artificial" for those that refuse to let us forget it.

We will pursue two orders of set as artifice in their relationship to narrative. The first has its origins in Georges Méliès's trips to the moon and to the bottom of the sea, and it extends through the distortions of German expressionism to the horror houses of Dr. Frankenstein, the spaceships, moons, and planets of *2001: A Space Odyssey*, "Tracy Town," and Batman's Bat Cave. To this level of design intensity belong films seminal in the history of art direction, *Das Kabinett des Dr. Caligari*, *Metropolis*, and *The Thief of Bagdad* (1924), films whose stylistic influence on design has been far-reaching. The second order designates the art direction of films whose subjects are the theatre and the cinema themselves. Many of these narratives are explicitly self-reflexive in that they feature performance and performers: movie adaptations of Shakespeare, *The Great Ziegfeld*, the Fred Astaire-Ginger Rogers musicals, ballet and opera films. Highly ornamented sites for spectacle and display, and often crucial to the conduct of the narrative, these stages of performance are designed to be eye-catching, memorable.

We do not mean to suggest that the artificial set challenges star and story for narrative supremacy. Dr. Caligari himself, Werner Krauss, is every bit as expressionistic as his lopsided sideshow wagon; Brigitte Helm's true and false Marias are a match for the machine-age energy of *Metropolis*; Fred and Ginger have the grace to share their glitter with the "big white set" of *Top Hat*. Except in the most unusual instances, the set as artifice achieves co-star status, not top billing. We may be inspired to exit the theatre whistling these sets, but only along with the other tunes—performers, plot, staging— that capture the viewer's fancy.

Invented Realities

Art directors exercise greatest freedom in the representation of the irrational and the fantastic. Decors appropriate to these modes are palpably invented realities. The distorted sets of *Frankenstein* and *Svengali* distance their narratives from the realm of reason. Fantasy is embodied in the splendid city in *The Thief of Bagdad* (1924) and the "stairway to Heaven" in *A Matter of Life and Death*, decors that desert verisimilitude for visions conjured from legend and eschatalogy. *2001: A Space Odyssey*, which belongs to a different zone of the fantastic, moves viewers beyond their knowledge of the past and experience of the present to speculations on "things to come."

The Irrational

German expressionism found a place on the screen immediately following World War I. It has been there ever since. In various degrees and manners, it prevails among the decorative strategies of art directors. To this privilege of practice corresponds the privilege of critical esteem we will explore in chapter 7. In fact, whatever attention decor commands in both scholarly and journalistic discourse is directed toward the artifical set in general and expressionist design in particular. It began, of course, with *Das Kabinett des Dr. Caligari* (fig. 57), a film that lends its title to the English-language version of one of the few book-length studies devoted to art direction, Léon Barsacq's *Caligari's Cabinet and Other Grand Illusions*. Siegfried Kracauer's formulation of *Caligari*'s style is particularly apt: "The canvases and draperies . . . abounded in complexes of jagged, sharp-pointed forms strongly reminiscent of gothic patterns. Products of a style which by then had become almost a mannerism, these complexes suggested houses, walls, landscapes. . . . The settings amounted to a perfect transformation of material objects into emotional ornaments."[2] The sets of *Caligari* rely, in good measure, on the modernist gestures of cubism; their nearly total refusal of conventional dimensionality radically dislodges the viewer from the familiar.[3]

Artificial sets mediate the narrative relationships between the material and the emotional; they objectify a nexus between exterior and interior, between the physical and the psychological universe. Pervasive in their narrative activity, the sets of *Caligari* are redolent of the characters' states of mind, feelings, and fantasies. Is Francis's story of murder and kidnapping the product of his madness? Is the evil Dr. Caligari also the direc-

57. *Das Kabinett des Dr. Caligari*: a street, Dr. Caligari (Werner Krauss)

tor of the insane asylum? The fevered imaginations of the characters shape the narrative of *Caligari* in terms of its unreal environments. In order to read the film, we must therefore read its sets.

A focal point in German cinema of the 1920s, *Caligari* lent its name to a visual style. In a discussion of Paul Iribe's decors, Louis Delluc wrote that caligarism is "the creative filmmaker's complete and magical replacement of nature, which seems so easily captured by the honest camera but which, however, is so elusive. . . . Let's imagine nature, construct life, stylize truth, because cinema is an interpreter."[4] This replacement of a natural with an invented reality, this endorsement of set construction and stylization, suits fictions imbued with enigma, menace, trauma, violence, the supernatural, the monstrous. The skewed staircases of *Raskolnikow* and the Gothic worlds of *Der Golem* and *Faust* are descendants of *Caligari*'s sets. Even the more regular geometries of *Metropolis* come from the antinaturalistic ethos that authorized filmmakers to lade decor with legibility. The play of decor in these works exemplifies the fourth level of design intensity, where sets show off their own artifice. Consistently and consciously foregrounded, the artificial set proffers itself as an opaque object in pursuit of the fiction effect—surely the case for the madhouse world of *Caligari*. That other locus classicus of German expressionism, *Metropolis*—with its dehumanizing machines and subterranean workers' quarter, city of

58. *Metropolis*: the tower and other buildings

the future, catacombs, pleasure palace, combination Gothic house and science-fiction laboratory, Tower of Babel, and cathedral—offers a repertoire of artificial sets that are predominantly descriptive, intent on defamiliarization, not only on detaching viewers from the ordinary and the everyday but plunging them into an alternative world, constructed for the fiction and the camera (fig. 58).

Nearly all horror films are heavily indebted to German expressionism for their design motifs. Hambley and Downing trace the lineage to Paul Leni, who brought his German experience as art director and director to Universal, the Hollywood studio that exercised a near monopoly on the genre.[5] Lotte Eisner remarks that *Caligari* shared part of its title and "fairground ambience" with Leni's *Das Wachsfigurenkabinett* [*Waxworks*].[6] Charles D. Hall was art director for three of Leni's four Hollywood thrillers. Hall also presided over the design of major productions in other genres at Universal (*Broadway*, *All Quiet on the Western Front*, *Show Boat*) and the decors of many Chaplin films. But it is his work on the horror film that ensures Hall's reputation. Even his German town, originally constructed for *All Quiet on the Western Front*, was recycled into *Frankenstein* (1931) and *Bride of Frankenstein* (1935).[7] Jack Otterson and Richard H. Riedel, responsible for Universal's third entry in the series, *Son of Frankenstein* (1939), were clearly inspired by Hall's work.

59. *The* Bride *of Frankenstein*: forest, the capture of the monster (Boris Karloff)

The Frankenstein movies exhibit the design elements that are the basis for the conventions of the horror genre. In the first, views of real life under a real sky are rare; in the second, they are minimal; in the last, they are absent. These are studio-bound films; their rocks and mountains belong to the art department, not to nature. In *The Bride of Frankenstein*, a forest of leafless and nearly branchless trees provides a carefully composed site of fear for the capture of the monster (fig. 59). Most of the out-of-doors scenes in the first two films are backed by a cyclorama that shows an unmoving, threatening sky whose artificiality is apparent to even the most gullible viewer (fig. 60). The design scheme of all three emphasizes the distorted and the disproportionate.

The series opens in a cemetery, its gravestones and crosses askew. Dr. Frankenstein performs his secret experiments in an abandoned old watchtower that looms high on a hillside. The interior walls dwarf the actors; the stone steps climb vertiginously; the dungeon tilts. In this universe devoid of right angles, the modern laboratory and its apparatus appear as demented as the scientist—who is repeatedly declared mad by the other characters (fig. 61). A windmill, turning and burning in Charles Hall's mountainscape, a demonic structure out of all control, is the apt final image for a fiction about monstrous, Heaven-defying ambition. The film's environment is manifestly controlled by the filmmakers, its "created" exteriors and interiors fit settings for Dr. Frankenstein as he creates his monster before our very eyes.

60. *Frankenstein*: rocky pass, Dr. Frankenstein (Colin Clive) above, on right

The first shot of *The Bride of Frankenstein* is of a castle during a storm. This generic sign for horror is almost immediately ironized as we explore the comfortable interior where Mary Wollstonecraft Shelley, Shelley himself, and Lord Byron are spending a friendly evening. Byron's voiceover evocation of the events of *Frankenstein* conjure shots from the previous film, recalling its important decors and ending with the flaming windmill and presumed demise of the monster. From her early nineteenth-century frame, Mary Shelley (Elsa Lanchester) then proceeds to tell a story that, for all its dungeons and towers, and its stepped-up Gothic imagery, unfolds sometime in the twentieth century. In the series opener, Baron Frankenstein resided in town, in a large dwelling with comfortably appointed rooms. Its distinguishing feature was a two-story-high central hall with exposed bracing timbers. For the sequel, the house has been transformed into a true castle complete with moat and a very large courtyard; all of the interior ceilings are vaulted. The Frankenstein family now appears to be living in a Gothic crypt. An actual crypt serves the momentous meeting between the necrophilic Dr. Pretorius (Ernst Thesiger) and the monster (Boris Karloff) (fig. 62). The film ends with the explosion that destroys the watchtower/laboratory. As with *Frankenstein*'s windmill, narrative closure in *The Bride of Frankenstein* is effected by foregrounding a remarkable decor through its destruction.

61. *The Bride of Frankenstein*:
    Dr. Frankenstein's
    laboratory

729-P.100

The German town that provided short moments of sunlight in *Frankenstein* and even shorter ones in *Bride* is shown only in rain, fog, or darkness in *Son of Frankenstein*. Baroness von Frankenstein (Josephine Hutchinson) looks at the desolate landscape outside her train window and exclaims, quite accurately, "What a strange-looking country!" Here, two new generations of Frankensteins—the baron, the baroness, and their little son—will encounter menace and terror in the now cinematically familiar narrative of monstrosity. The baroness asks, "What's that queer-looking structure across the ravine?" It is none other than the remains of the watchtower, here shorn of its height but equipped with an array of unusual entries: a heavy door, a circular stone disk that is sometimes lifted from the floor, a ladder rising out of a sulphur pit. Ygor (Bela Lugosi) occupies a house suited to a fairy-tale goblin. But it is the transformation in the Frankenstein dwelling that pushes the decor "over the top," a not inconsiderable achievement given the pointed expressionism of *Son of Frankenstein*'s predecessors. It appears as a full-fledged castle looming in the background of the first shot. The interior boasts a wooden stairway precariously attached to the wall (fig. 63). Its steps cast ominous shadows; its railings and posts establish a pattern of unsettling angularity apparent also in the film's other decors. For the dining room, with its two promontories jutting over the table and bare wall

62. *The Bride of Frankenstein*: the crypt, Dr. Pretorius (Ernest Thesiger), two graverobbers, and the monster

63. *The Son of Frankenstein*: sketch of entrance hall

64. *The Son of Frankenstein*: the dining room, Baron Frankenstein (Basil Rathbone), his son (Richard Nichols), and his wife (Josephine Hutchinson)

slashed with thick shadows, the designers attain a level of defamiliarization unusual even at the artificial level of design intensity (fig. 64). The staircase and the dining room are striking to a degree that transcends the conventions of the horror film genre. Indeed, the eccentricities of decor in *Son of Frankenstein* provide necessary relief to a plot overburdened by convention.

Anton Grot, chief designer at Warner Bros. in the 1930s, could claim to deploy the "crazy house" planes as skillfully as any art director. In fact, he adopted antirealist slants and skews for films and genres of all kinds, some, like the Malibu beach house he designed for *Mildred Pierce*, remote in spirit from the insanity of *Caligari* and the monstrosity of *Frankenstein*.[8] Grot's work on *Svengali* extends expressionism to a subject more accurately defined as uncanny than horrific. *Svengali* opens with a shot of a city street, deep in shadows, its planes distorted. We find ourselves in fin-de-siècle Paris. Not the elegant capital familiar to most moviegoers, the French metropolis is here a place of mystery where mood enjoys a vastly greater imperative than geography. In the film's first interior, Svengali's garret room, a chair that has no specific function in the plot casts a gigantic shadow, a prefiguration of the altered proportions and planes of all the major sets. *Svengali* sustains the tenor of its expressionism to serve its protagonist (John Barrymore), whose hypnotic powers shape this narrative of obsessive love and mind control.

The rooming house inhabited by Svengali and a group of young artists is a study in imbalance. The building itself, an architectural anomaly, could not possibly contain within so narrow a frame its many small rooms and disproportionately wide landings. The arches bear down on the characters, who are forced to bend when, on raked floors, they endeavor to pass through implausible doors. The crypt, broad and low with wide arches and short columns or walls, the analog for this hallway/landing, is the film's dominant motif, repeated wherever we see Svengali and his beloved protegée, the singer Trilby—in a Paris concert hall, a Neapolitan theatre, a Cairo café. Grot has imposed on garrets, dressing rooms, and stages the look peculiar to horror films.

Nearly six decades after *Frankenstein* and *Svengali*, the expressionistic designs of three big-budget comic-book films, *Batman*, *Batman Returns*, and *Dick Tracy*, drew rare critical attention and exceptional audience approval. Batman and the Joker fight for dominion in an urban nightmare of oversized, irregular buildings whose exposed structural articulations are signs of threat as they overpower the inhabitants. This studio-bound, sunless Gotham City embraces high and low, rich and poor, good and evil in the coherence of its decors. Hero Bruce Wayne/Batman (Michael Keaton) lives in a castle; his Bat Cave is as terrifying as the factory/lair of the evil Joker (Jack Nicholson). Skyscraper, luxury apartment, offices, public square, and museum are equally menacing. As in *Metropolis*, the film's perilous climax is played out on the roof of a Gothic cathedral, a site whose grotesque statues and sharp angles are incorporated into the conventions of expressionism (fig. 65).[9] Although there is no denying the authority of the over-the-top performances of Jack Nicholson, Danny De Vito, Michelle Pfeiffer, and Robert De Niro in the *Batman* films and in *Dick Tracy*, the set as artifice rivals these actors for narrative appeal.

The Fantastic

The demented, the horrific, and the uncanny liberate art directors from the everyday; the fantastic gives them yet greater license to construct alternative worlds in the service of the fiction effect. Mary Corliss and Carlos Clarens locate the true advent of art direction in the mid-1920s when a fantastic film, *The Thief of Bagdad*, helped establish the career of William Cameron Menzies, the future dean of art direction in the United States.[10] Menzies designed this silent film in black and white in 1924; he was also associate producer of Alexander Korda's 1940 sound-and-Technicolor remake.

The Thief of Bagdad, vintage 1924, demonstrates the function of art direction in support of the fantastic narrative. Decor, in fact, roots the fiction in the tangible world necessary to the performance of the unreal.[11] Corliss and Clarens comment on the debt owed by Menzies to Bakst's scenery for Les Ballets Russes.[12] In sets inspired by dance decor, Douglas Fairbanks, as Ahmed the thief, disports himself like a phenomenally graceful athlete, a "dancing" actor who exploits the physical environment to enhance the rhythm and scope of his movement.[13] All walls are there to be scaled, staircases to be vaulted. The mammoth scale of the structures both dwarf the earthbound actors and afford the gravity-defying hero vast frames for the exhibition of his dynamic command of

65. *Batman*: the roof of the
cathedral, the Joker (Jack
Nicholson)

space (fig. 66). And when the level of the fiction rises to the peak of fantastic invention, only a flying carpet is adequate to display the expanse of this imaginary city, construct of an art director's fancy—"Bagdad, dream city," as one of the film's earliest intertitles tells us. It is also Bagdad, colossal city, a city of monumental walls and turrets. The primary in-film viewer, Ahmed, gazes across unusually deep vistas at the wonder of Bagdad and its beautiful princess, inviting moviegoers to enjoy the same spectacle. Here, nothing is of normal scale. Emblematic of the city's unusual dimensions, both as fantastic locale and movie set, is its gate, whose four parts meet and separate like a giant's jaw, a fearsome threshold for the awestruck tiny creatures who pass through it.

Near the film's beginning, a miniature model of Bagdad is presented to Cham Shang, the Mongol prince who aspires to conquer the city itself. Although Cham Shang does become master of Bagdad briefly when his army infiltrates the city, Bagdad truly

66. *The Thief of Bagdad* (1924): the walls of Bagdad

belongs to Ahmed the thief. It is he who has access to all its zones, who climbs its balconies, ferrets into its hidden recesses, penetrates the palace. His explorations lead him repeatedly to the outer walls, the courtyard, the eunuchs' room, each decorated with one or two striking, defining, and memorable design elements that themselves become the means of Ahmed's accessions: the grillwork on the wall, the curve of the staircase in the princess's bedroom (fig. 67). A stage for the single figure of the hero in the first half of the film, in the stupendous climax the now familiar palace is filled with groups and violence when it is first occupied by the hordes of Cham Shang, then reclaimed by Ahmed's army. The sets finally become the decorative elements that subsume narrative recapitulation, recalling their initial and subsequent appearances. The narrative of *The Thief of Bagdad* depends as much upon the fantastic invention and the extraordinary beauty of its sets as it does on their affinity to its star, Douglas Fairbanks.

   With Vincent Korda for art director (he won an Oscar for the effort) and Menzies as associate producer, Alexander Korda's 1940 version of *The Thief of Bagdad* did not stint on its sets either. Each of the two principal locales, the cities of Bagdad and Basra, has a large public square and walls rising to its palace. The 1940 *Thief* is a narrative of the fantastic film, and some of its sets would have adorned its predecessor: the garden where

67. *The Thief of Bagdad* (1924): the princess's bedroom, the three suitors (Noble Johnson, Mathilde Comont, So-Jin), the princess (Julanne Johnston), her father (Brandon Hurst)

the princess (June Duprez) first meets Ahmad (here, the King of Bagdad, played by John Justin); the temple and the giant idol from whose forehead the thief Abu (Sabu) steals the "all-seeing eye" (fig. 68). Soaring minarets and graceful cupolas render the "Arabian fantasy" promised by the film's initial title card. Yet the realism of speaking actors, even as they enunciate the deliberately archaic "Arabian Nights" dialogue, has an inhibiting effect on the fantastic. The voices of Sabu and the other actors mandate a moderate degree of verisimilitude; the balletic mime of Douglas Fairbanks is as marvelous as the marvelous sets of his Bagdad.[14]

Fantasy worlds are not necessarily located in the distant past. Intercut with contemporary reality, the fantasy of Heaven depicted in *A Matter of Life and Death* is congenial to contemporary speech. The film's title captures the core of its subject and foreshadows the long, hallucinatory debate that constitutes its climax; the release title in the United States, *A Stairway to Heaven*, makes prominent its most critical decor. *Matter/ Stairway* is, in fact, constructed around three fantastic decors that emanate from the imagination of Peter (David Niven).[15]

Heaven is composed of two distinct areas. The reception center recalls a mammoth office building with "a definite sweep, a modern, clean-cut elegance that seems quite appropriate to a repository for the sky-soaring souls of airmen." The amphitheatre

68. *The Thief of Bagdad* (1940): the temple of the idol with the all-seeing eye, the genie (Rex Ingram)

has "a vastness that seems to melt into space at the edges, so that one can readily imagine an ethereal domain beyond the heavier atmosphere of the Universe" (fig. 69).[16] Combining smooth and rough, its symmetrical tiers are for the judge and jury, its rocky outgrowths for the opposing advocates. The amphitheatre provides a space that accommodates not only the immensity of Heaven but also the debate on life and death. The former is revealed in a pullback at the end of this scene when the amphitheatre appears as the base of a much greater, endlessly rising ring of tiers that becomes the center of a galaxy, which is in turn only part of the universe. Neither the reception area nor the amphitheatre moves far, however, from the light-filled, airy iconography of other Heavenscapes. This paradise for pilots is prefigured in the white clouds and airplane of *Here Comes Mr. Jordan*.

The film's third fantasy decor is the stairway itself. Though there are, of course, precedents for a stairway to Heaven (Jacob's ladder, Dante's progress through the terraces of Purgatory), it is neither a celestial commonplace nor a necessary component of the Earth/Heaven topos. Shown twice in the film, first during the bantering exchanges between the dying Peter and his "conductor" (Marius Goring), a French fop guillotined during the Revolution, this is not truly a stairway but an escalator lined with statues of

69. A *Matter of Life and Death*: the court of Heaven, Peter's advocate (Roger Livesey) in the
foreground

the great men of history: Plato, Lincoln, Solomon, among others. A moving stairway is a
fit decor for moving pictures. It is also the site of a familiar cinematic mannerism: the
switch from Technicolor to black and white. As it crosses the boundary between Earth
and Heaven, the stairway and Heaven turn black and white. When it moves the heavenly
tribunal toward Earth, the stairway is in color.

Peter is on the operating table, hovering between life and death. The imagination
of the flyer/poet/lover suspends the surgical procedures as the staircase meets the operating room. June (Kim Hunter) is asked to prove her love for Peter by giving up her life
for his. She steps on the stairway; it begins to move up and then stops abruptly, halted by
the force of her devotion (fig. 70). Here, as it locates the crucial issues of the film in the
juxtaposition of the reality of the operating room and the fantasy of the stairway, *Matter/
Stairway* exhibits decor's narrative privilege.

Much of the fantastic imagery we have discussed issues from the stuff of myth and
legend, from retrospective, familiar iconography that obtains for imaginary worlds, after-
worlds, underworlds.[17] Based on shapes suggested by contemporary technology, fantastic
science-fiction decor has a prospective familiarity. Science fiction invites art directors to
discard the picturesque of fairy-tale city and metaphysical Heaven for the picturesque of
computerized spaceship and astronomical lunarscape. Posited on the tension between

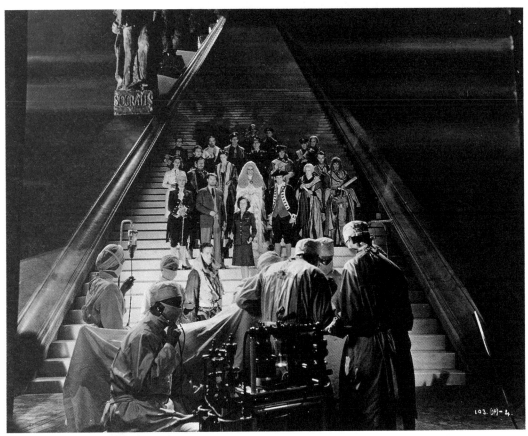

70. A *Matter of Life and Death*: the operating room and stairway, Peter (David Niven) in his pilot's gear, June (Kim Hunter) and the others on stairway

character (the fate of individuals, spaceship crews, whole populations) and technologically accessed environments, science-fiction narratives must, of necessity, foreground their decors. Whether dystopic or utopic, science fiction tests the values of contemporary society by altering relationships between human beings and their environment. As Susan Sontag asserts, "Things, objects, machinery play a major role in these films. A greater range of ethical values is embodied in the décor of these films than in the people."[18] In *Metropolis*, the machine feeds on enslaved humanity; with its rain-drenched streets, giant television screens, and immense buildings shaped like Mayan pyramids, *Blade Runner* proposes a crushing, chaotic vision of transnational styles; even the utopian city of the future shown in *Things to Come* harbors a society in revolt against technology (fig. 71, fig. 72, fig. 73).[19]

The status of decor as primary narrative marker in science fiction is perhaps best illustrated by *2001: A Space Odyssey*, a film in which the future seems, at first, to be hospitable. The Orbiter Hilton and the Bell Picturephone provide momentary brand-name comfort before the film's disquieting journeys are undertaken. True to its title, this is a narrative about voyage, but, distinct from other such fictions, it devotes more attention

71. *Metropolis*: the machine

to the vehicles than to the travelers. The odyssey is marked by a series of decors whose power to astound the viewer is enhanced by the persistence of their presentation. Here, human speech relinquishes its hegemony over plot for unusually long stretches of time, time enough for us to concentrate on environments and to allow those environments to overpower the characters. The interiors of the vehicles range from familiar to extraordinary: the cockpit of *Orion* and its gravityless passenger cabin; the gently curving floor of the space station; the conference room with luminous walls; the centrifugal command center/living space of *Discovery 1*, whose shape is forcefully inscribed when crew member Frank (Gary Lockwood) jogs laps around the inside rim (fig. 74). The various vehicles emerge with startling clarity in the blackness of space, usually in relationship with each other, the moon, or Jupiter. We first see *Orion* about to dock in a space station orbiting the moon. The space station is the core of two revolving wheels; *Aries*, the space shuttle, is pod-like; a moon bus transports the scientists to the monolith. Each of these shapes organizes a different phase of the narrative.

The most important vehicle is *Discovery 1*, spaceship for the Jupiter mission, whose uncommon design boasts a command module that resembles a bulb pulling a train with a giant caboose (fig. 75). That portion of *2001* governed by conventions of narrative

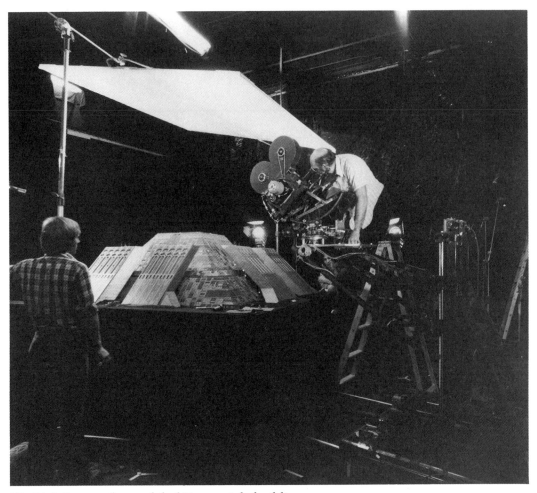

72. *Blade Runner*: the model of Mayan-style building

tension and suspense involves the positioning of the oversized *Discovery 1* and a tiny pod-like vehicle. The supercomputer HAL 9000, a camera-like element of decor, has "decided" to take control of the mission from the human agents, Frank and Dave (Keir Dullea). While Frank is performing a repair outside the vehicle, HAL sends him careening into space; Dave goes to his rescue in the pod. With Frank in its mechanical arms, the pod hovers near *Discovery 1*. HAL refuses to obey Dave's command to open the hatch. We measure the conflict between human and computer in this image of two very different vehicles poised in the silence of space. Finally, the human prevails; in yet another artificial decor, the computer's brain, Dave removes a sufficient number of data banks to "lobotomize" HAL.

Just as HAL narrativizes *Discovery 1*, the entire narrative of *2001* is organized by the monolith that first appears in the "Dawn of Man" section of the film.[20] The subsequent discovery of a monolith on the moon occasions the space odyssey. What does it mean? Who placed it there? The monolith has its own stage for display, a rectangular pit

73. *Things to Come*: the city of the future

74. 2001: A *Space Odyssey*: Frank (Gary Lockwood) and Dave (Keir Dullea) walking inside the hub of *Discovery* 1

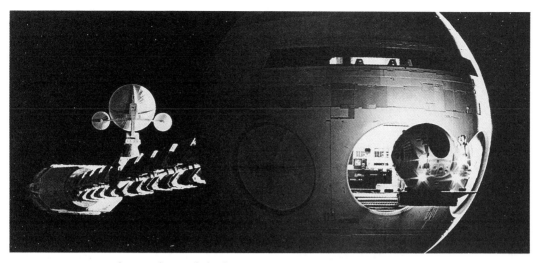

75. 2001: A *Space Odyssey*: the pod docking at *Discovery* I

76. 2001: A *Space Odyssey*: Dave in the Louis XVI–style hotel room

on the moon's surface. Men approach it from ramps and pose next to it as a photo op. When the rays of the sun strike it for the first time, the monolith emits a high-frequency radio signal. This object clearly has a life of its own; we know it as decor in action, and we will subsequently see it floating in space. Another cosmic convergence between monolith, spaceship, planet, and satellites creates the "star gate" through which Dave passes in an accelerated time trip.

The monolith makes its final appearance, most incongruently, in a Louis XVI–style hotel suite whose sole "futuristic" feature is a luminous floor (fig. 76).[21] The coolly formal room with its retrospective moldings, statues, and paintings constitutes the film's ultimate vehicle. Coming after more than two hours of gadgetry, this is indeed a decorative shock. As it conveys Dave through the ages of his life to a rebirth as a "star child" contemplating Earth, this hotel room claims for decor stunning power to signify with the play of its artifice.

Performance

On Stage/On Screen

In *A Double Life*, rehearsals and performances of *Othello* reflect, according to Harry Horner, "the magical atmosphere and illusion of the theatre" as well as "the sick mind of an actor on the verge of insanity."[22] The specific narrative premise of *A Double Life*—the contagious effect of a fictional character's jealousy on an actor who immerses himself completely in his role—is executed in locations and sets that depict contemporary New York, in film noir decors appropriate to murder, and in the scenery meant for a production of *Othello* (fig. 77). Shakespeare, the most revered playwright in the English language, is an obvious choice for a film whose subject is the impact of theatricality on the experience of life. His conventions of speech and dramaturgy are in radical opposition to stylistics of

77. A *Double Life*: audience and stage, the final scene of *Othello*, Othello (Ronald Colman) and Desdemona (Signe Hasso)

realism operant in mainstream narrative cinema. On the movie screen, Elizabethan theatre becomes a useful metaphor for the artifice of theatre itself.

In order to narrow the gap between theatre and film, Franco Zeffirelli situates his Shakespeare films (*Romeo and Juliet*, *The Taming of the Shrew*, *Hamlet*) in naturalistic sets, representations of lived realities, much the way he would were the actors speaking dialogue written by a twentieth-century screenwriter rather than a seventeenth-century playwright. Other movie adaptations of Shakespeare, however, use decor to emphasize the stylistic distance that separates the Globe Theatre from the movie palace. These approaches root Shakespeare's plays at their theatrical origin. *As You Like It* opens with a shot of a real sky and a real tree but then moves into the constructed universe designed by Lazare Meerson, a French castle and garden that recall the shallow perspective and shortened dimensions of miniature structures we see in medieval manuscripts (fig. 78). The breath of nature never rustles through Meerson's Forest of Arden, an artfully arranged cluster of fake trees that recalls the illusionism of the stage. While the movies have led us to believe that the trees on the screen have roots in the earth, no one expects to see a facsimile of a forest in the theatre. And when art directors flaunt the artifice of the stage, they force us to pay heed to the craft of the film designer.

78. *As You Like It*: Duke Frederick's castle, Rosalind (Elisabeth Bergner) and Celia (Sophie Stewart)

Laurence Olivier, who played Orlando in the screen version of *As You Like It*, found a solution for cinematizing Shakespeare in the decorative pattern of *Henry V*. Although decor belongs to the reality effect of a history play, *Henry V* is, in fact, far more insistent in its foregrounding of stagecraft than the pastoral comedy *As You Like It*. In *Henry V*, Shakespeare provided a Chorus to facilitate the imaginative leap required of an audience about to see the representation of historical events of great scope: the siege of Harfleur, the battle of Agincourt, events that are "cribb'd and confin'd" on the stage of the Globe.[23] Olivier writes, "So that when at last we leave the place, with a flourish of William Walton's music, and I speak my lines beginning with 'Now sits the wind fair, and we will aboard' realistically and with a modern tone, there's a tremendous feeling of relief and anticipation. The language may be archaic, but it's not strange. It's charming. It's sincere."[24]

Olivier was determined to make archaic words and expressions come alive for the movie audience. If he did not shoot the French court scenes at the castle of Kenilworth, it was precisely because it would have put into too sharp relief the gulf between the *past* of the language and the *present* of the setting. "I didn't want the eye to quarrel with the ear; what the eye saw had to bolster the seeming reality of the language. No eyesore like crumbling Kenilworth stone; but something artificial, very pretty and unreal, and yet real to the mind's eye's vision of a romantic tale of an heroic medieval king. . . . The difficulty was the language, and my only hope was for the background to be more unreal than it was, so that the language would seem real." Olivier and his designers, Paul Sheriff, Carmen Dillon, and Roger Furse, brought the moviegoer into ever-increasing familiarity with Shakespeare's language through decor. Their schemes were inspired by Dutch painting and medieval illustrations, "especially those of the Limbourg brothers, with their bright and pastel colors, prettiness, odd perspectives and, sometimes, no perspectives at all. I wanted the characters to spring out from the beautiful, stylized, almost cutout scenery, alive and kicking and speaking in a vigorous and varied language; the actors to dominate, to feel confident and sometimes to dwarf the scenery."[25] Through ironic reversal of proportion, we become acutely aware of the scenery that the actor dwarfs.

The first shot of *Henry V* is a protracted (nearly two-minute-long) aerial exploration of what is palpably a model of Elizabethan London. When the camera descends we enter a quite authentic reconstruction of the Globe Theatre, its audience waiting for the play to begin. We are then treated to pre-performance backstage activity that emphasizes the artifice of theatrical illusion. Olivier, as the actor Burbage, clears his throat just before making his entrance, then acknowledges the audience's applause. When the action moves to Southampton and to the imminent departure of the young king and his army, the decor acquires more realistic dimension without abandoning the patent artifice of the painted backdrop. The Channel crossing is accomplished in what are clearly model ships. Although images of water and a beach increase the reality effect, the mini-walls of Harfleur and the flatly rendered backdrops keep us from forgetting that *Henry V* is a movie as much about the stage itself as it is about Shakespeare's play (fig. 79). And if we had for a moment forgotten, Olivier reminds us of it pointedly at the film's conclusion when, during the wedding of Henry and Katherine, the actors are suddenly shown in different

79. *Henry V*: King Henry (Laurence Olivier) and his troops before the walls of Harfleur

costumes and makeup, thereby transporting us back to the decor of the Globe Theatre.[26] The centerpiece of *Henry V*, the spectacular battle of Agincourt, filmed on real fields with real horses, puts into sharp relief the artifice of theatre that brackets it.[27] The illusion of decor, here meant to naturalize Elizabethan English and stagecraft for a twentieth-century movie audience, is crucial to the very nature of narratives about one of cinema's favorite subjects: its own status as a performing art.

Song and Dance

The set as artifice finds a congenial home in the musical whose narrative explicitly pertains to the staging of musical numbers. The over-the-top, highly stylized decor of the conventional musical number occupies an eminent position within the naturalistic context of the larger diegesis. The city streets, theatrical boardinghouses, fancy hotels, and dressing rooms frame the patently false and fabulous sets designed for the unnaturalistic discourses of song and dance that define the genre's principal values.[28]

    The sets for musical numbers have a variety of connections to the narrative. They mark character (posh cityscapes for Fred Astaire's white tie and tails), ethnicity (south of the border for Carmen Miranda's headdresses and platform shoes), or race (an African

80. *Stormy Weather*: the jungle number (Lena Horne)

jungle for Bill Robinson and Lena Horne in *Stormy Weather* [fig. 80]). They comment on theme ("We're in the Money" opens *Gold Diggers of 1933*) or reflect indirectly on the encompassing film (the three spectacular numbers that conclude *Footlight Parade* are proof of the producing talent of the protagonist [James Cagney]).[29] Ostensibly, they relate directly to the mini-narrative of the particular song being performed (Fred Astaire and Eleanor Powell dance in the "tropical splendor" of "Begin the Beguine" in *Broadway Melody of 1940*; Gene Kelly and Vera-Ellen perform their "Slaughter on Tenth Avenue" in a suitably lurid dive in *Words and Music*). The sets devised for most musical numbers are emphatically descriptive in the profusion and artificiality of their decorative elements: jungle fronds made of cellophane; oversized bananas (*The Gang's All Here*), dimes (*Gold Diggers of 1933*), typewriters (*Ready, Willing and Able*); ramps and flights of stairs that lead nowhere and the mirrored and transparent floors seen in so many films. They engage the fiction effect. And just as the gate, the arena, and the forum focalize their narratives of ideological conflict on a scale of colossal realism, the movie musical often bursts beyond the confines of the stage proscenium to a colossally artificial display of its performance practices and narrative concerns.

The Great Ziegfeld is, as the credits put it, "suggested by romances and incidents in the life of America's greatest showman, Florenz Ziegfeld, Jr." The essence of that life is captured in the production values of the showman: what he wished to put on the stage and the means he used to put it there. At its opening and closing, the film is bounded by the staircase decor integral to Ziegfeld's obsession with spectacle. In the first sequence, he insists on changing the stage for Sandow the Strong Man, his attraction at the 1893 Chicago World's Fair: "There oughta be a lot more steps here. . . . I want this higher." At the conclusion of this exceptionally long film, as Ziegfeld lies dying, superimposed on his face are choruses marching down staircases. His last words are "I've got to have more steps. I need more steps. I've got to get higher. Higher." Ziegfeld's lifelong pursuit is for "more steps," not for a sideshow strong man or for his own way to Heaven but to "glorify the American girl." The staircase, the paradigmatic decor of a Ziegfeld show, is the privileged space for exhibition as performance, exhibition primarily of women.[30] Ziegfeld, the producer, spends lavish sums to satisfy his fantasies; he positions his spectators as he does himself. The price of a ticket buys the right to a safe place in the dark from which to engage in gendered fantasies of sexual fulfillment and luxuriance fired by the sumptuous decors that display sexuality.

In an early sequence, Ziegfeld says to a child, a little girl, that he loves "all the girls," that he's going to take the pretty girls and "put them together to make pictures with them." That desire becomes his *Follies*. On opening night someone asks, "Are the steps high enough for you this time, Mr. Ziegfeld?" No, he replies. He'd like to see a lot more, the more the better to "make pictures" with showgirls. What follows is an unusually long number that features what may be the most massive set ever created for a musical: it weighed one hundred tons, was seventy feet wide, had seventy-five steps, and held 192 performers (fig. 81).[31] Here, decor incorporates music and lyrics as it expresses Ziegfeld's preoccupation with women on staircases.

Irving Berlin's "A Pretty Girl Is Like a Melody" is the major theme in this nine-minute-long musical medley.[32] A tenor (Dennis Morgan, dubbed by Allan Jones) begins to sing; behind him a curtain opens slowly. A stage-filling turntable begins to move and continues to rotate until the number finally comes to a close. Against a background of white curtain and white pillar, the turntable brings into view groups of singers and dancers who represent different musical periods and styles: Dvorak's "Humoresque" in eighteenth-century costumes and wigs; Puccini's "Un bel dì" sung by a fabulously adorned soprano whose finery bears absolutely no relationship to the kimono of poor Madama Butterfly; nineteenth-century attire for Lizst's "Liebestraum" and a Strauss waltz. On an elevated section, a tenor in a clown's costume breaks into Leoncavallo's "Vesti la giubba." Then the white curtain begins to rise, following the contour of what we now perceive to be a giant cone-shaped spiral staircase. At the perimeter are men at keyboards, miming a rendition of Gershwin's "Rhapsody in Blue." The camera climbs along with the spiraling pillar and the rising curtain. Men in top hats and tails line the column; women in black and white descend the stairs, followed by more men in tuxedos and then more women in elaborate white and black headdresses—a contrapuntal up/down pattern of rising elevation and declining human figures. The tenor we saw at the start comes into view to reprise his song, a bevy of women seated at his feet and on the steps below and above him. The cone continues to revolve without interruption, camera and curtain continue to mount, and we finally come to the peak just as the tenor reaches his high note. There sits the single "pretty girl," Audrey Dane (Virginia Bruce), meant

81. *The Great Ziegfeld*: the spiral pillar, the "Pretty Girl Is Like a Melody" number

to be the sum of all of the pretty girls in the number. The camera pulls back until the entire set and its showgirls, dancers, and singers fill the screen. The curtain begins to fall.

This ascent up the spiral is accomplished in two extended shots: the first, more than three minutes long, ends during the *Pagliacci* aria; the second, three and a half minutes long, closes the number itself. The proscenium has been magnified by the sound-stage and the movie camera. But the filmmakers do not exploit the shot durations to dwell on the sheer size of the set. Rather, they make it the object of progressive movement and disclosure, momentary revelation, and rapid concealment.[33] The "pretty girl" at the apex is on view for one minute; the entire set for only thirty seconds out of the number's nine minutes. A figure of description as it is slowly unveiled, visibility itself is enacted in a set that, when we finally see its totality, becomes a figure of display. Stairs that move and turn in a regular rhythm vie for attention with the variously costumed performers arranged upon them. The cycle of disclosure and closure corresponds to the musical reprises. After all, melody is likened to a pretty girl who "haunts you night and day. . . . She will leave you and then come back again." In this linking of musical and visual refrain, the latter becomes a decorative spectacle when, at last, all the performers are seen in their relative positions on the spiral, turning into and then out of view. The narrative of the song and the narrative of the spectacle fold into the narrative of the biopic.

The Great Ziegfeld continues to explore the effects of decor that moves, of scenery that becomes a literally active part of the film text. For "You Gotta Pull Strings," the stage seems to take on a life of its own, aggressively advancing, then retreating. The in-film audience applauds the set for the next number, "You," a sumptuous white cottage that is eventually divided at the middle to reveal a series of couples, each one thrust before a different domestic interior. In another variation, scantily dressed showgirls are arranged in five rows of beds, four deep. Now, the five sections of the stage floor move separately, in a pattern that corresponds to the rhythm of the music and the dancers' steps. The scenery seems to dance no less than the dancers, in fact more, since scenery does not usually dance. But that's not all. Audrey Dane appears, first alone on stage, then serenaded by a chorus of men who assert, "You never looked so beautiful before." Showgirls parade in the exotic plumage typical of the Ziegfeld extravaganza, in costumes so esoteric and distant from conventional garb as to constitute a decor in themselves. A curtain rises to show the entire group of women we had been invited to admire one by one; then another curtain, this time black, parts on yet another "big white set," a disk with Audrey at the rim, her train ending in the feathers of eight more showgirls at the opposite perimeter (fig. 82). The staircase, here purely decorative since no one walks on it, curves up and behind the disk; the disk revolves.

The overwhelming succession of production numbers at the center of *The Great Ziegfeld* features scenery that performs and hordes of anonymous performers who function more or less like scenery. When we are meant to admire the talent of a performer, the impact of the scenery is lessened, sometimes minimized. The charm of Anna Held (Luise Rainer) and the talent of Fanny Brice (playing herself) require little decorative context. We are reminded of this in M-G-M's subsequent Ziegfeld movie, *Ziegfeld Girl*, where the distinction between the singing talent of Judy Garland and the showgirl appearance of Hedy Lamarr and Lana Turner becomes an important narrative thread. For its conclusion, *Ziegfeld Girl* reutilizes the giant spiral of *The Great Ziegfeld*, with Judy Garland replacing Virginia Bruce at the top. The film's "showgirl" staircase that has greatest narrative significance is, however, the one in the lobby. Her career and her life shattered, "Red" (Lana Turner) struts her way down that staircase the same way, early in the film, she descended the fantastic structure Ziegfeld had built to exhibit her as an aesthetic and sexual object.[34]

Busby Berkeley, who staged the numbers of *Ziegfeld Girl*, refers to the "immense sixty-foot-high spiral staircase in gold and silver, adorned with massive cut-glass chandeliers and fantastic trimmings. Each girl emerged from a misty cloud effect, dripping with silver sequins. With all due respect to the master, Ziegfeld could never have done on a stage what we did in that finale."[35] Berkeley is, in fact, something like the Flo Ziegfeld of the movies. He magnifies the prototypical Ziegfeld routine through the sheer number of people who figure in his formations. Berkeley arranges bodies, usually women's bodies, to express and to sometimes nearly replace the structure of the set. In *Gold Diggers of*

82. *The Great Ziegfeld*: the disk and staircase, Audrey (Virginia Bruce) and showgirls in the "You Never Looked So Beautiful Before" number

1933, the showgirls play illuminated violins on an enormous curving staircase; they sit at fifty-six moving pianos in *Gold Diggers of 1935*. The latter uses an enormous but particularly austere nightclub as the principal stage for the "Lullaby of Broadway" (fig. 83). Composed of steps and platforms exposed in their geometrical forms and relationships, the style of this nightclub could not be further removed from the "big white set." David Rubin speaks of its "haunted-house quality" and a style that is "unusually deco for Warner Bros. . . . Van Nest Polglase with a hangover." [36] The decor accommodates legions of stomping dancers who eventually chase the female protagonist of the song's narrative to her death. The fate of this "Broadway baby" serves as a moral to the gold diggers of the film's title. Rick Altman integrates the specific narratives of the Berkeley numbers and the overarching narratives of the films that contain them: "The Berkeley pattern is a simple one: develop the young couple's love simultaneously with the show (preferably by making

83. *Gold Diggers of* 1935: the nightclub, the "Lullaby of Broadway" number

the success of one depend on the success of the other), project the thematics of the couple into the thematics of the show by having the lovers outside the show play the lovers inside the show, then drop the thematic concerns in favor of graphic equivalents to the show."[37] This move from the thematics of romance to graphic representations is, in a large measure, accomplished through decorative means: the narrative of the number is reflected in the extraordinary set.

All the Berkeley movies have arresting decors: the dividing Pullman car of "Shuffle Off to Buffalo" (*42nd Street*), the three-tiered semicircle of "Remember My Forgotten Man" (*Gold Diggers of 1933*), the fountain and pool of "By a Waterfall" (*Footlight Parade*), the banana grove of "The Lady in the Tutti-Frutti Hat" (*The Gang's All Here*). In *Ready, Willing and Able*, a Berkeley-inspired number, "Too Marvellous for Words," is staged by Bobby Connolly on a gigantic typewriter (fig. 84). For Berkeley, for Ziegfeld, and for the art directors who made the movie musical a preeminent American genre, one of the principal functions of decor is to enhance the potential for display of performance space. What results is the display of the space as well as that of the performer. Decors that range from the geometric abstraction of the "Lullaby of Broadway" nightclub to the baroque convolutions of the "Pretty Girl Is Like a Melody" spiral, stationary sets and

84. *Ready, Willing and Able*: the giant typewriter, the "Too Marvellous for Words" number

moving sets, are insistent lures, frameworks that satisfy the audience's desire for the unusual, platforms that flaunt luxury and fix the gendered gaze on sexualized objects, figures for the song narratives that often mirror the narratives of the films that contain them.

The 1930s musical contributed to the movies a decor so distinctive that it acquired a name—the "big white set." The adjectives presume the positive values of size and whiteness, indices of class and wealth. The pillar of *The Great Ziegfeld* is a prototypical "big white set." Donald Albrecht notes the importance of abundant light in the representation of luxury: "While, as a visual device, large quantities of lighting added to the beauty of films' sets, they also suggested the abundance and the luxurious sheen of the high life. Light heightened virtually every element of decor in movie night clubs, making objects highly reflective, and stressing smooth surface over texture and mass." [38] Arlene Croce credits Van Nest Polglase and Carroll Clark with establishing the "big white set" as a "fixed architectural institution" at RKO in the 1930s and traces its appearance through all of the Astaire-Rogers musicals. [39] In these films, the advantage of wealth is played out in the artificial decors designed for swank hotels, transatlantic ocean liners, nightclubs, and theatrical productions. The misery of the Great Depression increased the audience's desire for images of luxury; the Astaire-Rogers romantic comedies, with their requisite trappings of comfort and ease, satisfied that desire. In most of the films, the couple suffers the peripeties of love in a pastoral landscape, far from the realities of life.

Even if, as in *Swing Time*, Astaire and Rogers are initially defined by their modest surroundings, the full expression and celebration of their feelings require the fabulous dance
floor of the "big white set."

Top Hat opens in London, where hotel suites, with their curved *white* walls and
oversized satin bedsteads, establish the ritz standard suited for characters blissfully igno-
rant of unemployment and breadlines. Even whiter, bigger, and more outlandishly decorated are the Venetian hotel rooms featured in the second part of the film. And the Lido
vaunts RKO's "biggest white set": two joined sound stages replete with canal and
bridges, and much closer in look to streamlined art deco than to the convoluted baroque
of the late Renaissance *veduta* (fig. 85). This Venetian never-never land, where people
actually swim in the canal, caps the high style that pervades the film as a whole. As Jerry
(Fred Astaire) sings, it's "an atmosphere that simply reeks with class," but class with a
fanciful flair.

The gigantic piazza/canal/hotel serves different phases of the protagonists' dance
to romance. First, the movement from restaurant/ballroom to private dance floor charts
the passage from public dancing to Jerry's private "cheek to cheek" wooing of Dale (Ginger Rogers). Eventually, the entirety of the set accommodates the jubilant confirmation
of the couple's love. "The Continental" number in *The Gay Divorcee* offers a variation
on this effect. During the couple's duet, we see only the dance floor and its immediate

85. *Top Hat*: dancing the "Piccolino" at the Lido

background. It is when hordes of other dancers take up the rhythm that the full scope of the set is revealed in an emphatic gesture of display. This gargantuan "esplanade," with its central pavilion flanked by balconies and terraces, is animated with people who not only dance but twirl inside four prominently featured revolving doors.

In the sets concocted for *Top Hat*, *The Gay Divorcee*, the Busby Berkeley musicals, and many others, we come to understand the exchange between dancer and decor, a partnership not unlike the relationship between the balletic Douglas Fairbanks and his fantastic Bagdad. Dancers explore and appropriate decor with insistence and rapidity, imposing their bodies on the shape of the physical world that participates in the definition of their grace. Tapping feet, swinging arms, jumping and bending, they inhabit space with greater intensity than mere talkers and walkers. Dancers endow hotel rooms and piazzas with their rhythms and postures; the high style of the hotel rooms and piazzas is a congenial setting for the high style of dance and the types of narrative it engenders, stories in which identity is a function of dance.[40]

In *Swing Time*, the "big white set" transcends its essential yet most obvious function as a sign of opulence. Where *Top Hat* opens in a posh London club and an even posher hotel, *Swing Time* foregrounds the deluxe by deferring it. We follow Lucky (Astaire) and then Penny (Rogers) through a series of modest sets—vaudeville stage, dressing room, tailor's shop, railroad station, freight car, city street, dance studio, apartment building—the exception being the nondescript upper-class dwelling of Lucky's fiancée (Betty Furness). As in all the Astaire-Rogers musicals, the narrative premise forms (or re-forms) the couple, in song and dance and love. *Swing Time* inflects this action in the decor of a spectacular nightclub.

This nightclub's narrative purpose is established by its alteration; an already striking set is modified to become yet more striking.[41] Although the first time we see the Silver Sandal we are denied an establishing shot of its full extent, we do get a sense of its unusual structure: tables set on tiers rising next to a staircase, the orchestra nestled in the curve of the staircase. The tablecloths are black, the table lamps have conventional shades, and the large wall panels are decorated with bird silhouettes. While the Silver Sandal is clearly a fancy nightclub, at this point in the film it is not ostentatiously exhibited. The remodeled Silver Sandal, on the other hand, is flaunted in a dizzying shot of the floor in front of the bandstand, its design an aerial view of New York skyscrapers. The camera climbs and finally shows us the expanse of the club, its two levels, its dual staircase, its star-studded wall panels (fig. 86). The cellophane table coverings and the unshaded globes add to the brilliance of the image. The dual staircase is narrativized when Penny's friend, Mabel (Helen Broderick), and Lucky's sidekick, Pop (Victor Moore), enter together but mistakenly walk down opposite sides, Mabel thinking she is continuing her conversation with the absent Pop.

The professional triumph and blissful union of Lucky and Penny seem to be heralded at the new Silver Sandal when Lucky performs "Bojangles of Harlem." Here, elements of decor—gigantic sliding panels, the stage-filling fake legs of Bojangles—extend the nightclub's amplitude.[42] But the number that defines the couple's love will be performed for the movie camera and for movie audiences, not for the patrons of the night-

86. *Swing Time*: the renovated Silver Sandal

club. We see Penny and her fiancé, Romero, reflected in a mirrored door, along with the sweep of the staircase; the door opens, effacing their reflection and revealing the dejected Lucky. A moment later, the Silver Sandal is empty, except for Penny and Lucky, in love yet on the verge of parting. The place shimmers with the cellophane table coverings and the dots of light that pierce the panels; the blonde Penny shimmers in her white gown. Lucky's song, "Never Gonna Dance," stops Penny in her tracks and summons her back to him, down the stairs. As they walk around the dance floor, the shape of the room—its various perspectives, its curves and sparkle, its contrasts of light and dark—anticipates the shape of the dance. In this empty nightclub, to the music they have sung and heard, Penny and Lucky dance the story of their relationship, apart and together on the black and white sections of the dance floor, in front of the twin staircases, structures that, however inviting for dance, lead to separation. Inevitably, Penny and Lucky waltz up the staircases, separately, and finish the dance on the constraining upper level, Penny whirling in and out of Lucky's arms with great force, finally whirling out of the dance, the space, the shot, and presumably the love affair. *Swing Time* is, of course, a romantic comedy. At its conclusion, Lucky and Penny are reunited in a nightclub—another nightclub—that provides panoramic windows for their joyous final dance before a snow-covered cityscape.

Many musicals are explicitly about putting on a show, so their protagonists are performers; hence the justification for singing and dancing that takes place on stage. There are other musicals in which the introduction of song and dance has no such pretext. The Merry Widow sings and waltzes simply because she is in operetta-land; in *Meet Me in St. Louis*, Esther Smith (Judy Garland) lifts her voice because she is thinking about "the boy next door" or about taking "the trolley"; Fred Astaire plays a singing and dancing psychiatrist in *Carefree*. The unnatural eruption of music into life prompts René Clair to advocate for decor that corresponds in style to the artifice of characters who sing rather than speak: "It's silly to see people burst out singing in realistic sets [in *Le Million*]."[43] Although a major section of *Le Million* takes place in an opera house and thereby justifies the characters' singing, episodes staged in a boardinghouse and a police station do not. Clair, designer Lazare Meerson, and cinematographer Georges Périnal "decided to paint everything white and grey in order to soften all the lines" and to hang gauze in front of the sets. "It gave a sort of third-dimensional effect to the actors, set them very clearly out and away from the sets because the sets were reduced almost to hazy outlines behind them. It gave us exactly the effect we wanted, one through which the characters could be real in vaguely unreal backgrounds, therefore capable of almost any sort of action."[44]

Clair and his collaborators did not intend that viewers of *Le Million* notice their trickery. "I had worked to create an atmosphere and an atmospheric style in which people could sing naturally; I didn't want to show any contrast, any disharmony, or rather any lack of appropriateness between the people and the décor. If the audience had noticed my technique for arriving at this goal, the whole correspondence would have been destroyed because they would have become aware of style."[45] Yet some musicals, with only a minimal show-business narrative justification, indulge in highly stylized decors that demand great attention. The diction of music and dance is meant to authorize the patently unreal New York City of *Guys and Dolls*, Latin America of *Yolanda and the Thief*, and American West of *Red Garters*. Although only the first began life on Broadway, the art direction of all three recalls stage artifice, the highly stylized decors created for ballet, opera, operetta, and musical comedy.

Many of the hit musicals that make their way to the screen detach themselves from the proscenium by exploiting cinema's affinity for the out-of-doors: corn that's "as high as an elephant's eye" in *Oklahoma!*, a New England fishing port in *Carousel*, city streets in *West Side Story*, the mighty Alps in *The Sound of Music*. Broadway, the matrix for *Guys and Dolls*, appears nothing like the actual Manhattan street (fig. 87). Even during the scenes staged in the more naturalistic interiors, the deliberate flatness of the adjacent, principal decor for Times Square dominates the film, recalling a city and city lives more imagined than experienced.[46]

Yolanda and the Thief is a fantasy about a con-man (Fred Astaire) who impersonates an angel in order to swindle the credulous, rich, and pretty Yolanda (Lucille Bremer) out of her fortune. In the fictional Latin American country of Patria, people and animals disport themselves both in patently false, painted landscapes and on real lawns. Among the principal sets, only the hotel is marginally verisimilitudinous. The main hall of Yolanda's mansion is florid baroque; her bathtub, with its trompe-l'oeil stream, bridge, and

87. *Guys and Dolls*: the weddings of Nathan (Frank Sinatra) and Adelaide (Vivian Blaine), Sarah (Jean Simmons) and Sky (Marlon Brando), in Times Square

waterfall, outdoes the most fanciful pools concocted for Cecil B. De Mille's sex comedies (fig. 88).[47] As we will show in chapter 7, the sets for the *Yolanda* dream world did not pass unnoticed.

The decor of *Red Garters*, the most extreme example of Hollywood stylization, makes not the slightest gesture toward the true-to-life. The film opens with this title: "You are about to see a new kind of 'Western.' We hope you won't take it too seriously, because our story takes place in a land that never existed, called, Limbo County, California." A few moments later, there is yet another disclaiming title: "Many people have said: 'The movies should be more like life.' And a wise man answered: 'No, life should be more like the movies.' " So much for realism. These paratexts attempt to justify a fantasy West where the hero (Guy Mitchell) rides in a contructed landscape, in front of a monochromatic backdrop cyclorama and stylized trees and bushes. He enters a town that has many of the articulations of buildings—moldings, stairs, doors—but no walls. A western/musical, in itself a Hollywood rarity, *Red Garters* goes far beyond the limits of genre. Viewers of westerns have high expectations of realism. The singing cowboys, Gene Autry and Roy Rogers, perform in the usual naturalistic contexts of the genre. Full-fledged musicals with western settings, *The Harvey Girls* and *Oklahoma!*, look like westerns, not like operettas.

88. *Yolanda and the Thief*: Yolanda's bathroom à la Tiepolo

Even the decor of *Whoopee!*, an early Ziegfeld musical with a western setting redolent of its Broadway origin, does not begin to match the artifice of *Red Garters*, certainly "a new kind of 'Western,' " a film that spawned no imitations.[48] The sets for *Red Garters* are anomalous; the filmmakers enjoin you to sing along with them.

Producer-directors Michael Powell and Emeric Pressburger need no preliminary titles to establish the high style of *The Tales of Hoffmann*, based on the Jacques Offenbach opera. Their song-and-dance film goes over the top along with the conventions of opera and ballet, with narratives that are the rich imaginings of a poet-hero, and with sets that fully acknowledge their artifice. Song, dance, story, and decor are meant to remind the viewer that the rules of the lyric theatre are not governed by the reality effect. Offenbach's opera has a fantasy narrative and therefore provides the art director great latitude. Designer Hein Heckroth says of the Olympia episode, for instance: "The action does not take place in Paris—it takes place in 'Yellow.' There are of course some other colours to play against the yellow. I will tell you another thing. Our biggest 'set,' the Grand Staircase, down which Moira and Robert waltz and Massine runs, is painted on the floor" (fig. 89).[49] The "yellow" episode to which the designer refers is that in which the poet Hoffmann (Robert Rounseville) wears glasses that make him see marionettes as real people. Hoffmann falls in love with a dancing doll, Olympia (Moira Shearer). They waltz

89. *The Tales of Hoffmann*: Hoffmann (Robert Rounseville) and Olympia (Moira Shearer) waltz down the Grand Staircase

in a decor of illusory walls made of yellow gauze; they descend an utterly flat floor cloth of stairs that is unrolled before our eyes. Yet our perception of the decorative illusion is simultaneous with our perception of the dancers in a ballroom, then moving down a staircase. We are thus made to share Hoffmann's own shifting perception.

The Antonia act and the epilogue of *The Tales of Hoffmann* further extend the film's emphatic exhibition of the artificial set. Antonia (Ann Ayers) is an opera singer who will die if she exercises her art. Summoned by the evil Dr. Miracle (Robert Helpmann), the ghost of Antonia's mother exhorts her to sing. This occasions a series of decorative transformations upon the stage of a Greek amphitheatre where mother and daughter move through several opera sets. Hoffmann's three other loves, Olympia, Giulietta, and Stella, then reappear and merge in the body of Stella, the ballerina. She and her partner perform, first against a dark background, then in a stage set that is an image of decor itself. Artificiality of depth is marked by vanishing perspective lines painted on the floor; four pylon-shaped framing pillars and superimposed curtain-like veils complete the theatrical conceit. The couple recedes toward the horizon as a curtain falls. Figures on the curtain materialize into Hoffmann and his drinking companions, the point of departure for the recital of the tales near the film's beginning. In the baldness of their artifice, in the wit and complexity of their transformations, Heckroth's sets reflect upon theatrical and cinematic illusion. Pertinent also to the illusions of the fevered tales lived and recounted by the protagonist, they repeatedly remind us how much all illusion owes to decor.

Hollywood/On Screen

At the climax of *Sunset Boulevard*, silent-movie diva Norma Desmond (Gloria Swanson) emerges from her bedroom in a trance of movie madness. She believes that she is about to appear before the cameras for the first time in twenty years and that the grand staircase of her mansion is a movie set. Her factotum and onetime director/husband, Max Von Mayerling (Erich von Stroheim), stationed between two newsreel cameras on the lower level, calls for "lights." Norma asks, "What is the scene? Where am I?" Max responds, "This is the staircase of the palace." And she, desperate to be part of this fiction, adds, "Yes, yes, down below they're waiting for the princess." Norma is ready to play her part, the Princess Salome, on the staircase of the palace. When Max signals "action, cameras," Norma begins her slow descent of the staircase (fig. 90). Franz Waxman's tango theme helps blur the line between the fictions here proposed: the film *Sunset Boulevard* and the film Norma thinks she is making. The music serves the style of Norma Desmond, movie queen of the 1920s; it serves the sensuality of Princess Salome. The grandiose staircase, fit for a movie queen and a Judaean princess, also exhibits this double affiliation.

Oblivious to the newspaper photographers, reporters, and policemen who line the staircase, Norma raises her arms seductively as she continues her descent. But before the end of the sequence (which is the end of the film), she adds yet another level of fiction. Overcome with happiness at being back in the "studio," once again in front of the movie cameras, Norma momentarily steps out of the character of Salome to announce that moviemaking is her life. In the final moments of the film, Norma Desmond is (1) an agent in the melodrama of *Sunset Boulevard*, (2) Salome, and (3) a movie actress working in an imaginary studio with other artists and technicians. What better place to satisfy these three roles than on a movie set that simultaneously represents the outlandish artifice of the star's domestic opulence and the harsh reality of the crime narrative.

Joe Gillis (William Holden), Norma's lover, acts as the viewer's surrogate. We share his curiosity about the star's mansion, its anachronisms, its excessive decorations, its oversized dimensions. Norma sleeps in a bed that belongs in Versailles; her living room is designed for a fictional character, as Joe is quick to point out. He compares her to Miss Havisham of Dickens's *Great Expectations*, another reclusive woman whose attempt to freeze time is doomed to failure. At first, Joe is lodged in a sparsely furnished room over the garage. From its window, he looks out at "the ghost of a tennis court" and a swimming pool drained of water, decors meant for the stars of the 1920s at play. Eventually he moves into the mansion itself, into "the room of the husbands" with its ornate bed and richly carved closets. His attention is drawn to the gaping holes in all the doors, their locks removed: Norma is, after all, suicidal. Joe opens the door to her room. "There it was again. That room of hers. All satin and ruffles. And that bed like a gilded rowboat. The perfect setting for a silent movie queen." Joe highlights Norma's world with his

90. *Sunset Boulevard*: Norma Desmond (Gloria Swanson) descends her staircase

articulate description of its accoutrements. We are made to see *Sunset Boulevard* as the story of an extraordinary mansion, the reflection of the star who inhabits it, and the image of a bygone Hollywood.[50] Joe Gillis belongs to the new Hollywood.

Joe is a screenwriter, and Norma, who has not appeared in a film for twenty years, has written a screenplay for what she calls her "return." Two types of set design are required by their respective scripts. Norma's *Salome* is a biblical epic that demands sumptuous decor, while Joe's baseball yarn, *Bases Loaded*, needs only modest sets. Historical colossal and contemporary sparse are the styles that inflect the narrative conflict between

Norma and Joe. She owns a fabulous mansion, an expensive wardrobe, and an Isotta-Fraschini touring car; Joe lives in a nondescript apartment, wears the same sports jacket every day, and drives a 1946 Plymouth convertible. Uncomfortable in the fancy tuxedo she has bought for him, Joe flees from Norma's New Year's Eve party, staged for just the two of them in her living room/ballroom, to a contrasting informal party at his friend Artie Green's (Jack Webb) apartment, in a room crammed to overflowing with a crowd of revelers.[51]

Joe's movement between old and new Hollywood is not, however, as aberrant as it first seems. After all, both Hollywoods are in the business of manufacturing fiction. *Sunset Boulevard* opposes the real and the fictional only to erase the line between them. Buildings and their rooms are in constant tension between their locational, denotative function (a movie queen's mansion, a writer's office) and their position as artifice in this movie about the "dream factory." Seen twice, the main gate of Paramount Studios is, indeed, the "real" gate familiar to many moviegoers, featured in a number of Paramount films.[52] It is also the gate to the place of fiction, the studio whose resources are dedicated to the illusion of moviemaking. The Paramount gate, a high-profile decor, a structure whose primary function is to identify the studio through its distinctive design, is not the *background* for scenes. It quite literally occupies the foreground in this narrative about moviemaking, specifically at Paramount.

Joe makes his second trip through the Paramount gate in the company of Norma, in her Isotta-Fraschini with its gold-plated intercom car phone and its leopard-skin upholstery. At this point, the studio takes on an aura of fiction, of Hollywood legend and magic that is shared by all the major characters in *Sunset Boulevard*. Norma enters the sound stage on which Cecil B. De Mille is shooting *Samson and Delilah* (fig. 91). As it foregrounds the set as artifice, the sound-stage sequence becomes a mise-en-abyme of cinematic illusion. We see the customary apparatus of a sound stage, its machinery and modernity, its functional elements, its lights and cameras, as well as the "biblical" tent set for the scene being shot. In one of the film's many ironies, De Mille warns Norma that movies have changed greatly since her day, but the contemporary moviemaking practice he touts is devoted to filming a subject not unlike the old-fashioned *Salome* she herself is proposing. More important to the priority of decor in *Sunset Boulevard* is, however, the way the sound stage itself is transformed into the decor for a film about the star who, according to Max, was "the greatest of them all." An old grip, high on his perch, notices Norma and shines a bright light on her. Extras recognize her and cluster around. A chair and a circle of light become a fitting, indeed a spectacular, decor for this movie about stardom.

Outside, on the lot, as Max indicates to Joe the utilitarian row of writers' cubicles that once constituted the former director's own wood-paneled office, Joe spies Artie Green's fiancée, Betty (Nancy Olson), a script reader who aspires to becoming a writer. It is to one of those cubicles that Joe will return night after night for his collaboration with Betty. During a break in one such session, Betty and Joe stroll through the deserted studio, down the streets constructed for the standing sets of a western and a nineteenth-

91. *Sunset Boulevard*: Norma Desmond and Cecil B. De Mille on the *Samson and Delilah* sound stage

century city (fig. 92).[53] Betty describes the make-believe of *her* Paramount decors in a manner befitting Norma Desmond: "Look at this street, all cardboard, all phony, all done with mirrors. I like it better than any street in the world, maybe because I used to play here when I was a kid." These sets are viewed as pure decor, stripped of the illusion invented by lighting and the presence of fictional characters who inhabit them. Betty acknowledges in the movie-made streets the power of the privileged set that is both a representation and a spectacle, a sight to behold, a value unto itself. Amidst the false fronts that manifest the work of art directors, two screenwriters fall in love.

The film's denouement is triggered when Joe summons Betty to 10086 Sunset Boulevard, where he catalogues, for her benefit, its particularities. Determined to send Betty back to the good-hearted Artie, untainted by the decadence of Norma and her mansion, Joe gives the young woman a tour of the downstairs floor. "Ever been in one of these old Hollywood palazzos? . . . Did you ever see so much junk? She had the ceiling brought from Portugal." The gigolo allies himself with the vulgarity of the palazzo; Betty finally leaves. From outside, we see Joe standing in the doorway. The camera tilts up, framing Joe downstairs and Norma on the upstairs landing in a shot that discloses the full

92. *Sunset Boulevard*: Betty (Nancy Olson) and Joe (William Holden) on the studio street

scope of the two-storied entrance. Then, from Norma's point of view, we see Joe slowly mount the stairs and, a few moments later, descend, on his way out. But, as Norma says, "no one ever leaves a star." She follows and shoots him in the back; he staggers forward and falls into the swimming pool. Then, still trapped in her fiction, Norma again transforms her home into a movie set. She leans seductively against a pillar, assuming the sort of movie-star pose that undoubtedly served her in many films: "The stars are ageless."

This is where we came in. Soon after the murder, Norma is lured downstairs by the cameras and the fiction that transforms her mansion's staircase into the "staircase of the palace." As she descends, we perceive this decor in terms of its multiple narrative functions: the policeman's factual "scene of the crime," the movie queen's exotic residence, her movie set, the studio itself. The patently constructed film decor and Hollywood locations are interwoven just as the film interweaves the movies as illusion and as industrial process. Commenting upon cinema practice in the late 1940s and reflecting upon that of the 1920s, *Sunset Boulevard* repeatedly draws the viewer's attention to codes of decor. Norma Desmond's "great white elephant of a place" is the principal artificial decor of a movie whose subject is the artifice of cinema itself.

It seems a long journey from Metropolis to Hollywood, from horror houses to outer space, from the stages of Shakespeare's London to Ziegfeld's Broadway. But, as

Stanley Kubrick taught us in *2001: A Space Odyssey*, the journey is the vehicle. For the self-reflexive realities of performance, as for the invented realities of fantasy, the vehicle is an illusion that emanates from the shop of the art director. The artificial set releases the art director from the need to replicate the true-to-life—present or past, tawdry or glamorous. In a legendary Bagdad palace and a legendary Manhattan nightclub, the set designer reflects upon the reality of his or her own art as unabashed artifice.

Chapter 6

Set as Narrative

We apply this final approximation of our taxonomy to films whose narratives propose a generally circumscribed spatial field and whose art direction disposes its actual limits. Here the script tells us clearly that the camera need not wander from place to place, at least not for the sake of the action. In fact, precisely for action's sake, the camera is asked to check its proclivity to turn up as it pleases and accept instead the confines of one dominant (and perhaps one or two ancillary) clearly defined perimeter. As the camera resists the temptation to roam, to show off set after set, decor, far from being suppressed, is foregrounded—not necessarily through the intensity of decoration as in the examples cited in previous chapters, but through a design strategy that calls for one set to be recurrently, insistently, and on occasion unfailingly present to the spectator.

This decor is either unitary or gives that impression through the conspicuous articulation of its separate parts. Its origins, whatever the film's source (screenplay, novel, or, most often, play), are solidly rooted in the theatrical unity of place that, like the unities of time and action, is one of the three unalterable prescriptions of classical dramaturgy. Time and action have been liberated for centuries, of course, from the doctrine that a single plot must unfold within a single day. The single place, on the other hand, continues to be the convention with which the scene, and certainly the proscenium, is obliged to reckon.[1] Why would cinema revert to the prescription of unity of place through the self-imposition of the unitary or quasi-unitary set? Why would it contest one of its fundamental properties, the power to transport the audience across distances bridged by the ellipsis of editing? How does the narrative function of the closely circumscribed set differ from that of the uncircumscribed decor?

For one thing, whatever its status, whether denotation, punctuation, embellishment, or artifice, by virtue of its very restriction, the circumscribed set enjoys a privileged relationship to the narrative. To a greater or lesser degree, it subsumes the narrative and is subsumed by it. Decor becomes the narrative's organizing image, a figure that stands for the narrative itself. Whether the set is a repeated figure to which the action is obliged to return (*The Magnificent Ambersons*, *Rebecca*), a persistent figure that accommodates an occasional, brief flight (*Hamlet*), or a ubiquitous figure that refuses to allow the camera to stray beyond its borders (*Street Scene*), the sets we consider here are inseparable from the narrative.

Second, the circumscribed decor enjoys a privileged relationship with the spectator. We come to know it intimately. The set in question may be as narrowly defined as a room (*Le Jour se lève*) or a public chamber (*Mr. Smith Goes to Washington*); it may be somewhat less restricted, for example, a mansion (*Rebecca*), a castle (*Hamlet*), a hotel (*Grand Hotel*); it may wander from interior to exterior by way of a street (*How Green Was My Valley*) or a courtyard (*Le Crime de M. Lange*). Where more than one space is described, the distance between them is charted and recharted by the camera until finally, through the insistent portrayal of their interconnections, the spectator understands the spaces to be contiguous.

And last, the narrative that demands a unitary or quasi-unitary set obliges the art director to restraint, of course, but also to ingenuity. Spatial limitation in the hands of a master art director is a necessity not only to be obeyed but to be exploited; to be, in fact, transcended. The result is often a design performance whose virtuosity is underscored by the obvious economy of the decorative means at hand. The strength of that performance rests, in the end, on the privileged relationship of decor to camera and to script that is the inevitable consequence of spatial constraint. That relationship, not freedom of movement or extravagance of design, if successfully negotiated, guarantees the quintessentially cinematic quality of the product.

Within the boundaries that most tightly restrict cinema's theoretically boundless space—repeated, persistent, or, in extreme cases, ubiquitous figures—we discover the artful manipulation of an intensive design vocabulary that tests the narrative's powers of concentration. Among these is cinema's capacity to describe as opposed to the capacity for display we considered in our discussion of *The Towering Inferno* and *The Gay Divorcee*. The opening of *Rear Window* describes, as we noted in chapter 2. So do the ball sequence of *The Magnificent Ambersons*, the initial exploration of Elsinore of *Hamlet*, and the first minutes of *Dead End*, to cite three examples we treat in detail below.

Repeated Figure

Nearly all of the action of *The Heiress* takes place in an elegant home—not just any home, or even a typical upper-middle-class home, but the home of Dr. Austin Sloper (Ralph Richardson), on Washington Square, in mid-nineteenth-century New York City. Its drawing room was designed for his beautiful, accomplished, and beloved wife, long dead, reflecting her excellent yet out-of-fashion taste. Now Sloper's plain, awkward, and unloved daughter Catherine (Olivia de Havilland) presides there. Harry Horner's art direction for *The Heiress* has been the object of considerable, indeed exceptional, comment.[2] The specifics of his design decisions have constant and direct impact on our reading of the narrative, here a film adaptation of a successful play based on Henry James's short

93. *The Heiress*: Catherine (Olivia de Havilland) on the staircase of the Sloper residence

novel *Washington Square* (fig. 93). In addition to positioning the appropriate signs of period and class, Horner provides for the psychological "space" the characters occupy and for the dynamics of their relationships:

> The staircase was a very dramatic effect. I designed it like the heart of a human being. It was the pivotal point of the house. I wanted Catherine to have certain feelings when she would go up or down the steps. There was a mirror placed on one of the landings, and you could see the rest of the house through it. To see her in the mirror when she rushed down to her lover gave the impression of extra speed. When she had to climb up at a moment of defeat—when she finally knew he was not coming to marry her—the climb was very dramatic. I thought the designer could help this by making a very steep staircase.[3]

Like most other films based on single-set plays, *The Heiress* opens out to a locale suggested by its original text. Catherine Sloper and Morris Townsend meet at a ball; in *A Streetcar Named Desire*, we follow Blanche and Mitch on their date; some scenes of *Casablanca* are played on the streets and, most memorably, at the airport of the Moroccan city. *The Little Foxes* shows the houses that neighbor the Giddens residence, the streets of the town, the bank, even a hotel in Mobile where Horace (Herbert Marshall) and his daughter Alexandra (Teresa Wright) stop on their trip back from Baltimore. But it is the stairway and parlor that define this fiction about family, greed, and power. Here, in the connective area between public and private life, with its vantage points from below and above, Alexandra witnesses her uncle (Carl Benton Reid) strike her aunt (Patricia Collinge); Regina (Bette Davis) slowly climbs and exhorts her husband Horace to die, and she climbs again to solitude at the end of the film. This decor is the site of the film's coup de théâtre: Regina remains immobile on a settee, refusing to fetch Horace's heart medicine, while he struggles into the depth of the parlor and collapses on the stairs.

Cinematic in their deployment of space and decor, these films are firmly anchored in the narrow limits of their theatrical origins. Transgressions to other locales do not undermine the focalizing effect of the film's central decors: Dr. Sloper's elegant residence on Washington Square, Kowalski's dilapidated flat in New Orleans, Rick's Café in Casablanca, the Giddenses' "good-looking" living room "in a small town in the South."[4] With the exception of Rick's Café, all of these decors represent living spaces (Rick's apartment is situated above his establishment). In fact, as we have seen, even narratives not derived from the stage may be deeply lodged in the decor of dwellings: Mildred Pierce's Glendale house, the class-coded domiciles of *Kings Row*, the horror castles of the Frankenstein series, the mansion of the demented movie star in *Sunset Boulevard*. These structures punctuate narrative and invest it with expressivity but do not locate all of its intersections. The stories of Mildred Pierce and Norma Desmond range over metropolitan Los Angeles; *Kings Row* is about a town with many houses; Frankenstein's monster spreads terror from castle and laboratory to village and countryside. Conversely, whatever wandering occurs in *The Magnificent Ambersons* and *Rebecca* is subordinate to the houses that both fill the center and limit the circumference of their respective fictions. These films, adaptations of novels rather than plays, illustrate how a specific decor, recurrent but not unfailingly present, comes to dominate, in fact, to embody a work's essential qualities.

Not unexpectedly, *The Magnificent Ambersons* boasts a number of elaborately staged sequences that take place out of doors; one of its subjects is the impact of motor vehicles on society. The film features a sleigh ride that required twelve shooting days in an ice plant and a "motorized" shot that uninterruptedly captures a carriage ride through the streets of a small city.[5] But it is the Amberson mansion that situates the relationships, that indicates the tensions, that governs our progress through the film's duration. The first facade we see belongs to a more modest house across the street. This sets up a sturdy middle-class reference point for judging the magnificence of the Ambersons, a family whose pride precedes its fall. And from across the street we share the view of assembled neighbors commenting on the luxurious and exceptional circumstances of the Ambersons: "$60,000 for the woodwork alone . . . stationary washstands in every last bedroom in the place!"

The film never explores the three-dimensionality of the mansion's exterior.[6] However, the deep interior spaces of interconnected rooms and levels capture three generations of Ambersons in a flux of speech, attitude, and feeling. First hidden behind a front door repeatedly closed in the face of Eugene Morgan (Joseph Cotton), the disappointed suitor of Isabel Amberson (Dolores Costello), the depth of the interior space is emphatically penetrated when a much older Eugene and his daughter Lucy (Anne Baxter) cross

162   *Set as Narrative*

the threshold to attend what turns out to be the last ball ever to be held by the Ambersons. Continuous space and contiguous decors are described in the extended duration of traveling shots of people walking, dancing, conversing, some positioned near the camera and some in the adjoining rooms. Isabel's son George (Tim Holt) sits with Lucy on an elaborate staircase; over their shoulders, we see the great depth of the hall and the ballroom beyond.[7]

Here, early in the film, we attend this last festive occasion in a house designed for such events. With the exception of the funeral of Isabel's husband Wilbur Minafer, all subsequent scenes are private encounters of agonizing intimacy. The aura of public ostentation, so carefully established, lingers through the whispered exchanges, the furtive gazes, the guilt, the recriminations, and the grief of a family whose decadence is measured by the empty, echoing rooms of their house. The integrity of the rooms is guaranteed by shot durations that accommodate fluid, unrushed camera movements. We come to know this house in its horizontal and vertical articulations.[8]

Again, as in so many films about families and domestic interiors, the staircase enjoys particular privilege. At the end of the party sequence, George and Lucy sit at its foot and watch Eugene and Isabel dance (fig. 94). After the death of Wilbur Minafer, the

94. *The Magnificent Ambersons:* the downstairs hall of the Amberson mansion, George (Tim Holt) and Lucy (Anne Baxter) seated on the stairs, Eugene (Joseph Cotten) and Isabel (Dolores Costello) dancing

relationship between Eugene and Isabel becomes the subject of gossip, or so Aunt Fanny (Agnes Moorehead) implies to George. George is resentful of Eugene, the intruder; Fanny is jealous of Eugene's affection for her sister-in-law. The emotions of Fanny and George mount as they ascend this remarkable staircase that rises through the core of the house in fits and starts, in six sections of alternating flights and landings. (fig. 95).[9] The progress of emotion is charted on the stations of the two characters, sometimes uncomfortably close on a horizontal landing, sometimes in positions of dominance and subordination on the inclined portion of the stairs, sometimes glaring at each other across the stairwell. Shortly afterwards, the disposition of the scene is restaged with significant emotional and spatial variation. In the interval, George has acted to sever the relationship between his mother and Eugene. Isabel and her brother Jack (Ray Collins) disappear behind a door on the main floor; the camera tilts up to George on the second-floor landing and to Fanny on the floor above. Aunt and nephew replay their previous scene over the full extent of the staircase, but this time the contrite Fanny tries in vain to repair the damage caused by her previous insinuations. And in a moving coda to this story of aborted romance, we see Eugene at the foot of the staircase, still denied access to his beloved Isabel, who is dying in an upstairs bedroom.

95. *The Magnificent Ambersons*: George and Fanny (Agnes Moorehead) on the staircase of the Amberson mansion

There is no way to avoid becoming aware of decor that is so meticulously and insistently presented. A stationary camera records a long scene in the kitchen, a conversation between Fanny and George, against a background of sharply silhouetted pots and pans. An ironic reversal of the initial entry into the house occurs near the end of the film, when the family fortune has been dissipated and the house must be abandoned. The camera followed Eugene and Lucy through the front door on the night of the last ball; it precedes George and Fanny as they make their way from the kitchen through the same public rooms, now filled only with sheet-draped furniture and deep shadows. The great house is fated to be divided into single-room apartments. The death of the Amberson mansion was underscored in the film's original 131-minute version. As George kneels in his dead mother's bedroom, the voiceover narration states that "the very space in which tonight was still Isabel's room would be cut into new shapes by new walls and floors and ceilings." [10]

The fundamental decor of *Rebecca* is another great house, Manderley, a building so splendid that it appears on postcards and is opened for public tours. And like the Amberson mansion, Manderley is not the sole locus of the fiction. Soon after the first sequence, nearly one-fifth of *Rebecca*'s 130-minute duration is devoted to scenes on the Riviera where the master of Manderley, Maxim de Winter (Laurence Olivier), meets and marries a shy young woman (Joan Fontaine); nearly as long is the protracted denouement, staged in a nearby town and in London. These excursions do not, however, weaken Manderley's grip on the narrative. The Amberson mansion provides a dynamic display for a saga of family and society; Manderley actively participates in the peripeties of a romantic melodrama. As Hitchcock himself put it, "In a sense the picture is the story of a house. The house was one of the three key characters of the picture." [11]

"Last night I dreamt I went to Manderley again." The film reiterates the famous first words of the popular novel. We dream along with the narrator, the second Mrs. de Winter, who is never named. We approach the dream object through a gate, down an overgrown drive. The silhouette of the ruined house looms ahead. Light appears from the windows, but it is only the reflection of the moon. When the moon is obscured by a cloud, the house becomes "a desolate shell." The narrator asserts, "We can never go back to Manderley again." But the film demonstrates that we can—in a dream, in a fiction. Thus, Manderley is a house that is not merely a house but a dream figure, a decor constructed for fiction, posited outside of time, exempt from the laws of reality. It will exert the power of that exemption throughout the rest of the narrative.

After their honeymoon in France, the de Winters return, through the gate, down the winding drive. There is a break in the trees, a crescendo in the music, and the eyes of Mrs. de Winter widen at the sight of the castle. Max exclaims, "That's it. That's Manderley." Manderley emerges as a threat to this unprepossessing woman who feels herself unequal to its size and nobility. She is dwarfed as the camera returns, again and again, to the vast central hall, its wide staircase mounting and then bifurcating on a landing that links the east and west wings (fig. 96). Late in the film, tricked into wearing a costume like one that belonged to Rebecca, the first Mrs. de Winter, she attempts a grand entrance down the staircase and thereby provokes her husband's wrath. This coincides with the

96. *Rebecca*: set still of the central hall and staircase of Manderley

discovery of Rebecca's body in the sunken boat. It is as if Rebecca had returned to humiliate the imposter wearing her dress, the interloper treading on a staircase made for a great lady, not a timid one.

In *The Magnificent Ambersons*, the disposition of rooms is manifest in the depth-of-field stagings that reveal their junctures and contiguities. In *Rebecca*, explicit verbal reference is made to the disposition of Manderley: the east wing, with no view of the sea, for the new Mrs. de Winter; the west wing and Rebecca's room, preserved just as it was the day she died. Each return to the landing between the two wings heightens the conflict between the two Mrs. de Winters. The camera follows the new wife from room to room in her tentative explorations of this overwhelming house. It pauses at Rebecca's door as she and Mrs. Danvers (Judith Anderson), Rebecca's fanatically devoted servant, disappear from the frame. On the main floor, poor befuddled Mrs. de Winter walks into the library and is directed to the "morning" room by the butler. During these episodes we imagine that we know our way around Manderley better than she does.

Manderley intimidates its insecure new mistress not so much by its scale as by the many reminders of Rebecca, a woman ostensibly adored by her husband for her exceptional beauty and social graces. Over and over, decor serves to make present the absent figure. Mrs. de Winter mounts the stairs and hesitates at the landing. We see Rebecca's door from her point of view, then a close-up of the handle. She enters and gapes in amazement at the room's enormity, measured by the great gauze curtain that separates the canopied bed and dressing table from the sitting room. The faithful guardian of the past, Mrs. Danvers, materializes: "A lovely room. The loveliest room you've ever seen." Mrs. Danvers proceeds to evoke Rebecca by fetishizing, by eroticizing the room and its objects with the caress of her voice and the touch of her hands. At the end of the shot we see the power of the decor in the relationship between the room and Mrs. Danvers, starkly outlined in her black dress in front of the white gauze curtain.

Rebecca is as much a fiction of Manderley as it is a narrative about those who inhabit it. We are, in fact, made to regret the absence of Manderley during Maxim's long confession to his wife in the beach house, following the discovery of Rebecca's body. Here, during the episodes related to the inquest, and in the scene in a London doctor's office, words must convey the complexities of a plot previously served by images of decor. But as soon as the mystery of Rebecca's death is solved, the former mistress of Manderley reclaims her rights. Just as in the film's opening dream shots, the windows are illuminated. Mrs. Danvers has set fire to the house. We last see her in Rebecca's room, still hieratic in her black dress, before the collapsing ceiling crushes her. The last image is an eroticized decor: Rebecca's burning bed, then a close-up of her pillow and her negligee case, an *R* embroidered on it by Mrs. Danvers.

Mr. Smith Goes to Washington and *Le Jour se lève* are films whose principal sets organize narrative without monopolizing screen time. Mr. Smith (James Stewart) goes to Washington in order to serve out a term in the Senate chamber. This exemplary tale of the democratic voice is played out in the forum whose structure and rules of order are laboriously spelled out to Smith, the naive idealist, who eventually commands both structure and rules to serve his cause (fig. 97). The floor of the Senate with its semicircular tiers of desks, the podium of the President of the Senate, and the visitors' gallery are brought into verbal and visual exchange during Smith's three speeches, with greatest intensity in the last, his filibuster, a speech that validates his life and the narrative, a speech that requires a decor of the Senate chamber in Washington for its proper voicing and hearing.

François's room in *Le Jour se lève* is a highly narrativized decor from which the entire fiction radiates. The room—set and props—triggers the memories that unleash François's retrospection, flashbacks that comprise the better part of the film's duration. The rooms into which François's working-class apartment building is divided are all similar in size and appearance, we suspect. Yet his, on the uppermost floor, occupies a place of priority accentuated by the disproportion, actually a decorative paradox, between the building's elongated facade, the film's liminal image, and François's cramped quarters (fig. 98). As the narrative unfolds and the last hours and minutes of François's life draw to their end, this living space becomes progressively reduced. Decor quite literally marks the narrative. The walls of the room, pocked by bullet holes, modify the narrative present; as the furniture and objects—the heavy armoire, the cracked mirror, the teddy bear, the locket—are realigned during the police attack, they too recapitulate the events of the film. The other characters and decors of *Le Jour se lève*—Françoise, Clara, Valentin, the factory,

97. Mr. *Smith Goes to Washington*: the Senate chamber, Jefferson Smith (James Stewart) standing at center

98. *Le Jour se lève*: François's room, the death of François (Jean Gabin)

the greenhouse, the bar and stage—are all inscribed in François's room, a set that captures the form and substance of an entire narrative.

Persistent Figure

We posit a distinction between a set like that of François's room, whose repeated foregrounding sums or even elides the disparate elements of a narrative, and a set (or a cluster of sets) that monopolizes all of screen time. Brief forays outside of the persistent set serve only to emphasize its persistence. We are seized by the certain knowledge that the narrative cannot stray long from the confines of the familiar decor. That decor is the functional Parisian building and courtyard of *Le Crime de M. Lange*, a figure for community, for work, love, and fiction as well as for M. Lange's pardonable crime. It is three adjacent spaces—a lurid back alley, a labyrinthine kitchen, and an exquisitely appointed restaurant—that constitute the site for the brutal clash of moral and political values in *The Cook, the Thief, His Wife, and Her Lover*.[12] In *Black Narcissus* it is an exotic palace high in the Himalayas where a group of nuns fail the test of their vocation. It is as extensive as a Welsh mining village (*How Green Was My Valley*), as complex as a castle in Denmark (*Hamlet*). Its borders, like those of a painting, locate all the narrative data in a field immediately accessible to our eye.

The gigantic mining village built for *How Green Was My Valley* inflects a narrative of unusually broad dimensions.[13] First seen through the window of the narrator, Hew Morgan, as he packs his belongings in his mother's shawl prior to leaving his valley, the houses and street that climb the hill toward the framework of the mine elevator constitute the film's liminal set and central locus (fig. 99). The sharp definition of the row of nearly identical houses is favored by the configuration of the other side of the the street—not a like row of similar houses but rather a low wall, beyond which spread the rest of the village and the valley. This is a comprehensive image of home and work. The mine entrance dominates, at the apex; the dwellings are accented by small walled plots that front them.[14] If the street is the domain of men, the houses, with their front doors, tiny yards, and gates, belong to the women. The elevation of the set displays women, men, and children as separate characters, as family groups, and as parts of an entire community. Throughout the film, the set supplies a shape and a stage that take into account different aspects of individuality, plurality, gender, and age, hence different aspects of the narrative.

Showing the street both in its integrity and in fragments, the initial shots correspond to Hew's laments about the encroaching mountain of slag in his once beautiful valley. Grime-covered working boys wearily descend part of the street; a solitary girl walks up it in the opposite direction. In refusing to accept that the past is dead, Hew initiates the flashback that occupies the remainder of the film. We see the valley as it was when it was green, some of the principal characters, and the village street, reinscribed as the men descend it after work. With the women standing at their doors and within the little walled plots, the set exhibits its size and spatializes family and community. We know that the Morgan family will be given priority by the narrative when we observe Beth Morgan (Sara

99. *How Green Was My Valley*:
the village street and the
mine elevator

Allgood), the matriarchal figure, seated at the front gate, receiving in her lap the pay of
husband and sons as they enter the house, singing. Positioned opposite the church, at the
foot of the street, one side unattached to the other identical houses, the Morgan house
also enjoys spatial priority.

The only excursion out of the village is Hew's, to a school on the other side of the
mountain. Otherwise, whatever occurs in *How Green Was My Valley* is related to the articulations of the main set, the exits from and entrances into the principal interiors: house,
mine, church. Often with the Morgan house as fulcrum, the totality of the set is called
upon for the major communal events: the strike, the celebration of Mrs. Morgan's recovery from her long illness. Moments of sadness and joy meet at the juncture of the private
and the public, house and street. Invited to perform for Queen Victoria, Ivor Morgan's
male chorus sings in front of the house; the camera pans right to two other Morgan sons
who, laid off from work, commence the first leg of their journey to America. The whole
length of the street becomes a scene of private and public sorrow when the whistle signals
a mine accident. The men descend the street; the Morgans' daughter-in-law moves from
her gate to her front door, screams her husband's name, and collapses. The street marks
young Hew's (Roddy McDowell) rite of passage, his first day in the mines, as he joins the

other men trudging up to work; it is on the street that he is mocked by the women of the village over the divorce of his sister Angharad (Maureen O'Hara) and her attachment to the minister, Mr. Gruyffyd (Walter Pidgeon).

The exterior set of *How Green Was My Valley* provides a model of integral exterior space that is reinforced by the film's use of interior space in the flow of action through the lower rooms of the Morgan house. There, the framing of low ceilings and wide portals emphasizes connections between zones and characters. As the shape of the Morgan dining room becomes familiar, its grouping of the family members becomes crucial to our reading of the narrative. *How Green Was My Valley* is the story of comings and goings (mostly goings), of children who marry, of sons who leave the Morgan table because they disagree with the head of the family, who return at a moment of great happiness and honor to the family, and who leave for good, in search of work.

Life and narrative connect on the connective street, memorable in its arrangement of the places where meaning is generated. Intended to appear as a naturalistic representation of a Welsh mining village, the set nevertheless serves as an emblem for the dynamics of a fiction that oscillates between the harsh necessities of work and the emotional centers of home and hearth. Looming over the village is the machine, the elevator that carries each miner down to hard labor and, twice in *How Green Was My Valley*, to death. The elevator is the summit, its image inescapable. The line of houses is an accumulation of human abodes, collected at the bottom, in the Morgans', next to the church. Thus, the dimensions of the narrative, the life in the mine and the life of the family, are commensurate with the set. Satisfied with their paychecks, glum and out of work, happy in their song, griefstricken over death: this is how we see the characters on the *How Green Was My Valley* street, a movie set that seems, in fact, to produce the attitudes it displays.

When *How Green Was My Valley* is through with the daily life of the Morgan family, with the thwarted love of Angharad and Mr. Gruffydd, the global configuration of the village disappears from the film. The final sequence—the public disgrace of Angharad, the resignation of Mr. Gruffydd, the mine disaster that claims the life of the family patriarch Gwilym Morgan (Donald Crisp)—withholds the familiar set, an image that is too much of the everyday world for the dramatic conclusions of this fiction, for the transcendental force of memory that brings back the departed and the dead at the very end.

At the conclusion of Laurence Olivier's film of *Hamlet*, the persistent set is a sign of death and transcendence. Beneath the opening credits, the castle of Elsinore stands high atop a promontory; a moment later, we see it from above as it materializes out of swirling clouds. The camera descends toward a frozen image of the highest tower at the moment of Hamlet's funeral, then pulls up to place the tower within the context of the castle. The funeral procession vanishes, leaving behind the now deserted maze of battlements and towers. The decor remains uninhabited as the camera traces its descent down one flight of steep steps, then another.

Following the scene of Horatio's encounter with the Ghost, the camera continues its construction of Elsinore as an architectural object. It spirals down the castle's interior, again beginning at the topmost battlement, bringing into its field nothing but decor—

100. *Hamlet*: Elsinore's assembly hall, Hamlet (Laurence Olivier) seated at center

stairs and stone walls, landings, archways, ending with a plunging look at the bottom-most level, the unoccupied assembly hall (fig. 100). There is a dissolve to a close-up of what we later learn is Hamlet's chair. The camera reverses its journey, now rising level by level to show Ophelia's archway in the depth of the frame, approach it, then spiral upwards to the open doorway of Queen Gertrude's chamber, her canopied bed illuminated in sharp focus in the distance. We advance with the camera and pass through the door toward the bed.

This series of shots, systematically devoted to the mode of description, lasts nearly a minute. It establishes most of the significant playing spaces within the castle; more important, it establishes their relationships to each other. The camera has demonstrated the interconnections, has "walked us through" the sets. We are thus able to follow in the steps of the characters, imagine their itineraries, spy on them from a variety of vantage points, just as they spy on each other: in very sharp focus, across long distances, down the corridors and through the archways of this sparsely furnished castle.

There are two very brief scenes played outside the confines of Elsinore: Hamlet's journey to England and Ophelia's drowning. The rest of the film hovers in and next to

TE133-276.A.

101. *Hamlet*: Hamlet mounting Elsinore's battlements

the castle (fig. 101). Along with the characters, again and again we retrace the steps taken by the camera in the opening sequence. Hamlet repeatedly ascends and descends the steep flights of stairs; Ophelia's "As I was sewing in my closet" speech is framed in her archway; Hamlet confronts his mother on the Oedipal bed we approached during the exposition; the assembly hall, scene of many encounters, is the site of spectacle for the play within a play and the theatre of final carnage.

The conclusion of *Hamlet* circles to its beginning, the camera's initial mappping of the sets now laden with the intervening narrative. With a camera-glance back at his empty chair, Hamlet's body is borne from the assembly room through the sets we have come to know so well, past Ophelia's empty archway, past his mother's empty bed. At times, the cortege is absent from the shot; we know it is proceeding upwards, however, as the camera pans and climbs the spiral route, over the familiar stones. Horatio and his four companions carry Hamlet's body to the uppermost tower of Elsinore. The final shot shows the group from a side angle, in silhouette against a darkening sky, thus adding yet another dimension to the liminal decor, the castle fit for tragedy, the monument fit to display the nobility of the dead prince. The closed system of Elsinore, initially positioned as a figure of density, elevation, and complexity, is now merely a shadow structure, an immaterial decor appropriate to the cathartic transcendence of tragedy.

Ubiquitous Figure

At its extreme, the set that stands as a figure for the narrative is ubiquitous, present to the viewer from opening to closing shot. Often the film's very title carries the message: such is the case in *Grand Hotel* and *Weekend at the Waldorf*, where the camera does not stray from the eponymous buildings, and in *Dead End* and *Street Scene*, where it is confined to a river slip that forms an urban cul-de-sac or to the facade and stoop of a single building in a working-class neighborhood. A courtyard, an attic, and an apartment are the charts on which the narrative is plotted in *Rear Window*, *The Diary of Anne Frank*, and *Rope*. Present to the story with the same insistence they are to the viewer, these sets transcend the notion of narrative function. They become, in fact, inseparable from the narrative; what happens (the action) cannot be separated from where it happens (the place). The definition of that place is left to the agency of decor.

Street Scene (directed by King Vidor) and *Dead End* (directed by William Wyler) are separated by six years (1931 and 1937). They feature the same star (Sylvia Sidney), the same producer (Samuel Goldwyn), and the same art director (Richard Day) (fig. 102, fig. 103, fig. 104, fig. 105). Both are based on New York plays, Elmer Rice's *Street Scene* and Sidney Kingsley's *Dead End* (screenplay by Lillian Hellman); both advance a progressive social message. In each case, the film's decor imitates a celebrated stage production of the play. Both observe unity of time; no more than twenty-four hours elapse from

102. *Street Scene*: stage production, the murder of Anna Maurrant

103. *Street Scene*: film, Frank Maurrant (David Landau) defies the crowd

exposition to climax.[15] Both observe unity of place and make that known at the outset by locating through their titles the generic urban spaces that frame and define the narrative.

Street Scene announces with a touch of ingenuousness that what we are about to witness, however startling, is in fact a realistic representation of quite ordinary events: before us will unfold a scene that has been played out repeatedly on any number of like and indistinguishable neighborhood streets. The street and the narrative demand only the most generic identification. We can, therefore, expect the decor to reflect an essentially denotative generality. *Dead End*'s title has more complex metaphoric weight and its set a design sufficiently elaborate to punctuate the narrative at moments of heightened tension. This particular dead end is a slip that reaches into New York's East River. It is also a slum from which few escape, a literal and ideological impasse. Both sets, street and dead end, are unitary spaces that determine the conduct of their narratives. The characters converge, observe, and are observed from the confines of titles from which there is, in the life of the narrative, no exit. The violent deaths of Anna Maurrant and of Baby Face Martin brand the decors, street and dead end, as sites of narrative endgames.

Shots of the city skyline open and close *Street Scene*. Between the first sequence and the last, essentially without interruption, we have before us the street, facade, and stoop of a solidly working-class apartment building—only one step grander than a tene-

104. *Dead End*: stage production, the death of Baby Face Martin

ment. The facade provides the frame and backdrop for character and action, both of which are bound by the El station at the end of the block. *Dead End*, too, opens with a cityscape, followed by a cut to the set that, like *Street Scene*'s, will be exhibited to the viewer throughout the film. A protracted crane shot describes the expanse of the playing space, scaffolding on the right, luxury high-rise apartment building on the left. The street that occupies the center of the set is lined by tenements and stores. It disappears into the background; in the foreground it stops abruptly at the wharf and the river.

Like *Street Scene*, the set of *Dead End* is unitary; unlike *Street Scene*, it is ununified. It is, in fact, composed of several discrete adjoining sections. If *Street Scene*'s decor is conspicuously shallow and horizontal, *Dead End*'s set is strikingly deep and vertical. And just as the seamless shallowness and horizontality of *Street Scene* support the set's denotative intention, the depth and verticality of *Dead End* promote the punctuative potential of its decor. Richard Day's version of Jo Mielziner's stage design of *Street Scene* allows for some pavement-level and other sharply angled shots. In general, however, the set favors a frontal, eye-level point of view, and it is from that point of view that much of the action is captured. Day's version of Norman Bel Geddes's *Dead End* Broadway set is clearly intended to invite the virtuosity of photography in depth.[16] Moreover, the set's literal and figurative verticality elicits the dramatic and visual potential of elevation: in low angle

105. *Dead End*: film, the Dead End Kids (Billy Halop, Huntz Hall, Bobby Jordan, Leo B. Gorcey, Gabriel Dell), Baby Face Martin (Humphrey Bogart, leaning over dock), and his accomplice, Hunk (Allen Jenkins)

from street level and in high angle from the tenement roofs, luxurious balconies, windows, and scaffolding. These radical camera angles, responsive to the geometry of a dynamic twentieth-century urban decor, are specifically expressive of the narrative: its high/low economic conflict; its climactic chase up and down the scaffolding, fire escapes, and ladders; the fall to the street of the villain shot dead on a fire escape. Much of *Street Scene* could be, and in fact is, witnessed by bystanders up or down or across the street from the building's front stoop. In order to see the whole set of *Dead End*, one would need to be suspended above the East River.

Despite the acute stylistic differences of staging, cinematography, and editing, the decors of *Street Scene* and *Dead End* fulfill the promise of the best of ubiquitous sets: standing as figures for the whole of their narratives, they determine character and action and represent the work's ideology. The omnipresent front stoop, windows, street, and dead end serve the violent and melodramatic encounters of their respective narratives; as the dominant and essential constructs of social life, they also contain and display crucial conflicts of ethnicity and class. The facade in *Street Scene*, to take the first example, is pierced by windows, identical frames for people of differing ethnicities and political and social persuasions: radical Eastern European Jews; gregarious, music-loving Italians; industrious Swedes; underclass WASPs, some tolerant and others not of neighbors whose English is heavily accented. While the dialogue is rife with references to ethnic tensions (and with ethnic slurs), the single set insists upon the commonality of class. And if, in spite of their bias and hostility, the inhabitants of *Street Scene*'s apartment building manage to live together with some measure of harmony, it is because, the unified decor tells us, they share the same class status.

The set of *Dead End*, on the other hand, juxtaposing a posh apartment building and a row of tenements, demonstrates the unbreachable divide between rich and poor, despite spatial proximity. The rich look down in fear and disdain on their impoverished neighbors. The poor look up, often dreaming of a better life: Dave (Joel McCrea), the aspiring architect, thinks he loves Kay, a rich man's mistress, and hopes to earn enough to marry her; Drina (Sylvia Sidney), a working girl on strike for higher wages, is desperate to take her young and impressionable brother out of the dead end; Baby Face Martin (Humphrey Bogart), who years before turned to crime to escape the neighborhood, comes back to die. Here, as in *Street Scene*, the ubiquitous set constructs the film's ideological charge. It offers, indeed insists upon, the relentless representation of the effects of economic and social conditions on those who are its subjects.

Where the set is narrative, decor's topography, no matter how complex, becomes utterly familiar. We are positioned to track it in our mind's eye. Leaving the movie theatre after seeing the films we consider in this chapter, we may or may not feel the urge to whistle the sets. That depends on the extent to which they have captured our imagination. However, if pressed for a description, we know the decor well enough to describe it with accuracy, to trace and retrace our steps through it. We know it physically, materially. It has been before our eyes repeatedly, often persistently, sometimes ubiquitously. In the end, this decor takes on for the spectator a relationship to the narrative akin to that which it has for the characters themselves.

Chapter 7

Judgment and Prize

The preferences of professional spectators—scholars, critics, and reviewers who publish their assessments—constitute a body of films remembered for their direction, their performances, sometimes their dialogue or even their music, occasionally their originality. Unless reviewers are conditioned by advance publicity to the reception of some aspect of design, the art direction of a film, as we have seen, is not likely to be the subject of much discussion.

But if judgment with respect to art direction is uncommon in newspaper reviews, articles, essays, and books about the movies, negligible by comparison with the enormous bibliography on acting and directing, it is certainly not absent. In this chapter, we will first examine the explicit evaluative discourse generated by set design in newspaper and magazine reviews.[1] Our sample is, by necessity, selective. We have focused primarily on reviews of films treated elsewhere in this book or considered by others who have written on art direction. The second part of the chapter is an analysis of the systematic evaluation of art direction offered by the Oscar. What will emerge from both parts of this inquiry are the bases and biases of judgment and the degree to which that judgment relates decor to narrative.

Reviewers

We take as our point of departure the collected reviews of Graham Greene, Otis Ferguson, James Agee, and Dilys Powell, essayists who set a very high standard for film criticism during the period on which we have concentrated. Greene, for one, casts only a rare and oblique glance at design. He mentions the decor of *Fire over England* in passing, without naming Lazare Meerson; he offers only the laconic "This is the best production to come from Denham yet. The sets are magnificent."[2] He ignores sets in his favorable reviews of *La Kermesse héroïque*, *Winterset*, and *Dodsworth*, three films renowned for their decor; he takes *Romeo and Juliet* to task for its excessively sumptuous Hollywood style.[3] Although

Otis Ferguson, the *New Republic* reviewer from 1934 to 1941, is particularly sensitive to matters of staging and composition, he, like Greene, has little to say about art direction or art directors.

James Agee eventually provides the exception to the rule. Critic for *Time* from 1941 to 1948 and *The Nation* from 1942 to 1948, Agee begins to consider art direction with his reviews of *Henry V*. In *Time*, he indulges in this hyperbolic judgment: "The French court, in fragility, elegance, spaciousness and color, is probably the most enchanting single set ever to appear on the screen."[4] In *The Nation*, he offers a relatively extended analysis of the film's illusionistic effects:

> I very greatly like the anti-naturalistic, two-and-a-half-dimensional effect that is got by obtunding shallow perspectives in painted drops, and these drops are very pretty and clever; but too many of them are pretty and clever in a soft, almost travel-poster way which to some extent conflicts with and lets down the foregrounds. The night sequence in the English camp might, I think, have been still better if it had taken more of its country-night po-etic atmosphere straight from nature, and had wholly avoided the smell and look of a good, semi-naturalistic studio set.[5]

It is not surprising that Agee should take detailed notice of the sets of *Henry V*. Given its mixture of realism and theatrical illusion, Paul Sheriff's decor helps define the artifice of our taxonomy and is, therefore, indeed hard to overlook.[6] Yet Agee's sophisticated re-marks here, and in his review of *The Best Years of Our Lives* ("some of the best stages for the action that I have ever seen in a movie"), demonstrate his awareness of the effect of visual design on narrative and make one wonder about the absence of that awareness elsewhere in his writings.[7]

The quality of art direction in British cinema of the 1940s is no doubt responsible for the increased attention paid to the subject by movie reviewers. Dilys Powell, critic for the *Sunday Times*, begins to consider design when the collaboration of Michael Powell, Emeric Pressburger, and Alfred Junge results in a series of films whose striking decor we have defined as set as artifice. On *A Matter of Life and Death* [*Stairway to Heaven*]: "They [Powell and Pressburger] owe a great deal to the designs of Alfred Junge, whose sets for celestial High Court and stratospheric escalator have at once the precision and extravagance of hallucination."[8] On *Black Narcissus*: "But when place is allowed to dominate, this is a film of astonishing quality. The directors, the designer Alfred Junge, and the cameraman Jack Cardiff have painted with fine clear line and cool brilliant colour the palace on the cliff-crest, the sunny courtyard, the night shadows."[9] Dilys Powell is also enthusiastic about Oliver Messel's *The Queen of Spades*: "[His] settings and costumes are among the most beautiful I can remember seeing on the English screen."[10]

The persistent unitary sets for the Laurence Olivier/Roger Furse *Hamlet* are praised even by less eminent reviewers, usually oblivious to design: A. S. Barnes of the *New York Herald Tribune* says, "Roger Furse's production design is arresting."[11] Bosley Crowther of the *New York Times* mentions "the rich designing of Roger Furse."[12] In

The New Yorker, John McCarten refers to the film's "remarkable sets."[13] Vague and generalized evaluation of this kind is symptomatic of the way daily reviewers treat most aspects of the film text, with the occasional exception of narrative and performance. Bosley Crowther, from his influential desk at the *New York Times*, usually disregards art direction altogether. Even when he is struck by it, as in *Henry V* or *The Red Shoes*, Crowther seems unable to enter into any detail. He returns to art direction no fewer than three times in his review of *The Red Shoes* without managing one meaningful comment: "and despite the beauties of the settings"; "spectacular décor"; "much could be said of the whole décor."[14]

The case of *The Red Shoes* is instructive in the variety of critical reaction to art direction the film generated. Its depiction of the *designed* world of ballet cries out for notice, and, on some level, Crowther responds; Barnes in the *Herald Tribune* and McCarten in the *New Yorker* remain impervious.[15] Eric Newton dismisses the "lamentable ballet sequences," invoking no criterion other than his sense that "the colours were unimaginative."[16] The very literal reviewer for *Newsweek* is generally disappointed by the film; he brings himself to praise the overall production but objects to the patently artificial sets for "The Red Shoes" ballet, citing their lack of verisimilitude: "The resulting sequences float through a good half-dozen dreamlike and almost surrealistic settings which could not possibly have been fitted into the most elaborately equipped theater"

106. *The Red Shoes*: "The Red Shoes" ballet (Moira Shearer)

(fig. 106).[17] For C. A. Lejeune, on the other hand, "the highspot of the film is unquestionably the 'Red Shoes' ballet, specially devised for the film. . . . To my mind, the wedding of movement and colour here is almost perfect, and to Hein Heckroth, who designed the production, I would gladly award the finest red rose in my garden."[18] Dilys Powell concurs: "We must thank . . . Hein Heckroth, to whom we owe the designing of the whole production, but whose composition in form and colour is, naturally, most free and most beautiful in the limitless world of cinema ballet."[19] These widely diverse, pervasively unsupported opinions betray not only an insufficient critical vocabulary but also the lack of a standard for judgment. The consequence is an essentially unexamined reliance on the vagaries of personal taste.

Most daily and weekly critics have neither the interest nor the ability to comment on the positive relationship of decor to narrative; they are, however, struck by sumptuous visual design. The richly appointed *Jew Süss*, for instance, was considered by some the great hope of the British film industry in the mid-1930s (fig. 107). A sketch for one of the film's decors appears in the *Evening Standard* on December 30, 1933, nearly a year before the gala premiere in October 1934, attended by Prince George and Queen Marie of Rumania. The London reviewers respond with nationalistic fervor: "In production values—settings, lighting, cutting and the rest—it can put a chip on its shoulder at most that Hollywood has to offer."[20] "No American film has had more magnificent settings.

107. *Jew Süss*: the execution of Jew Süss

No better 'prestige' film has ever been sent out as an ambassador from these shores."[21] An article in London's *Daily Telegraph* on October 6, 1934, reports the film's success at New York's Radio City Music Hall. Even critics in the United States take special notice of the production, offering enthusiastic evaluations of the decor: "accurately mooded"; "imposing"; "the many lavish settings are a feature in themselves"; "opulent in period decoration and stunning backgrounds"; "handsome historical settings"; "backgrounds are beautifully executed."[22]

Jew Süss also provoked the more customary negative response to exceptionally lavish productions that compete with or that distract from narrative: "The illustrations stand out, but the text is blurred. On the pictorial side the film is of the highest quality. Here it can challenge comparison with the best the world studios have produced. . . . *Jew Süss* is the most ambitious film ever made in a British studio. But it is a long way from being the most convincing drama."[23] "Alfred Junge . . . has designed really impressive sets. In fact, they are some of the most beautiful I have seen from any studio. . . . Despite the importance of the actors and their parts, the acting, beside the settings, takes a second place."[24] "There may be a considerable number of people who will furiously resent the assault on their senses in the brilliant but cheerless last reel. . . . I don't grudge a little extravagance for a picture that, like *Roman Scandal* [*sic*], is going to make a million people laugh and be happy."[25]

The negative reception of *Jew Süss* prefigures the postwar reaction to the calligraphic period films produced in Fascist Italy.[26] Giulio Cesare Castello attacks what he considers to be the excessively decorative films of Mario Soldati, Alberto Lattuada ("formal, compositional, picturesque preoccupations"), and Renato Castellani ("the baroque *Zazà*").[27] Julien Duvivier's British version of *Anna Karenina*, with embellishing sets by Andrei Andreyev, arouses similar attitudes. According to one reviewer, it is "a triumph of production over spirit. . . . Tolstoy seems to have been mislaid. Decor dominates. Set after set of multitudinous detail which can never be absorbed overwhelm the players and tire the optic nerve"; another asserts, "Andreyev's magnificent, sublimely elegant interiors, his railway stations, his sad (surely too clean?) streets, Beaton's entirely adorable feathers, fans and laces, and Miss Leigh's beauty have pushed between us and a story which was of the heart above everything."[28] Bosley Crowther complains about "expensive Russian scenery" in a lifeless film, and A. S. Barnes calls *Anna Karenina* a "tedious succession of tableaus."[29] The critic for *Newsweek* places the blame on the director: "Julien Duvivier has made the going a little harder by slacking his pace in favor of sets, atmospheric abracadabra, and Cecil Beaton's striking costumes."[30] A decade later, the French New Wave critics make parallel objections (in more inflammatory prose) to the fastidious design of cinematic adaptations of "great" books and plays—the "cinema de qualité."[31]

One would think that manifestly artificial fantastic sets, exempt from the burden of realism, would also be exempt from criticism about decorative excess. But, in fact, *The Tales of Hoffmann* and *Yolanda and the Thief* draw considerable negative comment. *Variety* is alone in praising *The Tales of Hoffmann* ("Production, designed by Hein Heckroth, is lavish and distinctive").[32] The reactions of other reviewers range from annoyance to dislike to outrage. For Philip Day in the *Daily Express*: "The settings scream at all points for an Oliver Messel, whose flocculent artificiality would have suited this story of a poet's Cloud-Cuckoo-Land far better than the hard artifice of Hein Heckroth's décor."[33] Crowther is confused and contradictory. On the one hand, he appears to admire Heckroth's "décor of incredible magnificence." On the other, he calls the designs "sleek and tricky . . . academic, empty and overdone."[34] The reviewer for *Time* captures the consensus: "Settings and costumes seem overripe and ostentatious enough to pass for a Hollywood producer's dream of paradise."[35] Virgil Thompson stands at the vituperative end of the spectrum: "The sets are of a vulgarity to outdo Hollywood at its worst."[36]

With a musical score and book less venerable than the one provided by Offenbach and his librettists for *The Tales of Hoffmann*, *Yolanda and the Thief* is even more thoroughly trounced by most reviewers. Bosley Crowther, an exception, hates the script but likes the "show": "For brilliance and color of the settings and costumes are nigh beyond compare—as rich and theatrically tasteful as any we've ever seen. . . . Sharaff, who did the costumes, and Edwin Willis, who fashioned the sets, are much more deserving of mention than Irving Brecher who wrote the script. . . . However, the visual felicities and the wackiness of the main idea hold the show together and make it something most profitable to see."[37] Others like neither the script nor the decor. The critic for *Time* calls *Yolanda* "overstuffed."[38] Jack Grant finds the art direction "more often old-fashioned than imaginative."[39] The piece in the *Hollywood Review* is a bit more balanced: "The Daliesque settings for the dream were excellently conceived by Cedric Gibbons and Jack Martin Smith. The same cannot be said for most of the other settings, which are opulent to the point of bad taste. Their heavy ornamentation further depresses a gossamer tale."[40] Few reviewers neglect the sets in almost universally negative notices of the film.[41] Virginia Wright sums it all up: "Trappings . . . don't make a motion picture."[42]

More surprising than the notice, whether praise or blame, accorded some extraordinary sets are the numerous instances in which these very same sets draw no attention at all. How is it that some reviewers fail to mention the glaring instances of artifice in the emphatically stylized decors of *Red Garters* and *Guys and Dolls*?[43] The critic for *Newsweek* got it right. His favorable review of *Red Garters* describes how "realism has been jettisoned in favor of subtle fantasy." He notes the "conventionalized trees," the buildings that satirize "those seen in the conventional Western movie," the facades that obviously have "nothing behind them."[44] All of this escapes the *Time* critic, who likes the film but can find to say of the production only that he admires the colors.[45] The nonrealistic sets of *Guys and Dolls* are Oliver Smith's reinterpretion of Jo Mielziner's original Broadway production of the musical. Jean Simmons, one of the film's stars, thinks "the style got confused in the disparity between the sets and performance"; as Kenneth Geist puts it, "Particularly jarring is the juxtaposition of real police cars and other vehicles against the abstract backdrops of Times Square's signs."[46] Yet the critic for *Time* and Bosley Crowther pass over the film's unusual production, and William K. Zinsser of the *Herald Tribune* can only describe it as "gaudy," McCarten as "damnably cute," and the critic for *Newsweek* as expensive.[47] These reviewers seem not to grasp that the fiction effect is one of the distinguishing features of *Guys and Dolls* or, more important, that no other major musical released in 1955 saw fit to dispense so radically with the reality effect. Even the fairy-tale Bagdhad created for *Kismet* preserves conventional spatial proportions. In fact, 1955 is the year in which the pursuit of realism is taken to the extremes of *Oklahoma!*, the film version of a musical that abandons Broadway for actual fields of corn "as high as an elephant's eye."

Some reviewers are unable to suspend disbelief, whatever the genre, musical or not, fantasy or not. In his negative review of *Brigadoon*, a musical that is also a fantasy, the critic for *Newsweek* objects, "Its methodically distributed quotas of heather, mist, and moonlit church ruins are effective principally in fogging up the plot."[48] The critic for *Time* complains about "the multimillion-dollar reconstruction on the Williamsburg plan, with every plastic daisy on the village green set in by hand."[49] Bosley Crowther, who likes *Brigadoon*, accepts it on its own terms: "To be sure, it does look artificial, but it is scenery. That, too, is okay."[50] Stephen Harvey locates the general dissatisfaction with the *Brigadoon* production more accurately, that is, in sets whose artificiality is undermined by their realism: "The painted-scrim Scotland erected on Metro's Stage 15 was too literal for wistful fancies, and less vivid than any one-reel travelogue. . . . George Gibbon's diorama looks like the world's biggest *nature morte*; distant lochs glint like silver cardboard, unseen clouds cast static shadows on a flat sea of heather."[51]

Judgments are most persuasive, as we have attempted to demonstrate, when they integrate narrative and decorative functions, when value is gauged in terms of the effectiveness of the set, of the relationship between story and art direction. According to the parameters of practice and theory we drew in previous chapters, these are, in fact, the terms in which decor is conceived by art directors and, more important, received by viewers. We have referred to the casual, unsubstantiated value judgments expressed in reviews of *Hamlet*; the Olivier/Furse film also inspires apposite connections between art direction and narrative. Eric Newton protests that the excellence of the sets is detrimental to the text: "The result—a highly satisfactory result if one is content to think of a film as a purely visual creation—was that the décor and not the Prince of Denmark became the hero of the piece."[52] But Dilys Powell is full of admiration: "In a setting designed to give both space for composition in movement and the sense of a society enclosed, the stream of speech has been preserved; the images, too, have a long, poetic flowing. . . . I should be less than fair if I failed to praise . . . the designs of Roger Furse."[53] The *Newsweek* critic concurs: "Many factors contributed to make this *Hamlet* a memorable motion picture; as important as any is Roger Furse's imaginative concept of a rock-hewn Elsinore—the endless corridors, the craggy flights of stairs, and the battlements that glower into nothingness and supply the visual grandeur that sets off the oral beauty of Shakespeare's poetry."[54] James Agee is even more effusive: "The great, lost creatures of the poem move within skull-stark Elsinore like thoughts and the treacherous shadows of thoughts. (Roger Furse's sets, as nobly severe and useful as the inside of a gigantic cello, are the steadiest beauty in the film. Next best: the finely calculated movement and disposal of the speakers, against his sounding boards.)"[55] Agee's remarks demonstrate the rare ability to articulate the integrity of the film text, to treat the separate elements of that text within a dynamics of complementarity. In principle, the systematized evaluation of art direction applies the same sophisticated standard.

The Oscar for Art Direction

Between the first Oscar presentation, in 1929 for films made in both 1927 and 1928, and 1960, the conventional terminus for the studio era, a mere ten films won Oscars for both Best Picture and Art Direction: *Cimarron, Cavalcade, Gone with the Wind, How Green Was My Valley, Hamlet, An American in Paris, On the Waterfront, Gigi, Ben-Hur, The Apartment.* This handful of dual winners have in common the successful negotiation of the conjunction of decor and narrative: a stunning office set punctuates the depiction of contemporary alienation in *The Apartment*; the actual city streets and docks of *On the Waterfront* are expressionistic reflections of powerful emotions; *Gigi* lovingly recreates the belle époque Paris necessary to an understanding of the film's moral universe; the epic ideological tensions of *Ben-Hur* are played out in its spectacular arena; unitary decors give shape to the narrative of community in *How Green Was My Valley* and the tragic confines of *Hamlet*.

A more meaningful pool is constituted by the 272 art direction nominees and the fifty-three winners chosen at the thirty-three awards ceremonies held from the late 1920s through the 1950s. The number of nominees varied from year to year, as did the number of awards when separate Oscars were bestowed for black-and-white and color films.[56] For the remainder of this chapter, we will consider the impact upon Art Direction awards of other Oscar categories, studio affiliation, genre, and the talent and reputation of specific art directors.[57]

In 1929, at the first awards ceremony of the Academy of Motion Picture Arts and Sciences, Interior Decoration was among twelve categories of merit. By the following year, three of those categories, Artistic Quality of Production, Comedy Direction, and Engineering Effects, had disappeared; three subdivisions, Adaptation, Original Story, and Title Writing, had been reduced to the single rubric of Writing. The total number of categories has continued to fluctuate over the years, but from the very beginning the function of decor in cinema, called Interior Decoration until 1947 when it was renamed Art Direction—Set Decoration, has been recognized by an Oscar. Given the short history of Hollywood, the industrial award for achievement in decor can claim considerable longevity. It has generated a list of titles sufficiently extensive to support an analysis of both trends and anomalies.[58]

The original definition proposed by the Academy for the category of Art Direction (the designation we will use in this chapter) forms a succinct and reasonable set of criteria for judging excellence: "the best achievement in set designing, with special reference to art quality, correct detail, story application, and originality."[59] Achievement is to be measured by adherence to conventional artistic norms, fidelity to historical and geographical documentation, consonance with the narrative, and the special character of the designer's inspiration. Realism and narrative coherence are to be served by "correct detail" and "story application," artistic distinction by "art quality" and "originality." The winners are to be rewarded for bending their technical skill to the collaborative effort of filmmaking as well as for the uniqueness of their vision.

The establishment of tenets of excellence is, of course, no guarantee that the nominators or voters will always, or even often, feel bound to observe them. Indeed, the list of winners in the category of Best Picture suggests that excellence was not always the deciding factor. Along with the acting awards, the Oscar for Best Picture was, as it still is, the most prestigious, most newsworthy, and most readily translated into box-office receipts. Obviously, some of the choices for Best Picture were determined by standards other than those prescribed by the category: financial success, industry politics, modish taste in art and narrative, and popular appeal. Do *Cavalcade* (1933), *Going My Way* (1944), and *The Greatest Show on Earth* (1952) represent, in their respective years, the Academy's standard—"the most outstanding motion picture considering all elements that contribute to a picture's greatness?"[60] The members of the Academy either thought so or voted according to other than the official criteria. Was it anglophilia for *Cavalcade*, an homage to box-office success for *Going My Way*, and for *The Greatest Show on Earth* the sense that it was time to reward Cecil B. De Mille? These three films bested the nominated *I Am a Fugitive from a Chain Gang*, *Little Women*, *Double Indemnity*, and *High Noon* in years in which *Trouble in Paradise*, *Meet Me in St. Louis*, *Laura*, and *Singin' in the Rain* were not even in the running.

The adjective in "Best Picture" has relevance to our discussion of the award for Art Direction. One might well expect that the "best achievement in set designing," if judged in terms of "story application," will serve "the most outstanding motion picture considering all elements that contribute to a picture's greatness." This is not necessarily the case. As we know, many vote for a film and pass over its director and/or its writers, as happened in nearly half the instances during the period in question and occurs to this day. After all, the rationale for separate categories is to reward individual merit—filmmaking as a fundamentally collaborative process notwithstanding. To what degree have the Academy Awards determined that there is a relationship between the best in Art Direction and the best in other award categories? Fewer than a third of the 272 films nominated for Art Direction were nominated for Best Picture; the coattails or bandwagon phenomenon does not appear to be at work. *Just Imagine*, *The Magnificent Brute*, *Vogues of 1938*, *Bitter Sweet*, and many others received Art Direction nominations *solely* for the merits of their design.

The percentage of dual nominations and awards for Best Picture and Art Direction is only marginally lower than that for Best Picture and Cinematography. More significant is the higher correlation between directing, writing, and Best Picture. The Academy membership was frequently able to distinguish the visual excellence of design, lighting, and photographic image in a film that did not qualify as "best." Less obviously pictorial, direction, script, and dialogue were more obviously necessary to the overall quality of a given film. A comparison of the connection between Art Direction and Cinematography shows that different standards apply even in pictorial categories where one might expect more commonly shared judgments. The best design was displayed by the best cinematography only slightly more than a third of the time.

How are we to interpret these discrepancies? The processes of nomination and voting in the category of Art Direction may have been skewed by many of the same personal, financial, and political pressures brought to bear on other categories. In the case of Best Picture–winning *Cimarron*, the bandwagon effect helps explain its award for Max Ree's unremarkable decor when the competing nominees included the universally admired and frequently cited sets designed by Anton Grot for *Svengali*. But it is also important to make distinctions between the procedures for nominating and voting in the categories of Best Picture and Art Direction. Since the third award year, the entire membership of the Academy has been eligible to nominate and to vote for Best Picture. This is not true for the Art Direction competition; there, with the exception of 1946 through 1956 when all members of the Academy voted in each category, participation has been restricted to design practitioners. From 1929 to 1934, each branch of the Academy made its own nominations and the entire membership was entitled to vote. In 1934, each art director was enjoined to nominate one of her/his own works and at least one film designed by someone else.[61] Two years later, the rules created a nominating committee of fifty members charged to receive the choices made by each of the eligible art directors. The committee then made up a list of nominees.[62] In the following year, 1937, the rules were changed once again. The voting as well as the nominations for Art Direction was limited to members of the Academy branch.

We can reasonably expect that the choices of art directors, like those of any cohesive group, will inevitably reflect biases: for example, preferences for style and genre, studio allegiance. And the fact of life membership in the Academy, we might speculate, will predispose them to a certain conservativism. These assumptions will be tested in the analysis that follows. We have at our command a highly controlled sample, a finite set of films by which to measure and understand the assessments of those responsible for decor. What did they notice, admire, imitate perhaps? Can we explain their judgments?

Studio

The studios had a high stake in the Oscar ceremonies. They paid for the event until 1948 and only withdrew financial support when British films seemed to be gaining a large percentage of the prizes. On April 1, 1949, the *New York Times* applauded the end of studio sponsorship, asserting that this would "remove any suspicion of company influence" and that henceforth merit alone would would be recognized.[63] Studio sponsorship of the awards ceremonies was viewed by many as window-dressing for the real purpose of the Academy of Motion Picture Arts and Sciences: the strict control of labor. So much was clear to many stars, directors, and writers who protested by boycotting the awards ceremonies in the 1930s. In fact, in order to draw a sufficient crowd to the 1936 event, Frank Capra, then president of the organization, had to inveigle D. W. Griffith into accepting an honorary Oscar. Capra hoped thereby to ensure the attendance of many who would want to be present to applaud one of the founding fathers of the movie industry.[64]

There is, of course, no denying the influence of studio allegiance on nominations and voting. Emanuel Levy goes so far as to declare that in the 1930s "film workers" voted the company line in order to advance the interests of their home studios, hence to defend their jobs: "At times, to assure the nomination of colleagues, they were placed as first choice, followed by unlikely candidates from other studios, which guaranteed that there would not be serious competiton in the selection of winners."[65] Like other "film workers," art directors stood to gain when the films produced by the studios that paid their salaries were those that prospered. They were also subject to the normal incentive to vote for their own work, or that of their closest colleagues. How did they, in fact, nominate and vote?

The statistics do not exclude the connection between studio affiliation and the way people nominated and voted in the category of Art Direction. The numbers and percentages give an edge to two of the big studios, M-G-M and 20th Century–Fox. But the strength shown by prestigious independent and foreign productions—overwhelming strength through 1948—is persuasive evidence that choices were not made primarily on the basis of studio affiliation. The difference in the percentage share by studio for Art Direction and Best Picture offers additional evidence of a significant degree of impartiality in the former category. Between 1927 and 1948, United Artists and British-produced films won nearly one-third of the Oscars in Art Direction but fewer than one-tenth of those for Best Picture. If bloc voting had an impact on the awards earned by art directors, it was not nearly as predictable as one might have suspected. If patterns emerge, they are likely to be in areas not strictly related to the contract that bound voter to studio.

Auteur

The case of Cedric Gibbons is the extreme example of the vexing relationship between the high number of Oscar nominations and awards received by certain art directors and their actual achievements. Gibbons, undoubtedly the most famous art director in the United States from the late 1920s until his retirement in 1956, was head of M-G-M's art department. As we noted in chapter 1, his contract guaranteed that he would receive credit for nearly every film produced at M-G-M during this period. Most art directors and certainly some other practitioners knew that Gibbons worked primarily as an administrator and supervisor. While Gibbons imposed his taste on the design of others, he did little or no designing himself. Was the prestige of M-G-M sufficient to win for Gibbons so many nominations and awards? Or was it the other way around? Did his celebrity bring attention to M-G-M's art direction?

The data reveals at least one striking fact. From 1946 to 1956, when the entire membership of the Academy became eligible to nominate and vote in the Art Direction category, Gibbons garnered nearly a quarter of the nominations, almost twice the percentage of his success in the previous period. The influence of Gibbons's celebrity on nominators who were nonspecialists is difficult to ignore. Their choices were no doubt influenced by the prestige of one of M-G-M's most powerful figures. The number of nominations and awards bestowed on Hans Dreier and Lyle Wheeler is no doubt also inflated by the fact of their position as department head. But, unlike Gibbons, Dreier and Wheeler remained practicing art directors throughout their careers. Their contributions to the prizewinning films are therefore less problematic.

If, in terms of numbers, the career of Cedric Gibbons makes a strong claim for the name-recognition factor in the annals of the Academy Awards, Richard Day's success is unquestionably based on the quality of his work. In the late 1920s, Day was at M-G-M, where he designed many of the films for which Gibbons received credit, including *The Bridge of San Luis Rey*, award winner in 1929, and *The Hollywood Review of 1929*, nominee in the same year. During most of the 1930s, Day freelanced at United Artists, designing primarily for Samuel Goldwyn. Between 1927 and 1938, Day won two awards and was nominated seven times (he was uncredited for the two nominations and single award he contributed to Gibbons's total) while Gibbons and his staff at M-G-M received the same number of awards and only one more nomination. Following the general practice, Day shared credit with other art directors when he was supervising art director at 20th Century–Fox in the early 1940s, but he was certainly responsible for much of the design of the films that bore his name. After his stint at Fox, he went on to win two more awards out of four nominations between 1948 and 1954. Day's frequent commendation by the Academy is no surprise since he was one of the most universally admired art directors throughout a career that spanned nearly five decades.[66]

William Cameron Menzies earned only four nominations and two awards, all before 1930, during the first years of the Oscars. Several factors explain the low tally of the designer many consider the most influential art director in the history of American cinema. Some of Menzies's greatest designs predate the formation of the Academy; he later made uncredited contributions to films that were nominated and received awards.[67] He preferred to freelance, never established a strong affiliation with a studio, and often bent his energies to direction and production. His duly recognized impact on the design of *Gone with the Wind* was rewarded with a special Oscar for "outstanding achievement in the use of color for the enhancement of dramatic mood."[68]

More interesting than the relative neglect of Menzies are the blatant omissions from the list of winners. Not a single Oscar went to Van Nest Polglase, despite eight nominations in the years when, as head of the art department at RKO, he took a share of the credit for the extraordinary work of Carroll Clark (the Astaire-Rogers musicals) and Perry Ferguson (*Winterset, Citizen Kane*). Anton Grot's absence from the winners' circle is surprising for very different reasons. In nearly every discussion of major designers, of the function of the art director, of the creativity of the art director, Grot occupies a prominent position. If any art director can be thought to have a coherent oeuvre, to be an auteur, it is assuredly Grot. Yet he won not a single Oscar, and his total of five nominations is meager considering the quality and quantity of his designs. More nominations went to William Horning, Paul Groesse, Roland Anderson, and Joseph Wright, designers whose names were associated with strong supervisory art directors at the richest studios, M-G-M, 20th Century–Fox, and Paramount.

Thus, if the prestige of authority influenced the choices of some voters, it had an uneven effect on the history of the Academy Awards. For Gibbons, bolstered by the power of M-G-M and his own public image, it was clearly operant; it won no Oscars for Polglase, whose situation resembled that of Gibbons, albeit on a reduced scale. Richard Day's name and achievement carried decisive weight in the voting; Anton Grot's were insufficient. With the exception of Day's case, the factors of studio stability and studio policy are determining: the prosperous, well-organized power structure of M-G-M suc-ceeds where the shifting managements and fortunes of RKO and the frugality of Warner Bros. do not. But there is one more variable to be examined: the kinds of films whose art direction pleased the voters. Is there a style appropriate to a specific and beloved genre that tends to win the Oscar?

Genre

We have defined the borders of genre loosely for the purpose of measuring its effect on nominations and awards. The premises that govern genre classification vary greatly, from structural, stylistic, and content determinations to journalistic labels, publicity catch-words, and the lexicon in current use by the general audience. In classifying the data that serves our analysis, therefore, we have not hesitated to place a film in as many different categories as seem appropriate to the ways in which it might be perceived. *Lives of a Bengal Lancer*, for instance, is included in the lists of "action-adventure," "exotic," and "period" films; *Foreign Correspondent* under "suspense," "drama," and "exotic"; *Sergeant York* under "war," "biopic," "drama," and "period"; *Ben-Hur* under "biblical," "historical," "spectacle," "colossal," "exotic," and "period."

Among these genre categories, only "exotic" is unconventional, but because it relates closely to decor we consider it valid for inclusion. We have designated a film "exotic" when it is emphatic in representing a locale unfamiliar to the experience of audiences in the United States. Thus, in addition to films that feature non-Western locales, the extended Dutch windmill sequence of *Foreign Correspondent*, for example, seems sufficient to qualify this title as "exotic." The Paris of *Seventh Heaven* is not particularly unfamiliar to urban dwellers in the United States; because the Paris of *An American in Paris* is defamiliarized by the ballet sequence, we consider this title "exotic" as well.

At times, some of the designations relate naturally to each other. "Period" films are those in which the representation of the past is foregrounded; "historical" is a further refinement of "period" since it features specific events and often specific figures from the past: the Civil War, the Battle of Agincourt, Jesus, Zola, Marie Antoinette. Nearly every "biopic" is also a "period" film and a "drama." Other subgenres might have been added to the list, but they would not have altered the dominant patterns.

The results of the genre breakdown for Art Direction are, to some extent, predictable. The work of the art director appears to most obvious advantage at the level of embellishment, particularly in the picturesque reconstruction and representation of environments not contemporary to the viewer. Nearly half of the nominations and three-fifths of the winners are "period" films. "Period" is, however, a much less significant factor in the Best Picture list. The preponderance of films in the "drama" category reflects the Academy's bent for the serious, demonstrated by the overwhelming 73.7 percent of films in this category that were nominated simultaneously for Art Direction and Best Picture. The "musical" and the "exotic" figure strongly in Art Direction due to the rich opportunities they present for the play of artifice; they fare markedly less well in Best Picture nominations. The "historical" earns a smaller share than one might expect. The poor showing of the "western" is to be expected given the genre's frequent location/back-lot shooting and the transparent denotation of its modest frontier sets. The artifice of "fantasy," on the other hand, should have had more success since it exploits the full range of the designer's resources, but the genre itself is not popular in American cinema. "Spectacle," a genre that by definition demands the art director's maximum effort of embellishment, suffers from low critical esteem. "Horror," another low-culture genre, challenged Hollywood's art directors to refine the set as artifice; it is represented by only two nominations (*Svengali* and *The Phantom of the Opera*), clear evidence of the connection between genre and design in Academy voting. Despite the punctuative use of their fascinating noir stylistics, the total absence of "gangster" or "crime" films, extraordinarily popular genres, is certainly due to their contemporary, realistic settings.

It is difficult to assess the relationship between genre and the Oscar success of most of the major art directors. Statistics based on the total filmographies of the supervising art directors are meaningless since they include the entire output for the respective studios during the years in which Gibbons, Polglase, Dreier, Wheeler, and, to some extent, Day were in charge. However, the percentages of Oscar nominations for these department heads within the different genres offer some interest. Only Polglase falls significantly below the share enjoyed by the others in the all-important "drama" and "period" rubrics, a fact that may explain his deficient total of nominations.

Grot's situation differs because, though he was a figure of at least equivalent stature, he was never head of an art department. We may therefore assume that the total of his attributions accurately reflects his personal efforts. All of his Oscar nominations were in the "drama" and "period" groups. His disproportionately low total of nominations may then be ascribed to the high number of films he designed in the "horror," "crime," and "gangster" genres that rarely, if ever, found favor with the Academy. The nominators ignored Grot's expressionistic *The Mad Genius*, *Doctor X*, and *The Mystery of the Wax Museum* and the contemporary high style of *Mildred Pierce* and *Deception*, to cite only the most obvious examples. Even more surprising is the absence of Grot's Busby Berkeley musicals from the list of nominees. With the exception of *Svengali*, an anomalous (for the Academy) "horror" film of artifical design intensity, only *Anthony Adverse*, *The Life of Emile Zola*, *The Private Lives of Elizabeth and Essex*, and *The Sea Hawk* were placed in contention for awards. These are big-budget "period-historical" films whose decor functions primarily at the level of embellishment.

The pattern of Grot's successes and failures with the voters demonstrates the connections among studio, art director, and genre in the Oscar derby. Grot worked at Warner

Bros., where the stark expressionism that was his trademark provided economical decorative and narrative configurations, often for genres that require punctuative contemporary settings. The Academy consistently rewarded genres that could be taken "seriously" and films that boasted the extravagant means of the studios or independent producers that made them: M-G-M, 20th Century–Fox, United Artists, and Samuel Goldwyn. Four of five of Anton Grot's nominated films, all "period" films, flaunt lavish budgets, uncharacteristic for Warner Bros. Thus, despite the merits of a beach house skewed for murder, an ocean pier that invites suicide, and houses and restaurants that mark the various stations of the protagonist's life, Grot's *Mildred Pierce* was not among the ten films considered in the 1945 crop of nominations.[69] Seven are "period" and/or "exotic," their art direction predominantly embellishing.[70] Of the three with contemporary settings, *Blood on the Sun* (winner for black and white) also qualifies as "exotic," and *Leave Her to Heaven* was the rare melodrama to be shot in Technicolor. The only contender roughly comparable to *Mildred Pierce* in genre was *Love Letters*. Evidently, the Academy preferred a Hans Dreier/Roland Anderson/20th Century–Fox quaint English cottage to Grot's Malibu moderne (fig. 108).

108. *Love Letters*: the cottage, Singleton (Jennifer Jones) and Alan (Joseph Cotten)

The Winner

There is, of course, no denying the effect of self-interest, novelty, tradition, snobbery, and publicity, in addition to the principal factors of studio, auteur, and genre, on voters' opinions. Nevertheless, the history of the Art Direction Oscar cannot be accurately understood only, or even primarily, in these terms. Most often, voters selected the film they considered, quite simply, to have the best design. So many of the winning titles summon up memorable images of narrativized decor, surely reason enough for their triumph: the *Merry Widow*'s witty boudoir (1934), Sam Dodsworth's progressively American office and factory; Conway's utopian Shangri-La (1937); the staircase at Twelve Oaks down which Scarlett steals to declare her love to Ashley and the one that Catherine Sloper mounts in Washington Square after rejecting Morris Townsend. What would have prompted a majority of Hollywood art directors to vote for *Black Narcissus*, *Great Expectations*, *Hamlet*, and *The Red Shoes*, all British productions, if not their admiration for Alfred Junge's Himalayan palace/convent, John Bryan's Dickensian graveyard and moldering banquet hall, Roger Furse's Elsinore, and Hein Heckroth's fantasmagoric world of

109. *Black Narcissus*: the palace interior, the Young General (Sabu) and the seductive Kanchi (Jean Simmons)

110. *Great Expectations*: Miss Havisham's banquet hall, Miss Havisham (Martita Hunt) and Pip (Anthony Wager)

ballet (fig. 109, fig. 110, fig. 111, fig. 112)? They even broke with their own practice to give Richard Day an award for *On the Waterfront*, a film shot entirely on location. Thus, in spite of the power of extraneous factors—studio affiliation and self-interest, ossified taste—emerge many Oscars that exemplify the ideals of those who defined the award. These Oscars celebrated, in fact, the nexus of art direction and narrative.

It has not been our objective to establish a pantheon for art direction. We have engaged in the very different enterprise of proposing and illustrating a matrix with which to advance the elusive discourse on decor and narrative. Still, our own evaluations are implicit in most of the decors we have chosen to explicate. They frequently coincide with those of Oscar at three of our levels of design intensity: embellishment, artifice, narrative. We have also chosen to privilege punctuative sets, powerful markers less apt to win awards

111. (Opposite, top) *Hamlet*: Elsinore's assembly hall, the death of Laertes, from left to right, Osric (Peter Cushing), Laertes (Terence Morgan), Horatio (Norman Woodland), Hamlet (Laurence Olivier)

112. (Opposite, bottom) *The Red Shoes*: Hein Heckroth's sketch for "The Red Shoes" ballet

than conspicuous, exotic, glamorous, "star" decors. The art direction we prize satisfies a criterion for judgment absent from the guidelines of the Academy: legibililty. Legible sets are integral to the dynamics of the film text. Whether at the brink of opacity like Mildred Pierce's Glendale house or on blatant display like Flo Ziegfeld's staircase, these are decors that engage us all in the pleasure and complexity of reading. The specific shape and texture of rooms, houses, streets, temples, and stages are inextricable from the sign system that allows us to make sense of a story. And often, after the screening is long over, we are able to replay the narrative only because we still inhabit its decors.

Staffing Charts of Three Major Art Departments

Table 1   Staffing Charts of Art Departments at M-G-M, 20th Century–Fox, and Warner Bros., July 1944

	M-G-M	20th Century–Fox	Warner Bros.
Supervising art director	Cedric Gibbons	James Basevi	Max Parker
Executive assistant	William Horning	Joseph C. Wright	—
Art directors	17	9	9
Assistant art directors	4	4	8
Draftspersons	43	23	31
Sketch artists	10	6	14
Total	**76**	**44**	**63**

Note: All three studios had similar schedules: seven or eight pictures shooting and five or six in preproduction. All three found that an art director could design only two super-A productions (films with exceptionally high budgets) a year.

Appendix B

Histories of
Set
Design

This review of the literature on the history of art direction is informed by two questions: What is the relationship between the history of film decor, as it has been written, and the general history of film? To what extent do histories of film take account of the history of set design?

While general histories of film allude in greater or lesser detail to art direction (typically they acknowledge individual designers within an organizational schema that features the period and then the national cinema), no single text of cinema history treats the subject of set design to any significant degree. The discourse on the history of film decor remains, therefore, essentially disjoined from the discourse on the general history of film. Examples of total exclusion include Ann Lloyd's reference work *The History of the Movies*, an alphabetical listing under categories such as stars, individual films, genres, national cinemas, and technical areas. None of its 159 entries is devoted to film decor or to individual art directors. Gianni Rondolino writes a history of cinema in several volumes in which he discusses, for example, *La Kermesse héroïque* without mentioning Meerson and *Le Jour se lève* without referring to Trauner. (In an extensive chapter on poetic realism, Rondolino does cite both in passing.) The index to Douglas Gomery's *Movie History: A Survey* omits references to art direction and art directors entirely; the discussion of *L'Inhumaine*, a film whose place in cinema history is ensured by its design, includes no allusion either to Mallet-Stevens's exteriors or to Fernand Léger's laboratory. Brief discussions of art direction are related to expressionism and poetic realism in Kristin Thompson and David Bordwell's comprehensive textbook, *Film History: An Introduction*.[1]

Specialized histories of the silent period attend to settings far more consistently and extensively. In *The Parade's Gone By*, Kevin Brownlow considers the design of individual films (*Ben-Hur* and *Robin Hood*, to cite two) at some length, discusses set design aesthetics (successful when it is transparent, failed when it is opaque), and the place of art direction in the evolution of modes of production during the silent era (design was one of the last functions to develop). The most influential designers of the period—Buckland, Urban, Ballin—are acknowledged. In *American Silent Film*, William Everson commits a chapter to "Art Direction and Production Design" in which he charts the history of set design from 1915 to the coming of sound. Everson underlines the influence of expressionism and art deco and introduces the question of the narrativization of decor (*The Thief of Bagdad* and *The Kiss*). He proposes that specific art directors (Ben Carré and Anton Grot, for example) had a determining effect on the directors with whom they had repeated collaborations.[2] In his long study of the period 1915–1928, *An Evening's Entertainment: The Age of the Silent Feature Picture*, Richard Koszarski singles out Anton Grot, the first art director not to come up from the ranks of the carpenter shop, and *Intolerance*, the film that marked the melding of two traditions—that of the master carpenter

(Huck Wortman) and of the theatrical designer/graphic artist (Walter Hall). He refers to Robert Haas as the founder of the era of the architect and discusses the organization of the art department along corporate, specialized lines.[3]

General introductions to film that define themselves as textbooks also treat matters of set design, particularly set-design praxis, more consistently and with greater breadth than do general histories of film. In *Understanding Movies*, Louis Giannetti has an unusually long section on settings and decor in which he raises many of the issues that inform the discourse on cinematic set design. Giannetti contrasts design for stage and design for film, the poetic set and the realistic set, location and studio decor, and spectacle sets and expressionistic sets. He discusses the Hollywood studio and the "look" the head of the art department created for its major productions in back lots and standing sets far removed from the studio itself, and finally he treats the affiliations of set and story. Joseph Boggs devotes a section of *The Art of Watching Films* to production design/art direction and defines, as does Dennis DeNitto in *Film: Form and Feeling*, the role of the art director as part of the "filmmaking team."[4] Giannetti, Boggs, and DeNitto mention art directors and their most distinguished films, as do Gerald Mast in *A Short History of the Movies*, Thomas W. Bohn and Richard I. Stromgren in *Light and Shadows*, and David A. Cook in *A History of Narrative Film*. David Bordwell and Kristin Thompson accord a few pages of *Film Art: An Introduction* to setting and especially to the relationship of decor and narrative, taking as their example Keaton's *Our Hospitality*.[5] They distinguish two approaches that disclose decor's realist intention: the historically authentic (*Greed*, *All the President's Men*) and the personal image (*Intolerance*, *Ivan the Terrible*). According to Bordwell and Thompson, setting can be striking by its presence, even overshadowing the actors (as in *The Scarlet Empress*), or striking by its absence (as in *The Passion of Joan of Arc*).

Thus, even if briefly, in text after text addressed to the college film-studies classroom, the academic design canon is formed: Griffith and Buckland; German expressionism in general, Lang and *Das Kabinett des Dr. Caligari* in particular; for Hollywood during the studio era, Gibbons and M-G-M, Dreier and Paramount, Van Nest Polglase and RKO; and, of course, the famous ceilinged breakfast room of *Citizen Kane*.

We consider the first extensive history of set design to be the shorter section of the theory/history published in 1945 by Baldo Bandini and Glauco Viazzi, *Ragionamenti sulla scenografia*. In the almost half-century since, only three other histories have appeared: Léon Barsacq's *Caligari's Cabinet and Other Grand Illusions*, Donald Albrecht's *Designing Dreams: Modern Architecture in the Movies*, and Beverly Heisner's *Hollywood Art: Art Direction in the Days of the Great Studios*.

The history section of Bandini and Viazzi's *Ragionamenti sulla scenografia* is a well-illustrated survey of set design arranged chronologically through the silent era (Méliès, the early westerns, the reconstruction of locales) and then by national cinema (Germany, United States, Britain, France, Italy, Czechoslovakia, Denmark, Soviet Union). Bandini and Viazzi adopt a schema for the history of art direction that mimics in its distribution of topics a conventional general history of film. In this respect, *Ragionamenti sulla scenografia* anticipates the Barsacq text, which remains the standard reference for the field.

Part 1 of *Caligari's Cabinet*, the section on praxis, is clearly inflected by Barsacq's experience as art director over the course of a long and distinguished career.[6] Part 2, like the work of Bandini and Viazzi, is a history of film decor organized chronologically and, within each period, by national cinema, the most prominent nation for each period appearing first and others following in order of importance. The table of contents replicates the chapter breakdown of most histories of film from 1895 to the New Wave: early French film, the Italian silent spectacle, the U.S. silent film, Sweden and Germany in the silent era, German expressionism, France from 1918 to 1926, Russia from 1914 to 1930, Hollywood after 1920, France after 1926, Great Britain after 1930, the Soviet Union after sound, postwar trends, and so on.

Donald Albrecht's *Designing Dreams*, which we have cited numerous times in this study, is an important inquiry into the influence of modernist architecture on cinematic set design. The connection between the history of decor and Hollywood studio history has been pursued more recently by Beverly Heisner. Heisner organizes her material chronologically by genre within the production history of the major studios: the musical at M-G-M; the epic at Selznick International; crime at Warner Bros.; history, dance, and comedy at 20th Century–Fox, RKO, and Columbia, respectively; horror and melodrama at Universal. This unequivocal association of genre and studio compromises Heisner's argument at the very outset. In fact, except for Universal's domination of the horror film, no single genre was the province of any single studio. If M-G-M specialized in musicals, so did Warner Bros. and RKO in the 1930s, and among the most significant designs for musicals are those that appear in the Busby Berkeley and Rogers-Astaire series produced at these studios. And for Paramount, a studio that Heisner could not marry to a specific genre, she invents the dubious rubric of "passion."

Less extensive attempts to historicize art direction—in pamphlets, articles, public lectures, and book chapters—have been undertaken by critics and practitioners, among these the set designers Edward Carrick and Hugues Laurent in the 1940s, the set designer and director Alberto Cavalcanti and the critic and historian Lotte Eisner in the 1950s, and Colin Crisp in the 1990s. These efforts are essentially occasional. Edward Carrick was the pseudonym of Edward Anthony Craig, an art director in his own right and the son of one of England's most influential theatre designers and theoreticians, Gordon Craig. While Carrick's *Designing for Moving Pictures* is focused on the practice of set design, he offers also the first, if brief, history of cinematic decor.[7] The discussion is divided into three schools and reflects the organization by period and school that marks the subsequent historization of set design: the spectacular or American school, the imaginative or German school, and the realist or Russian and British schools. At approximately the same time, Hugues Laurent, whose considerable influence was more strongly felt over several decades as a pedagogue than as a designer (he was professor of set design at the Institut des Hautes Etudes Cinématographiques, the French national film school), published *La Technologie du décor de film*.[8] Here, once again, questions of praxis are combined with questions of history. *La Technologie du décor de film* is, in fact, an academic history of film decor from 1900 to 1940, based on the evolution of craft and materials. Alberto Cavalcanti, in a talk entitled "Notes for a History of Cinematographic Set Design," provides a brief chronology of decor, concentrating particularly on the silent era, beginning with the Lumière brothers.[9] Lotte Eisner, in "The Development of Cinematic Set Design," begins her history with *Das Kabinett des Dr. Caligari*, a celebrated example of a film in which the set figures as a principal actor.[10] Eisner equates expressionist sets with expressionist acting style, gesture, and attitude and stresses the influence of the Ufa school of decor on American and European sound film. On the basis of Ufa's commanding authority, she constructs her canon of set design. And finally, in *Classic French Cinema, 1930–1960,* Colin Crisp devotes an extensive subsection of the chapter "Work Practices and Stylistic Change" to the evolution of the debate for and against realism within French discourse on set design.[11]

How, then, have the historians of film decor positioned art direction in the history of film? For Carrick, Bandini and Viazzi, Cavalcanti, and Barsacq, the history of decor is roughly parallel to the general history of film; it divides by period, by national cinema, by art director. For Laurent and others, this history is most intimately joined to the history of the development of the set designer's craft, the evolution of materials, technique, standards. For Lotte Eisner, the historical and the evaluative are joined; the influence of the master sets created by the German expressionist designers dominates the history of subsequent decades of European and U.S. decor. For Beverly Heisner, the history of Hollywood decor parallels most closely the history of American studios whose fortunes were dependent, in great measure, on the strength and talent of the guiding head of the art department. These approaches, however varied, are not incompatible. There is, at the very least, unanimity of view on the movements and practices that were principally responsible for shaping the history of art direction: expressionism, realism, and the Hollywood mode of production.

Carlo Enrico Rava and Italian Film Journals of the Fascist Period

Italian periodicals of the period 1936–1943 provide an intriguing exception to the neglect of film decor as an object of sustained critical and theoretical attention. If the terms of the discussion surrounding set design in Italy in the 1930s and 1940s were generally unremarkable, the energy and concentration of the debate waged on the pages of the film journals *Bianco e nero*, *Cinema*, *Film*, *Lo schermo*, *Primi piani*, *Schermi*, and *Stile italiano nel cinema*, as well as several publications specializing in interior design, were clearly exceptional. These terms were, in fact, similar to sporadic American and European controversy on the same issue: the set designer as painter vs. the set designer as architect, the backdrop vs. the constructed set, the theatrical set vs. the cinematic set; the inferior status of the art director within the production hierarchy; the promise held out by genuine collaboration between the art director and the director; the role and mission of set design with respect to the cultivation of the public taste for modernist architecture and interior decoration.

Most fascinating in the Italian example is its evolution. In the course of six or seven years, the polemic was rooted ever more fixedly and heatedly in a larger context, often ideological, sometimes explicitly Fascist. To champion the constructed set over the painted set, to further the position of the art director within the production hierarchy, to support set design's potential as an agent for the transformation of the audience's visual sensibility; these intentions, similar if not identical to those advanced by critics and practitioners on both sides of the Atlantic, become the goals of an aesthetic justified by its adherence to Fascist ideology. The principal spokesperson for this position was Carlo Emilio Rava.

Rava was an architect and occasional set designer who had a regular column in two magazines of home decoration, *Domus* and *Stile*.[1] Between 1938 and 1943, Rava's articles on cinematic set design and related subjects appeared also in *Bianco e nero*, *Primi piani*, and *Cinema*.[2] In the lead article of the first *Domus* series, Rava introduces the reader to the methodological and programmatic premises of the series.[3] His column, Rava writes, will be, above all, highly figured. It will be composed largely of drawings and frame enlargements. In fact, his method will subvert the accustomed relationship between general commentary and specific illustration: the commentary will accompany the illustrations, not vice versa. Moreover, Rava asks the reader to pay particular attention to the "subtitles," that is, to the extensive glosses that explicate and evaluate the illustrations, drawings, and frame enlargements. The glosses, not the general commentary, will carry Rava's program. They will allow him to identify those cases— those films—in which a superior cinematographic reality has been achieved; they will define the elements of that reality; and finally, they will facilitate the exchange between film decor and home decoration that, according to Rava, is essential to the advancement of his project: the formation and cultivation of the taste of his time.[4]

Rava's early writings on the formal values of set design, marked by the scrupulous integration of word and image, are among the most interesting—and least available—models of aesthetic discourse on this subject. He is, in fact, the earliest critic to offer a method for the close reading of sets. The frame enlargements in the opening column of the initial *Domus* series, to take one example, serve Rava's attempt to define the good and the bad set. A caption labels the first illustration (from *Il dottor Antonio*) as old-fashioned, a lesson in retrograde design to be carefully avoided; another (from *Gli Uomini non sono ingrati*) as falsely modern, equally bad; a third (from *Scipione l'africano*) as stereotypical. A frame from Cocteau's *Le Sang d'un poète* is defined as a decor with the clear potential to accomplish the important mission of influencing contemporary decorative style; the next, from Duvivier's *Carnet de bal*, represents a refined and completely successful decor; yet another, from an unnamed Italian film, is considered fresh, therefore good. And finally, there are several frame enlargements drawn from *Gli Ultimi giorni di Pompei*, a film Rava himself designed. The significant points of this decor are polish of detail, simplicity, contemporary inspiration, light colors, mixture of antique and modern, translation of the past through the free expression of what the designer understands to be its essence.[5]

By the last article of the first *Domus* series, October 1938, Rava's goals have undergone a radical transformation. He lists them in the summary that opens the second series: to encourage set designers "to take advantage of all those elements, suggestions, and inspirations, which though essentially, typically, exquisitely Italian, others abroad before us or better than us have exploited to make works of beauty" and to encourage "the trade unions to work collaboratively with the producers to assure that set designers are called upon regularly to participate in the filmmaking process in those areas in which they are truly competent."[6] The first series, launched only eleven months before as an original effort of critical method in the service of the lofty ideal of cultivating the public taste for the modernist aesthetic, concludes with a rehash of a familiar position within the terms of a familiar debate. The intentions that Rava announced prospectively in November 1937, essentially methodological and programmatic, resemble very little his final statement of purpose, essentially nationalistic and corporate. No longer is Rava's intention to analyze decor through the illustration of the set itself; to define the good and the bad set, whether Italian or foreign; to draw the connection between film decor and home decoration; to contribute to the elevation of public taste. His objective, as expressed at the series' conclusion, is first to urge Italian set designers to find in the past of their national tradition the key to beauty in set design, and second to plead the cause of the set designer within the power structure of the production team. The champion of close readings has replaced analysis with slogans.

The opening article of the second *Domus* series, March–August 1939, makes explicit the connection between the intentions of the critic and the agenda of the political regime. By way of example, Rava proposes what must have startled less doctrinaire readers: that they model their weekend homes after an illustration of a set for a sailor's bar, "essentially Italian in its simplicity and taste."[7] Two points are made here: that Fascist ideology supports Rava's theory and criticism; that his work has direct application to the formation of contemporary Italian taste. The second article, May 1939, is a diatribe against the tendency of Italian films and film journals to criticize expressions of modernist sensibility while applauding nineteenth-century bourgeois taste, particularly as represented so dominantly in American film. Rava considers this tendency seriously anti-Fascist. The films and film journals in question reject specialization, corporate structures, monopoly—basic tenets of state policy within the state-owned film industry consolidated in the state-operated factory, Cinecittà.[8]

In the third and fourth of the articles, June–August 1939, Rava continues his tirade against periodicals or producers or others who fail to insist that the architect-specialist be a true collaborator on the production team, who defend the role of the painter in set design, who reject modernism in film and in set design. Here Rava, as recently as the previous year a patient and original reader of sets, turns into a strident ideologue. He calls on the state to resolve once and for all, "in a manner both totalitarian and definitive," the question of the relationship between architecture and cinema.[9]

Appendix D

The Art Direction Oscar and Awards in Other Countries

Art Direction and the Other Oscars

Of the 272 films nominated for Art Direction, 29.4% were also nominated for Best Picture. These 80 films represent a 35.2% share of the 227 nominated for Best Picture. Ten films (29.4%) won in both categories.

Table 2 Comparison of Share of Nominees and Winners between Best Picture and the categories of Art Direction, Cinematography, Director, and Writing, 1927–1960

	Best Picture	Art Direction		Cinematography		Director		Writing	
	No.	No.	%	No.	%	No.	%	No.	%
Nominations	227	80	35.2	95	41.8	116	51.1	128	56.3
Awards	34	10	29.4	11	32.3	19	55.8	19	55.8

Note: The Academy has usually had more than one category devoted to writing, distinguishing between Story, Screenplay, and Story and Screenplay. For the purposes of this comparison, we have conflated all the nominees and awards for writing into a single category.

Table 3 Comparison of Share of Nominees and Winners between Art Direction and the categories of Cinematography, Director, Writing, 1927–1960, and Costume Design, 1948–1960

	Art Direction	Cinematography		Director		Writing		Costume Design	
	No.	No.	%	No.	%	No.	%	No.	%
Nominations	271	122	45.0	52	19.1	67	24.7	54	50.9
Awards	53	19	35.8	7	13.2	9	16.9	11	45.8

Note: The category of Costume Design was added in 1948. Between 1948 and 1960 there were 106 nominees and 24 awards for Art Direction. The Costume Design percentages are coordinated with the Art Direction percentages for these years.

Studio

From 1927 to 1960, M-G-M (50) and 20th Century–Fox (47) generated nearly the same number of nominations for Art Direction and together accounted for more than a third of the total. Paramount (30) had 11% of the total; Warner Bros., RKO, Columbia, and Universal had less than 10% each. (In order to clarify the results, we will elide the various mergers and changes in the studio names: Fox will be included in 20th Century–Fox; First National in Warner Bros.; Universal-International in Universal.) These results must be seen in light of the changing fortunes of several of the studios during these decades. RKO was out of the running altogether by the late 1940s; Columbia became increasingly competitive. But over this entire period, United Artists, a studio that, from the beginning, had been host to prestigious independent producers, accounted for 13.6% (37) of the nominations—more than the individual totals of Paramount, Warner Bros., RKO, Columbia, or Universal. This is an indication that the power of a permanent staff in a studio art department was less of a factor than one might imagine. Samuel Goldwyn's productions, for instance, distributed primarily by United Artists and RKO, garnered an extraordinary 14 (5.1%) nominations.

The data is more revealing when examined according to other temporal divisions. The years 1927–1941, from the beginning of the sound era to the outbreak of World War II, mark the consolidation of the studios' financial positions, their rising power, and the relative homogeneity of the classical Hollywood narrative and visual styles. The standings of the studios during these years differ significantly from those of the entire period, 1927–1960. United Artists with 25 (23.8%) far outdistanced M-G-M (although *Gone with the Wind* was an independent film, produced by David O. Selznick, it was distributed by M-G-M and is included in its total) and 20th Century–Fox, tied at 15 (14.2%), and Paramount at 13 (12.3%). Samuel Goldwyn's productions garnered 9 nominations (8.5%), nearly as many as RKO, and more than Warner Bros., Columbia, and Universal. The combined total of the nominations for productions of Goldwyn, Selznick, and Walter Wanger was greater than that of either M-G-M or 20th Century–Fox, major studios with large permanent staffs.

Using 1948 as the cut-off point adds several factors: the imminent Supreme Court decision to break the studio monopoly on exhibition, the advent of television, and the impact of neo-realism on set design. There is, however, no significant change in the percentages. Twentieth Century–Fox moved slightly ahead of M-G-M; United Artists lost some of its commanding lead; the positions of Warner Bros., RKO, and Universal became stronger.

British film, a recent newcomer into the lists, dominated from 1946–1948, with 6 out of a possible 14 nominations that, along with 5 out of 15 nominations for Best Picture, prompted the studios to cease financing the awards ceremonies. This act, applauded by some as a step toward greater impartiality, came after the fact for art direction. In this period, the hegemony of the big studios and their influence over their employees seemed to have had less effect than one might have expected. The more or less independent productions that bore the United Artists logo earned the most nominations through 1948; in the immediate postwar years of the Hollywood studios' greatest prosperity, British cinema received a disproportionate share of nominations. This, too, suggests that the nominations reflected independent taste rather than the mandates of financial gain or studio influence.

The 1949–1960 nominations would appear to support the thesis that studio affiliation had a great impact on the list: M-G-M (27, 26.4%), 20th Century–Fox (21, 20.5%), and Paramount (18, 17.6%) made up the bulk of the entries with 64.5%. RKO, Universal, Goldwyn, and British cinema were nearly eliminated. But, paradoxically, this was the decade of ever-waning studio influence. The correlation of studio with nomination and voting was thus strongest when the very notion of studio was being redefined. By the end of the 1950s, some of the major studios no longer required the permanent staffs needed to manufacture a profit-making volume of annual product. Their sound stages had, for the most part, turned into facilities leased by independent production teams organized for specific films.

Were the same laws of studio dependence and independence in force when it came to voting for the awards themselves? It is possible to imagine that members could afford to be impartial during nominations but that, when it came to voting, they expressed allegiance to their studio. Indeed, in the entire period under study, M-G-M won a much higher percentage of awards (14, 26%) than nominations (50, 18.3%). M-G-M and 20th Century–Fox (11, 20%) were responsible for nearly half of the awards in art direction. The combined share of these two studios was approximately the same for 1927–1948, with 20th Century–Fox slightly in the lead. Yet the notion that studio affiliation was the determining factor must be challenged by the total percentage (29%) of awards won by United Artists (5, 16.1%) and British films (4, 12.9%), far greater than the single Oscar that Paramount, Warner Bros., RKO, Universal, and Columbia each succeeded in winning during this two-decade span. If 1945 is used as the cut-off point, to remove the unusual weight of the British successes from 1946–1948, the position of United Artists appears even stronger, with 5 awards, only two fewer than 20th Century–Fox and one fewer than M-G-M.

Another chronological slice, 1946–1956, is significant because these were the years in which the entire membership nominated and voted in the Art Direction category. Coinciding with the decreased activity and power of Goldwyn, Wanger, and Selznick, United Artists slips to a single award. Universal disappears from the list altogether. Paramount and British cinema surge to second position with 4 awards each, against 6 for M-G-M; 20th Century–Fox wins 3, only half its percentage for the period 1927–1948. M-G-M's dominance reaches its peak in the 1949–1960 period with nearly a third of the awards (7). Its departments were among the last to be disbanded, and that may account for a cohesive voting bloc.

Table 4   Academy Award Nominations and Awards for Art Direction 1927–1960, by Studio

	Nominations		Awards	
	No.	%	No.	%
British cinema	7	2.5	4	7.5
Columbia	16	5.8	2	3.7
Goldwyn	14	5.1	2	3.7
M-G-M	50	18.3	14	26.0
Selznick	1	0.6	1	1.8
Paramount	30	11.0	5	9.4
Republic	4	1.4	0	
RKO Radio	20	7.3	1	1.8
Goldwyn	5	1.8	0	
20th Century–Fox	47	17.2	11	20.0
United Artists	37	13.6	7	13.2
Goldwyn	7	2.5	2	3.7
Selznick	4	1.4	0	
Wanger	5	1.8	0	
Universal	13	4.7	3	5.6
Warner Bros.	24	8.8	3	5.6
Total	**272**		**53**	

Note: One- and two-time nominees and winners are not included. The independent producers Goldwyn, Selznick, and Wanger are listed under the studios that were credited with distributing their films. Goldwyn's total is also listed separately. The attributions grouped in the rubric "British cinema" are Rank-Cineguild, Rank-Archers, Rank–Two Cities, Rank-Ealing, Rank–United Artists, and Powell-Pressburger-Lopert.

Table 5   Academy Award Nominations and Awards for Best Picture 1927–1960, by Studio

	Nominations		Awards	
	No.	%	No.	%
British cinema	4	1.7	1	2.9
Columbia	18	7.9	5	14.7
Goldwyn	8	3.5	1	2.9
M-G-M	50	22.0	9	26.4
Selznick	1	0.4	1	2.9
Paramount	29	12.7	5	14.7
Republic	1	0.4	0	
RKO	19	8.3	2	5.8
Goldwyn	4	1.7	1	2.9
Selznick	5	2.2	2	5.8
20th Century–Fox	33	14.5	4	11.7
United Artists	29	12.7	4	11.7
Goldwyn	4	1.7	0	
Selznick	3	1.3	1	2.9
Wanger	3	1.3	0	
Universal	4	1.7	1	2.9
Warner Bros.	34	14.9	2	5.8
Total	**227**		**34**	

Note: One- and two-time nominees and winners are not included. The independent producers Goldwyn, Selznick, and Wanger are listed under the studios that were credited with distributing their films. Goldwyn's total is also listed separately.

Table 6 shows that, with the exception of Warner Bros., the difference of percentage share of nominations is insignificant. In the attribution of Oscars, however, there are obvious discrepancies. Here, Columbia does appreciably better in the Best Picture category than in Art Direction; 20th Century–Fox does appreciably worse. The discrepancies are more marked in the 1927–1945 period, when M-G-M received a 10.4% greater share of nominations for Best Picture than for Art Direction, and United Artists 7.5% less. The number of awards given in these years is, of course, much smaller, and therefore percentages are less meaningful, but Paramount's greater share of Best Picture awards (17.0%) and the lesser shares earned by United Artists (− 14.8%) and 20th Century–Fox (− 18.5%) cannot be ignored. These results argue for a clear distinction between studio and types of achievement in the voters' minds.

Table 6   Percentage Relationship of Nominations for Best Picture Award to Nominations for Art Direction Award, 1927–1961

Nominations	%	Awards	%
Warner Bros.	+6.1	Columbia	+11.0
M-G-M	+3.7	Paramount	+5.3
Columbia	+2.1	M-G-M	+0.4
Paramount	+1.7	Warner Bros.	+0.2
RKO	+1.0	United Artists	−1.5
United Artists	−0.9	Universal	−2.7
Goldwyn	−1.6	20th Century–Fox	−8.3
20th Century–Fox	−2.7		
Universal	−3.0		

Note: Studios and producers with fewer than 10 nominations and fewer than 3 awards are not listed.

Table 7   Percentage Relationship of Nominations for Best Picture Award to Nominations for Art Direction Award, 1927–1945

Nominations	%	Awards	%
M-G-M	+10.4	Paramount	+17.0
Warner Bros.	+6.4	M-G-M	+6.5
Columbia	+1.2	Warner Bros.	+6.5
Paramount	+1.1	Columbia	+6.5
RKO	−0.2	RKO	+1.2
20th Century–Fox	−2.9	United Artists	−14.8
Goldwyn	−4.1	20th Century–Fox	−18.5
United Artists	−7.5	United Artists	−14.8

Note: Studios and producers with fewer than 8 nominations and fewer than 2 awards are not included.

Because only 10 films received Oscars both for Art Direction and Best Picture out of a possible 53 (1927–1960), the number of awards and percentage share by studio are not statistically relevant.

Table 8   Films Winning Oscars Both for Art Direction and Best Picture, 1927–1960

Year	Film	Studio
1930	*Cimarron*	RKO
1932	*Cavalcade*	Fox
1939	*Gone with the Wind*	Selznick/M-G-M
1941	*How Green Was My Valley*	20th Century–Fox
1948	*Hamlet*	Rank–Two Cities
1951	*An American in Paris*	M-G-M
1954	*On the Waterfront*	Horizon/American
1958	*Gigi*	M-G-M
1959	*Ben-Hur*	M-G-M
1960	*The Apartment*	Mirisch/United Artists

Auteur

From 1927–1945, films that bore Cedric Gibbons's name received 20 nominations out of a possible 150 (13.3%). From 1946–1956, Gibbons had 20 nominations out of a possible 86 (23%), nearly double the percentage of the previous period. The discrepancy between the number of Oscars he won in the two periods is less dramatic (5 out of 25 [20%] in 1927–1945; 6 out of 22 in 1946–1956 [27.2%]). Hans Dreier, head of the department at Paramount until 1950, had his name on 23 nominations and won 3 awards; Lyle Wheeler received 20 out of his 28 nominations and 3 out of his 5 awards when he was supervising art director at 20th Century–Fox, from 1947 until the end of the period under consideration.

***Table* 9**   Art Directors with Multiple Academy Awards and Nominations, 1927–1956

	Nominations	Awards
Cedric Gibbons	40	11
Richard Day	18	7
Lyle Wheeler	28	5
Hans Dreier	23	3
William A. Horning	9	3
Paul Groesse	8	3
Edward Carfagno	6	3
Joseph Wright	8	2
Preston Ames	6	2
Alexander Golitzen	6	2
Wiard Ihnen	3	2
Hal Pereira	14	1
Roland Anderson	11	0
Jack Otterson	8	0

Note: Day's totals do not include the nominations and awards for the M-G-M films of 1929 for which he was uncredited but on which he worked. Horning's include nominations with Gibbons. All Groesse's awards and nominations were with Gibbons. Cargfagno shared 2 awards and 5 nominations with Gibbons; 1 award and 1 nomination with Horning. Wright shared both awards and 4 nominations with Day. Ames shared 1 award and 4 nominations with Gibbons. Anderson shared 7 nominations with Dreier; 4 with Pereira.

Genre

***Table* 10** Genre Breakdown: Oscar Nominees and Award Winners, 1927–1960

	Art Direction				Best Picture			
	Nominations		Awards		Nominations		Awards	
Genre	No.	%	No.	%	No.	%	No.	%
Drama	144	52.9%	36	67.9%	142	62.5%	23	67.6%
Period	129	47.4%	32	60.0%	76	33.0%	10	29.0%
Musical	54	19.8%	8	15.0%	24	10.5%	4	11.7%
Exotic	51	18.7%	13	24.5%	24	10.5%	4	11.7%
Comedy	42	15.4%	3	5.6%	42	18.5%	7	20.5%
Historical	33	12.1%	8	15.0%	21	8.3%	5	14.7%
Biopic	27	9.9%	6	11.3%	19	8.3%	2	5.8%
Action	19	7.0%	4	7.5%	12	5.0%	2	5.8%
Western	10	3.6%	1	1.8%	7	3.0%	1	2.9%
Fantasy	9	3.3%	2	3.7%	6	2.6%	0	
Suspense	7	2.5%	0		3	1.1%	0	
Biblical	7	2.5%	3	5.6%	4	1.7%	1	2.9%
War	6	2.0%	1	1.8%	14	6.0%	3	8.8%
Spectacle	6	2.2%	2	3.7%	4	1.7%	2	5.8%
Noir	4	1.4%	2	3.7%	4	1.7%	1	2.9%
Sci-fi	4	1.4%	1	1.8%	0		0	
Horror	2	0.7%	1	1.8%	0		0	
Disaster	2	0.7%	0		2	.8%	0	
Sports	1	.3%	0		1	.4%	0	
Gangster	0		0		2	.8%	0	
Crime	0		0		3	1.3%	0	
Total	**272**		**53**		**227**		**34**	

Table 11 Genre Breakdown: Simultaneous Nominations and Awards in Categories of Art Direction and Best Picture, 1927–1960

Genre	Nominations		Awards	
	No.	%	No.	%
Drama	59	73.7%	6	60.0%
Period	40	50.0%	7	70.0%
Exotic	14	17.5%	2	20.0%
Historical	12	15.0%	4	40.0%
Musical	11	13.7%	2	20.0%
Biopic	9	11.2%	0	
Comedy	9	11.2%	1	10.0%
Biblical	4	5.0%	1	10.0%
Action	2	2.5%	0	
Western	2	2.5%	1	10.0%
Spectacle	2	2.5%	1	10.0%
Fantasy	2	2.5%	0	
War	1	1.2%	0	
Suspense	1	1.2%	0	
Noir	1	1.2%	1	10.0%
Sports	1	1.2%	0	
Crime	0		0	
Disaster	0		0	
Horror	0		0	
Sci-fi	0		0	
Gangster	0		0	
Total	**80**		**10**	

Awards in Other Countries

We have been able to discover, for purposes of comparison, no value/award system among the dominant Western cinemas parallel to the Academy Awards in terms of time frame, continuity, or voter pool. The most similar awards are those of Great Britain and Italy. The correlation between Best Picture and Art Direction awards in Great Britain is 30.7%; in Italy, 15.5%. The Hollywood Oscar correlation for the same period as Great Britain is 34.6%; as Italy, 37%. When the British awards included Art Direction they were conferred by the Society of Film and Television Arts from 1964–1974 and the British Academy of Film and Television Arts from 1975–1989. The Italian awards were conferred from 1945–1989 by the Sindacato Nazionale Giornalisti Cinematografici Italiani (Italian Film Journalists' Union). After 1949, the Italian award for Best Picture was abolished; the award for Best Director is widely considered also the prize for Best Picture. The dual award winners in Great Britain: *Dr. Strangelove*, 1964; *The Ipcress File*, 1965; *The Spy Who Came in from the Cold*, 1966; *A Man for All Seasons*, 1967; *Cabaret*, 1972; *The Elephant Man*, 1980; *The Killing Fields*, 1984; *A Room with a View*, 1986. The dual award winners in Italy: *Romeo and Juliet*, 1968; *Death in Venice*, 1971; *Gruppo di famiglia in un interno* [*Conversation Piece*], 1974; *Città delle donne*, 1979; *E la nave va*, 1983; *Once Upon a Time in America*, 1984; *The Last Emperor*, 1987.[1]

Appendix E

A *Canon*
for
Art Direction

Does a set-design canon emerge from the judgments of critics and scholars? If so, does it correspond to the canon formed by film culture at large? These questions have no fixed answers, of course, given the fluctuating parameters of the corpus designated at any particular moment as canonical. But some models can be tested, and to that purpose we offer as a sample all of the films that competed for the Academy Award for Best Art Direction and Best Picture between the inception of these awards in 1927 and 1989, as well as the twenty-five films designated as "landmark" by the Producers Guild of America in 1991.[1] We flag the mention of these films in Barsacq's general survey of the history of art direction and in the less systematic histories of Bandini and Viazzi, of Cappabianca, Mancini, and Silva, and of Lotte Eisner. We have flagged them also in studies focused on Hollywood alone: Heisner's book, the extensive catalogue of Hambley and Downing, and the article by Corliss and Clarens in *Film Comment*—seven sources in all.

The most obvious limitation of our sample is the exclusion of the first three decades of cinema history and of most European films. Another restriction is that the seven critical works we cite have approaches that differ widely in dimension, scope, and ideology. Still, they offer ample evidence of convergence of opinion. It is that convergence, and its relationship to the prized Oscar and to "landmark" designation, that points us, however tentatively, toward a canon for art direction in the sound era.

1. Five films, *Citizen Kane*, *The Great Ziegfeld*, *The Informer*, *The Merry Widow* (Lubitsch), and *A Midsummer Night's Dream*, are mentioned in five of the seven sources. Only *The Great Ziegfeld* won an Oscar for Best Picture; *The Informer* and *Citizen Kane* were labeled "landmark" by the Producers Guild; only *Kane* is indisputably part of the general canon.

2. Nine more, *The Goldwyn Follies*, *The Magnificent Ambersons*, *Marie Antoinette*, *On the Waterfront*, *Samson and Delilah*, *San Francisco*, *A Streetcar Named Desire*, *Sunset Boulevard*, and *Top Hat*, appear in four of the seven sources cited. Here we find a single Oscar winner, *On the Waterfront*, which, along with *Sunset Boulevard*, makes the "landmark" list. Of the nine, *The Magnificent Ambersons* has secured a place in the general canon, and a persuasive case can certainly be made for the inclusion of *Sunset Boulevard* and *Top Hat*, the latter a representative Rogers-Astaire musical.

3. Nineteen films are cited for their art direction in three of the seven sources. Designated both Best Picture and "landmark" are *All Quiet on the Western Front* and *Gone with the Wind*; designated Best Picture are *An American in Paris*, *Hamlet*, and *How Green Was My Valley*. The canonical status of all but *How Green Was My Valley* is clear. Of these nineteen films, those that neither won an Oscar (Oscar nominations are marked [n]) nor achieved "land-

mark" designation are *Anna and the King of Siam*, *Conquest*, *David Copperfield* [n], *Dead End* [n], *Dodsworth* [n], *Henry V* [n], *The Little Foxes* [n], *Morocco*, *Romeo and Juliet* (1936), *Svengali*, *The Tempest*, *The Thief of Bagdad* (1940), *Winterset*, and *Wuthering Heights* [n].

4. Oscar and "landmark" films cited for art direction in fewer than three sources, or not at all, are *Ben-Hur* (1959), *The Best Years of Our Lives*, *Casablanca*, *From Here to Eternity*, and *Mutiny on the Bounty* (1935). It should be noted that three others, *The Godfather*, *Midnight Cowboy*, and *One Flew over the Cuckoo's Nest*, postdate some of the sources we have cited.

In sum, there is no obvious match between the general canon of film, as established by prize, and the canon of set design, as established by prize and critical reception. Of the films mentioned by the majority, that is, four or more of our sources, only four of fourteen, *Citizen Kane*, *The Magnificent Ambersons*, *Sunset Boulevard*, and *Top Hat*, are securely part of the general canon. Of the films cited by three or fewer of our seven sources, eight of twenty-five, *All Quiet on the Western Front*, *Gone with the Wind*, *An American in Paris*, *Hamlet*, *Henry V*, *Morocco*, *The Best Years of Our Lives*, and *Casablanca*, also belong to the general canon.

Notes

Introduction

1. Michael Powell, *A Life in the Movies* (London: Heinemann, 1986), 343.
2. For the films that we discuss extensively, we provide pertinent credit information (director, art director, release date) in the index entries of their titles.

Chapter 1   Systems and Praxis

1. "Pictorial Beauty in the Photoplay," lecture, 10 April 1929, in *Introduction to the Photoplay*, ed. John C. Tibbetts (Shawnee Mission, Kans.: National Film Society, 1977), 179.
2. "You Can't Stump an Art Director: He Has to Find the Answer," *Hollywood Reporter*, 24 Oct. 1938.
3. *Motion Picture*, 1930–1939 (34 issues); *Movie Mirror*, 1933–1939 (8 issues); *Movie Classic*, 1931–1936 (20 issues); *Movies*, 1939–1951 (16 issues).
4. Jack Holland, "Bette Davis Turns Softie," *Hollywood* (May 1940):29, 43.
5. 1945–1948 (all issues).
6. "What Are the Sets Like?," *Lion's Roar* 1 (n.d.).
7. Margaret Herrick Library, Academy of Motion Picture Arts and Sciences and Academy Foundation.
8. *Saturday Evening Post*, 5 Feb. 1921, cited in John Hambley and Patrick Downing, *The Art of Hollywood: A Thames Television Exhibition at the Victoria and Albert Museum* (London: Thames Television, 1979), 11.
9. Margaret Herrick Library.
10. Samuel W. Morris, "Balcony Scene Will Be Gorgeous in Film Romeo and Juliet," *Detroit Times*, 7 March 1936.
11. Virginia Wright, *Los Angeles Daily News*, 1941.
12. *Les Belles Affiches du cinéma, seconde époque, 1950–1980* (Paris: Atlas, 1986).
13. Pier Marco De Santi, ed. and comp., *Immagini in movimento: memoria e cultura* (Rome: Biblioteca Nazionale Centrale, 1989).
14. Ralph Flint, "Cinema's Art Directors," *New York Times*, 22 Nov. 1931.
15. W. R. Wilkerson, "Trade Winds," *Hollywood Reporter* (20 Feb. 1939): 1.
16. *Monthly Bulletin of the Society of Motion Picture Art Directors* (March 1951):4.
17. In 1924, Ben Carré, William Cameron Menzies, William Darling, and Robert Odell formed the Cinemagundi Club, which evolved, some years later, into the Society of Motion Picture Art Directors, and subsequently into Local 876 (Beverly Heisner, *Hollywood Art: Art Direction in the Days of the Great Studios* [Jefferson, N.C., and London: McFarland, 1990], 38–39).
18. "The Set Designer," *Unifrance Film* 20 (Oct. 1952):3.

19. "D'une Exposition à un colloque," *Le Technicien du Film* (June 1955):24–25.
20. "Le Décor," in *Le Cinéma par ceux qui le font*, ed. Denis Marion (Paris: Arthème Fayard, 1949), 192.
21. *L'Architecture-décoration dans le film*, proceedings of the Second International Meeting of the Schools of Film and Television, organized by the Institut des Hautes Etudes Cinématographiques, Cannes Festival April–May 1955, mimeo (Paris: Institut des Hautes Etudes Cinématographiques), 9.
22. "Scenografia, problema vitale," *Cinema* (25 Sept. 1941):198. Unless otherwise indicated, all translations are ours.
23. "The Artist and the Film," *Sight and Sound* (Sept. 1934):13.
24. Letter, 3 April 1946, Cinémathèque Française.
25. Letter, 13 Oct. 1961, Margaret Herrick Library. Arthur Knight's review, "Romeo Revisited," appeared in *Saturday Review of Literature* (14 Oct. 1961):40.
26. Mike Steen, *Hollywood Speaks!: An Oral History* (New York: Putnam, 1974), 226.
27. Vern Clark and George Stoica, "Set Builders," *Warner Club News* (April 1942):3.
28. Hambley and Downing, *The Art of Hollywood*, 15.
29. "Art Direction by Cedric Gibbons," *What's Happening in Hollywood*, 1 Feb. 1947.
30. "The Artist and the Film," 13.
31. "Le Décor," 192.
32. (pseud. Edward Craig), *Designing for Moving Pictures*, "How to Do It" series (London and New York: Studio Publications, 1941), 17.
33. Aljean Harmetz, *Round Up the Usual Suspects: The Making of Casablanca—Bogart, Bergman, and World War II* (New York: Hyperion, 1992), 76.
34. "The Art Director," in *Behind the Screen: How Films Are Made*, ed. Stephen Watts (New York: Dodge, 1938), 43–44.
35. Interview by Hugh Fordin, 1972, Doheny Library, University of Southern California.
36. In fact, relatively few women have worked as art directors at all. During World War II, when the draft depleted the pool of qualified men, women were not considered acceptable even as temporary replacements. Cedric Gibbons writes an internal memo to William R. Walsh in 1942 regarding draft deferments for art directors: "A short while ago you requested information on what, if any, positions now held by men in this department might be held by women. I might say at this time that the only possibility might be those positions now held by the Clerks and Blue Print men. But even there it is unlikely, because these people should have some architectural education or background. It is useless to hire people in these jobs who have no leaning toward the specialized work of architectural designing—because without it, it is impossible to advance them. And without advancement we find ourselves eventually with disgruntled and frustrated employees" (Margaret Herrick Library). European art directors held similar biases. Giuseppe Sala asserts, "We believe this not to be a feminine line of work. There are women among the costume designers" (*L'Architecture-décoration dans le film*, 27). There were, however, a few exceptions. Natacha Rambova designed *Camille* and *Salome* for Nazimova in the 1920s. In the late 1940s at least one woman made a reputation as art director in Great Britain; Carmen Dillon's credits include *The Browning Version*, *The Importance of Being Earnest*, *Accident*, and *The Go-Between*. In the United States, since the late 1960s, several women have been able to advance to the rank of production designer, among them Jane Musky (*Ghost*, *Glengarry Glen Ross*), Polly Platt (*The Last Picture Show*, *Terms of Endearment*), Patrizia von Brandenstein (*Amadeus*, *The Untouchables*), and Kristi Zea (*The Silence of the Lambs*, *Lorenzo's Oil*). Other recent women art directors are Setsu Asakura, who works in Japan, and Anne Terselius Hagegard, who works in Sweden.
37. Interview by Charles Affron, 21 June 1989, Los Angeles.
38. Interview by Charles Affron, 20 June 1989, Los Angeles.
39. Interview by Charles Affron, 20 June 1989, Los Angeles.
40. Hambley and Downing, *The Art of Hollywood*, 7.
41. Interview by Hugh Fordin, 1972, Doheny Library.
42. Kevin Thomas, "Art Director Carré: Perspectives of a Proud Craftsman," *Los Angeles Times*, 6 Feb. 1977.
43. Interview by Hugh Fordin, 1972, Doheny Library.
44. Letter to Patrick Downing, 16 Oct. 1982, Margaret Herrick Library.
45. Interview by Charles Affron, 20 June 1989, Los Angeles.
46. Interview by Charles Affron, 21 June 1989, Los Angeles.
47. David Thompson demonstrates fully Selznick's obsessive attention to both the largest issues

and the smallest details of the films he produced (*Showman: The Life of David O. Selznick* [New York: Knopf, 1992]). Goldwyn's impact on his films seems to have been less pervasive. Story editor Irene Lee, who worked for Goldwyn for two years, states, "I sat in a projection room with him for hours and never heard him say a creative word" (Harmetz, *Round Up the Usual Suspects*, 167).

48. Raymond Klune, interview by John Dorr, 1969, An Oral History of the Motion Picture in America, Regents of the University of California, Special Collections, University of California at Los Angeles, 102–103.

49. Ronald Haver, *A Star Is Born: The Making of the 1954 Movie, and Its 1983 Restoration* (New York: Knopf, 1988), 88.

50. *My Work in Films* (San Diego: Harcourt Brace Jovanovich, 1985), 8.

51. Howard McClay, "Pre-production Planning," *Los Angeles Daily News*, 26 Dec. 1951.

52. Interview by Hugh Fordin, 1972, Doheny Library. Arthur Freed appears to have been one of the few producers to successfully challenge Gibbons's power. Due to the success of his production unit, which made musicals primarily, Freed was able to import talent from Broadway. Oliver Smith, who designed *The Band Wagon* (1953), states: "There was enormous resistance to Broadway production designers" (Interview by Hugh Fordin, 1972, Doheny Library). Smith acknowledges that he would not have gotten credit as production designer if Freed had not pressured Gibbons and others at the studio.

53. Pete Martin, "Big Set," *Saturday Evening Post* (8 Dec. 1945): 22–23, 98, 100. Hal Wallis memorandum, 3 April 1937, Doheny Library. In their back lots the major studios had permanent sets—for example, the New York street, the Paris square—that were modified to fit the requirements of the specific script. In addition, they frequently redressed or reconstructed other sets that had been built for individual films. One of Hollywood's most famous sets, the Welsh mining village in *How Green Was My Valley* (1941), was altered with different houses and a slightly different mine for the Norwegian locale of *The Moon Is Down* (1943). This set was needlessly leveled for *Hello, Dolly* (1969), a film whose sets were eventually constructed elsewhere. *Frankenstein* (1931) used sets created for *All Quiet on the Western Front* (1930). *Show Boat* (1951) floated on Tarzan's lake. These standing sets often had a long afterlife. The battlefield constructed for *All Quiet on the Western Front* was redressed thirty years later for *Spartacus* (1960). The Roman slum of *Spartacus* was recycled from the Casbah Charles Boyer inhabited in *Algiers* (1938) (*Spartacus*, souvenir program, 1960).

54. Thomas Schatz, *The Genius of the System: Hollywood Filmmaking in the Studio Era* (New York: Pantheon Books, 1988), 421.

55. Memorandum, 11 Dec. 1946, Margaret Herrick Library.

56. "Hollywood Inside," *Daily Variety* (20 March 1953):4.

57. Charles Higham, in his 1993 biography of Louis B. Mayer, perpetuates the myth of Gibbons's herculean designing activity. Only near the end of the book, after many references to Gibbons, does Higham signal the work of another M-G-M art director, William Horning, for his design of *Quo Vadis*? (*Merchant of Dreams: Louis B. Mayer, M.G.M., and the Secret Hollywood* [New York: Donald I. Fine, 1993], 394).

58. Some critics have still not resolved the question of Gibbons's role as art director. As recently as 1991, Peter Hay credits Gibbons with the design of *Grand Hotel* and many other films (*MGM: When the Lion Roars* [Atlanta: Turner Publishing, 1991], 107). Yet elsewhere in Hay's book we read, "Gibbons did not have to lift a pen in order to be a creative force. If it was up on the screen, it was because Gibbons approved it" (187).

59. Interview by Hugh Fordin, July 1972, Doheny Library.

60. David Shipman, *Judy Garland: The Secret Life of an American Legend* (New York: Hyperion, 1993), 82.

61. *A Life* (New York: Knopf, 1988), 312.

62. Thomas, "Art Director Carré," 37.

63. Interview by Charles Affron, 21 June 1989, Los Angeles.

64. *A Life*, 312.

65. Margaret Herrick Library.

66. Stephen Harvey, *Directed by Vincente Minnelli* (New York: Harper & Row, 1989), 16. The St. Louis street was reused in *Valley of Decision, Two Sisters from Boston, Living in a Big Way,* and *Summer and Smoke* (Howard Mandelbaum and Eric Myers, *Forties Screen Style: A Celebration of High Pastiche in Hollywood* [New York: St. Martin's, 1989], 45).

67. Interview by Charles Affron, 21 July 1989, Los Angeles.

68. Interview by Hugh Fordin, July 1972, Doheny Library.

69. Mary Corliss and Carlos Clarens, "Designed for Film: The Hollywood Art Director," *Film Comment* (May–June 1978):39.
70. Ibid., 46.
71. Interview by Charles Affron, 20 June 1989, Los Angeles. More surprising, Zuberano identifies the designer of the acclaimed Rogers-Astaire musicals not as the man usually listed as Polglase's collaborator, Carroll Clark, but as either Al Abbott, an illustrator, or Charlie Ullman, a sketch artist.
72. Hambley and Downing, *The Art of Hollywood*, 3.
73. Interview by Rich Cheatham, 1 Nov. 1980, Doheny Library.
74. Interview by Charles Affron, 21 June 1989, Los Angeles.
75. Interview by Charles Affron, 21 June 1989, Los Angeles. Donald Albrecht relates Dreier's organization of Paramount's art department to a specific school of design: "Under Dreier's supervision the Paramount art department became a Bauhaus-like workshop of local architectural school graduates and fellow émigrés, most notably two of southern California's leading modernists, Jock Peters and Kem Weber. . . . Paramount's modern of the 1930s was the studio style most closely aligned with the Bauhaus repertory: White, unadorned surfaces; horizontality; and elegant simplicity are hallmarks of both styles" (*Designing Dreams* [New York: Harper & Row, 1986], 79).
76. Letter to Patrick Downing, 16 Oct. 1982, Margaret Herrick Library.
77. Lecture, University Extension Film Study, Columbia University, 11 Jan. 1938, typescript in library of Museum of Modern Art, New York, 55–56.
78. Mordecai Gorelik, "Hollywood's Art Machinery," *Sight and Sound* (Autumn 1946):90.
79. Ibid., 91.
80. Memorandum to Charles Chic, 4 Jan. 1941, Margaret Herrick Library.
81. Letter to Patrick Downing, 16 Oct. 1982, Margaret Herrick Library.
82. Interview by Rich Cheatham, 1 Nov. 1980, Doheny Library.
83. Ibid.
84. Patrick McGilligan, *George Cukor: A Double Life, a Biography of the Gentleman Director* (New York: St. Martin's, 1991), 98.
85. "The Production Designer," in *Filmmakers on Filmmaking*, ed. Joseph McBride, American Film Institute Seminars on Motion Pictures and Television, no. 2 (Los Angeles: J. P. Tarcher, 1983), 153.
86. "Visualization of *Reap the Wild Wind*," interview by Roland Anderson, *What's Happening in Hollywood* (12 Jan. 1942):2. While De Mille certainly took a great interest in the sets of his films, there is reason to suspect that Tyler's assessment is a product of press-agentry: "They call me his art director, but C.B. De Mille's art director is C.B. De Mille. I just make the sketches and see to the details, such as the mountains he wants moved and the ships he wants sailed thirty miles inland" (Ibid., 1).
87. Interview by Hugh Fordin, July 1972, Doheny Library.
88. *My Work in Films*, 80.
89. "The Set Designer," 3.
90. Interview by Charles Affron, 21 June 1989, Los Angeles.
91. Letter to Patrick Downing, 16 Oct. 1982, Margaret Herrick Library.
92. Interview by Charles Affron, 21 June 1989, Los Angeles.
93. Letter to Patrick Downing, 16 Oct. 1982, Margaret Herrick Library.
94. "The Production Designer," 157.
95. Ibid., 158.
96. Interview by Jacques Kermabon, *L'Avant-scène Cinéma* (Oct. 1988):17.
97. *Caligari's Cabinet and Other Grand Illusions: A History of Film Design*, ed. and rev. Elliott Stein, foreword by René Clair, trans. Michael Bullock (Boston: New York Graphic Society, 1976), 169.
98. Interview by Jacques Kermabon, 18.
99. *Le Décor de film* (Paris: Editions Seghers, 1970), 202.
100. *L'Architecture-décoration dans le film*.
101. Interview by Jacques Kermabon, 124.
102. These percentages are taken from production records of Universal and Warner Bros. housed at the Doheny Library and of M-G-M housed at the Margaret Herrick Library.
103. Leo K. Kuter, "Case of the Empty Stage," *Hollywood Reporter*, 11 Oct. 1948.
104. Philippe d'Hugues and Dominique Muller, eds., *Gaumont: 90 ans de cinéma*, with Renée Carl et al., La Cinémathèque Française (Paris: Ramsay, 1986).

105. Charles Merangel, "Décors en uniforme," *Le Technicien du Film* (July–Aug. 1955): 9; Umberto Sacca, "Uno scenografo e un arredatore," *Cinema* (25 April 1940):281–282.

106. Interview by Philippe Carcassonne and François Cuel, *La Cinématographie Française* (May 1965):20.

107. Cossa, "Scenografia, problema vitale," 198–199.

108. *L'Architecture-décoration dans le film*, 29.

109. Ibid., 23.

110. Ibid., 12.

111. "Seule la crise sauvera le cinéma français," *Arts* (8–14 Jan. 1958):1.

112. "L'Avenir du décor," *Le Nouvel Observateur* (29 April 1965):29.

113. "La Lutte contre l'amateurisme est ouverte," *Le Technicien du Film* (Oct. 1959):8.

114. "Long Live Movie Sets," *Unifrance Film* (Oct.–Dec. 1959):17.

115. "L'Oubli des leçons de Méliès," *La Technique-L'Exploitation Cinématographique* (April 1966):12–14.

116. Patrick Séry, "La Crise des studios cinématographiques: Fermés pour (r)évolution," *Le Monde*, 7 Oct. 1971.

117. Jean André et al., "Les Décorateurs du cinéma français défendent leur profession," *Le Film Français* (12 Nov. 1971):12–13.

118. Interview by Charles Affron, 21 June 1989, Los Angeles.

119. Marie-Paule Marchi, "Ken Adam: La Nostalgie des studios," *Le Film Français* (24 Dec. 1976):12.

120. *The Nation*, 16 Aug. 1947, in James Agee, *Agee on Film* (New York: Wideview/Perigee, 1958), 271.

121. David O. Selznick, *Memo from David O. Selznick*, ed. Rudy Behlmer (New York: Viking, 1972), 152.

122. Alan David Vertrees documents a different view of Menzies's contribution to *Gone with the Wind*. Vertrees discusses the various estimates of storyboard sketches (from as few as fifteen hundred to as many as three thousand) but goes on to state that only about two hundred original drawings survive ("Reconstructing the 'Script in Sketch Form': An Analysis of the Narrative Construction and Production Design of the Fire Sequence in *Gone with the Wind*," *Film History* 3, no. 2 [1989]:91). The relatively small number challenges the contention that a complete visual script ever governed the shooting. In addition, he notes discrepancies between the sketches and the finished film. Vertrees concludes that "it cannot be said even of this most memorable and demanding episode [the burning of Atlanta] in the motion picture that the film was precut, as had been the expressed intention of its producer, Selznick" (99). He positions Menzies's storyboard sketches as part of an ongoing production process, from script to final edited version. Vertrees's findings, however, should not minimize the importance of the production designer's impact on *Gone with the Wind*. Menzies was, after all, emphatically acknowledged by Selznick.

123. A ninth, Wilfred Buckland, is the one "who helped prepare the ground" for the others (Hambley and Downing, *The Art of Hollywood*, 9).

124. Ibid., 8–9.

125. Léon Moussinac privileges not the designer but the single set in putting forth the extraordinary idea that each character must have his or her own decor. The director must not allow one set designer to do all the interiors, because an original designer will mark everything with his own signature and all the characters of the drama would then appear to have the same taste ("Intérieurs modernes au cinéma," *Cinémagazine* [25 Feb. 1921]:7).

126. "Hein Heckroth," *Bianco e nero* 12 (1952):42.

127. "Quadernetto del cinema," *Domus* (Jan. 1940):61.

128. William K. Everson, *American Silent Film* (New York: Oxford University Press, 1978), 8.

129. "Designed for Film," 31, 27. Corliss and Clarens structure their assessments and choices around the following rubrics: "1) the creation of a visual style through the collaboration of director, producer, and art director (notably in films associated with David O. Selznick and Cecil B. De Mille); 2) the creation of a studio style (Paramount Art Deco, Universal Gothic, M-G-M grand bourgeois), which was, more often than not, established by the studio's Supervising Art Director (Hans Dreier, Charles D. Hall, Cedric Gibbons); 3) the personal styles of independent art directors such as Robert Boyle (*The Birds*), Boris Leven (*West Side Story*), Dale Hennesy (*Young Frankenstein*), and George Jenkins (*All the President's Men*); and 4) the work of the matte artist" (Ibid.). In addition to those already mentioned, their article is illustrated by the work of Warren Newcombe, Ed Graves, Carroll Clark, Mitchell Leisen, Perry

Ferguson, Hal Pereira and Walter Tyler, Herman Rosse, John De Cuir, Walter L. Hall, Alexander Golitzen, Eugene Lourie, Ted Haworth, James Basevi, and Jack Martin Smith.

130. Alexandre Trauner, *Décors de cinéma*, with Jean-Pierre Berthomé (Paris: Jade-Flammarion, 1988), 22; Baldo Bandini and Glaudo Viazzi, *Ragionamenti sulla scenografia*, pref. Aldo Buzzi (Milan: Poligono Società Editrice, 1945), 6.

131. *Le Décor de film* (Paris: Editions Seghers, 1970). The five other films are *Gribiche*, *Carmen*, *Les Nouveaux Messieurs*, *Le Grand Jeu*, and *Knight without Armour*.

132. Michel Ciment and Isabelle Jordan, "Entretien avec Alexandre Trauner," *Positif* (Oct. 1979):17.

133. For discussions of *Quai des brumes* and *Le Jour se lève*, see chapter 3; of *Les Enfants du paradis*, see chapter 5.

134. Corliss and Clarens, "Designed for Film," 57.

135. We assume that Wheeler excludes Minnelli from his list of art directors who made good as directors because he designed for Broadway shows rather than for the movies.

136. Steen, *Hollywood Speaks!*, 233. Ames collaborated with Minnelli on *An American in Paris*, *The Band Wagon*, *Brigadoon*, *Kismet*, *The Cobweb*, *Lust for Life*, *Designing Woman*, *Gigi*, *The Bells Are Ringing*, and *Home from the Hill*.

137. Harvey, *Directed by Vincente Minnelli*, 88.

138. Ibid., 242.

139. Occasionally art directors tried their hand at directing on a one-time or occasional basis, among these Eugene Lourié and Cedric Gibbons. Lourié directed several monster films in the 1950s and 1960s. "I stopped directing after *Gorgo* in 1961. No one was interested in what I wanted to direct; they all wanted more of the same comic-strip monsters. I'd made at least three of them, and I was tired of the formula. . . . But once you've had the responsibility of being a director, it's hard to turn back to just art direction. So in addition to designing films, I did second-unit direction and special effects: on *Crack in the World*, *The Battle of the Bulge*, *Custer of the West*, and *Krakatoa, East of Java*" (Corliss and Clarens, "Designed for Film," 53). Gibbons received a dubious credit for the direction of *Tarzan and His Mate* (1934). The caption to a photograph in Hay's *MGM: When the Lion Roared* reads that "he [Gibbons] receives assistance from veteran Jack Conway. Here, Conway guides the actors through the romantic tree nest scene" (113).

140. Peter Bogdanovich, "Edgar G. Ulmer," in *Kings of the Bs: Working within the Hollywood System, an Anthology of Film History and Criticism*, ed. Todd McCarthy and Charles Flynn (New York: Dutton, 1975), 377–409, 380.

141. Barsacq, *Caligari's Cabinet*, 152; Hambley and Downing, *The Art of Hollywood*, 46.

142. Hambley and Downing, *The Art of Hollywood*, 95.

143. "William Cameron Menzies," *Cinématographe* (Feb. 1982):32.

Chapter 2 Set Theory and Set as Denotation

1. Among the practitioners are the art directors Quenu ("L'Art de la décoration au cinéma," *Cinémagazine*, 26 Dec. 1924) and William Cameron Menzies ("Pictorial Beauty in the Photoplay," 162–180) in the 1920s, Virgilio Marchi (*Introduzione alla scenotecnica* [Siena: Ticci Editore, 1946]) and Michael Relph ("Designing a Colour Film," in *Saraband for Dead Lovers: The Film and Its Production at Ealing Studios*, ed. Michael Balcon [London: Convoy Publications, 1948], 76–84) in the 1940s; the filmmakers and painters Jean Epstein ("Le Décor au cinéma," *Revue Mondiale*, 1 Mar. 1923) and Paul Rotha ("The Art Director and the Composition of the Film Scenario," *Close Up*, 6 June 1930) in the 1920s and 1930s, Henri Alekan ("La Volonté de perfection n'existe pas, n'existe plus ou existe peu," *Le Technicien du Film et la Technique Cinématographique* [15 Jan.–15 Feb. 1974]:43–45, 64) in the 1970s, and Marcel Pagnol (*Cinématurgie de Paris* [Paris: Editions Pastorelly, 1980]) in the 1980s. Among the critics and scholars are Léon Moussinac ("Intérieurs modernes au cinéma," *Cinémagazine*, 25 Feb. 1921) in the 1920s, Eric Newton ("Film Decor," in *The Year's Work in the Film: 1949* [London: Longmans, Green, 1950], 55–61) and Anne Souriau ("Fonctions filmiques des costumes et des décors," in *L'Univers filmique*, ed. Etienne Souriau [Paris: Flammarion, 1952], 85–100) in the 1950s, and Claudio Terrana ("Scenografia come realtà e scenografia come illusione," *Bianco e nero* [Sept.–Dec. 1979]:65–97) in the 1970s. See appendix C for a discussion of the sustained attention to decor in Italian periodicals of the period 1936–1943.

2. (Madrid: Hermann Blume, 1986). Ramírez's effort to theorize set design is marginal to his discussion of Hollywood sets during the studio era. He is interested essentially in art direction

as an exercise in architectural replication, and his intelligent and thorough study is organized along the essentially chronological lines of a standard history of architecture: Antiquity, Medieval and Renaissance, Baroque, and so on.

3. Ramirez draws on the windmill sequence in *Foreign Correspondent* and the funhouse sequence in *Lady from Shanghai* to illustrate the connection between set design and the psychological state of the character (*Arquitectura*, 123–124).

4. *Ragionamenti sulla scenografia* (Milan: Poligono Società Editrice, 1945); *La costruzione del labirinto*, Cinema e Informazione Visiva (Milan: Gabriele Mazzota Editore, 1974).

5. Cappabianca, Mancini, and Silva, *Costruzione del labirinto*, 59–60.

6. Bandini and Viazzi also consider the relationship of set design to architecture. Set designers, they suggest, do not create architecture; they use architecture. Architects apply the real and immutable standard of being. Set designers apply the fictive and inconstant standard of appearing. In fact, outside of projection, set design, subject to the monocular law of the camera, has neither existence nor reason for existing (*Ragionamenti sulla scenografia*, 28–35).

7. Ibid., 17–19.

8. Ibid., 60.

9. In *Cinématurgie de Paris*, Marcel Pagnol makes the point differently. Film, he argues, frees us from the unity of space, from our servitude to the theatre (135ff.).

10. Bandini and Viazzi, *Ragionamenti sulla scenografia*, 58–59. See our chapter 6 for a discussion of *Street Scene*.

11. Epstein, "Le Décor au cinéma," 24. Quenu, "L'Art de la décoration," 562; Quenu was head of the art department for Pathé-Consortium-Cinéma in the 1920s. Arnheim, "Dettagli che non sono dettagli," *Cinema* (10 March 1937):180–182.

12. Morton Eustis, "Designing for the Movies: Gibbons of MGM," *Theatre Arts Monthly* (Oct. 1937):794.

13. Just as framing and decor are inseparable for Bandini and Viazzi, so are lighting and decor for both William Cameron Menzies ("Pictorial Beauty") and the cinematographer Henri Alekan ("La Volonté de perfection"). Not surprisingly, for Alekan in particular, emotion in the spectator can only be triggered through the coherence of form (that is decor) and of light (the illumination of the set).

14. Bandini and Viazzi, *Ragionamenti sulla scenografia*, 7–8, 49–51.

15. The many expressions of indebtedness by art directors to painting notwithstanding, Quenu maintains that there can be no influence of painting on cinema. The material of painting is color; the material of cinema is light and shadow ("L'Art de la décoration," 566).

16. "The Art Director," 377.

17. "Film Decor," 57.

18. We survey the more extensively discussed history of set design in appendix B.

19. "Classical filmmaking . . . considers edge-framing taboo; frontally positioned figures or objects, however unimportant, are seldom sliced off by either vertical edge. And . . . horizon-line isocephaly is common in classical filmmaking. Thus the human body is made the center of narrative and graphic interest: the closer the shot, the greater the demand for centering" (David Bordwell, Janet Staiger, and Kristin Thompson, *The Classical Hollywood Cinema: Film Style and Mode of Production to 1960* [New York: Columbia University Press, 1985], 51).

20. "Space becomes chiefly a container for character action; the story has appropriated it. That a locale is of little interest in its own right is shown by the fact that typically the exposition of space takes up the least time of any phase of the scene (often less than twenty seconds and seldom more than thirty). By this point, the characters have taken over the narration" (Ibid., 63).

21. Ibid., 54.

22. Menzies, "Pictorial Beauty," 166; Bandini and Viazzi, *Ragionamenti sulla scenografia*; Souriau, "Fonctions filmiques des costumes et des décors"; Tashiro, "'Reading' Design in *The Go-Between*."

23. Bandini and Viazzi, *Ragionamenti sulla scenografia*, 61–87. See our chapter 5 for a discussion of *Metropolis*, chapter 4 for *La Kermesse héroïque*.

24. "Fonctions filmiques," 100.

25. "'Reading' Design," 17–18.

26. *What Is Cinema?*, ed. and trans. Hugh Gray, foreword by Jean Renoir (Berkeley, Los Angeles, and London: University of California Press, 1967), 1:90–93.

27. In one of his many interviews, Trauner makes this observation: "Set construction should depend as much as possible on realistic details. But this is not realism. It is realism in the sense

that we try to achieve a reality effect [*un effet de réel*] through photography (Ciment and Jordan, "Entretien avec Alexandre Trauner," 17).

28. *Décors de cinéma*, 17.
29. It is in this film that Arletty delivers the famous line "Atmosphère, atmosphère, est-ce que j'ai une gueule d'atmosphère? [Atmosphere, atmosphere, do I look like an atmosphere?]" The two "atmosphères" became the title of a very popular French television show devoted to "old" movies.
30. Interview by Jacques Kermabon, 18.
31. Trauner justified the expense of the reconstruction of the Métro Barbès station on the grounds that shooting during the few hours the real station was closed would have been even more costly (Ciment and Jordan, "Entretien avec Alexandre Trauner," 14). The film cost 118 million francs. In applying the economic argument to an attack on the film's retrograde style, critic Louis Raitière contends that if Carné had had a budget of twenty million "he again would find in himself, in an atmosphere of constraint, the wellsprings of emotion and humanity that money has never given to anyone." He charges Carné, once "the director of reality," with having "hatred for the real decor," for being "primarily a painter" ("*Les Portes de la nuit*," *Bulletin de L'IDHEC* [March–May 1947]:18). The decor of *Les Portes de la nuit* demonstrates to Raitière, as it did to many in the audience, an insensitivity to the straightened circumstances of the French film industry and to the harsh living conditions suffered by the French in the immediate postwar years. (The British production of *Caesar and Cleopatra* was criticized for similar profligacy in similar circumstances [see chapter 4].) In addition, the negative response to Carné's studio-bound aesthetic was typical of French criticism at a time when the influence of Italian neo-realism was most strongly felt.
32. The Waldorf set was so exact a reproduction that Lucius Boomer, chairman of the Hotel Corporation, could not tell the difference between photos of the sets and photos of the real hotel (Arthur Hornblow, Jr., "Never Before Such a Backdrop," *Lion's Roar* [4 June 1945]:36).
33. *Coming to Terms: The Rhetoric of Narrative in Fiction and Film* (Ithaca, N.Y.: Cornell University Press, 1990), 40, 38, 39.
34. As Chatman points out in ibid., 45–46, the hero, J. B. Jefferies (James Stewart), sits sleeping, his back to the window that faces the courtyard, and cannot therefore be the agent through whose eyes the sequence is mediated.
35. *Cinémagazine*, 21 Jan. 1927.
36. "The Artist and the Film," 13–15.
37. "The Art Director," in *Working for the Films*, ed. Oswell Blakeston (London: Focal, 1947), 86.
38. "Art direction: une définition," *Cinématographe* 75 (Feb. 1982):22.
39. "Etude sur le décor," *Arts* 493 (8 Dec. 1954):5.
40. "The Art Director," 41.
41. Some years earlier, in a piece frankly entitled "Background Stuff," another designer, Harold Grieve, insisting that decor know and stay in its place, had likened the fit of the set to narrative to the fit of wallpaper to a room. "For a successful picture, there must be coordination of a most intimate nature between sets and story, for the sets must help get over the feeling of the story. Mere realism or beauty alone is not sufficient. The sets must be built to harmonize with the intention of the director. They must always remain in the background, but they must fit the plot just as exactly as paper fits the wall of a room" (*Motion Picture Director* 3, no. 3 [Nov.–Dec. 1926]:28, cited in Bordwell, Thompson, and Staiger, *The Classical Hollywood Cinema*, 220).
42. Horner, "The Production Designer," 152; Douy, "Long Live Movie Sets," 17; Barsacq, "Etude sur le décor," 5; Gibbons, "The Art Director," 41.
43. "The Set Designer," 3.
44. Scot Holton and Robert Skotak, "William Cameron Menzies: A Career Profile," *Fantascene* 4 (1978):4–11. Trauner too makes clear the importance of the subordination of the decor to the aspect of the human figure: "It is the human body and its proportions that must be supported above all; everything that surrounds it must submit to the success of the portrait" (*Décors de cinéma*, 24).
45. *Caligari's Cabinet*, 122.
46. Elena Boland, "Design Artist Models Moods: Atmosphere Established by Urban's Settings," *Los Angeles Times*, 23 Nov. 1930.
47. Ciment and Jordan, "Entretien avec Alexandre Trauner," 8.
48. Sets must eschew that other sign, written and therefore objectionable, according to Hilyard M. Brown: "I think this is the worst thing an art director could do, is have an insert that says 'Courtroom' and then you cut into the courtroom. If the scene and the courtroom doesn't tell

the audience that this is a courtroom without this sign, we're in a lot of trouble. I avoid signs like the plague because I think it is just the cheapest, corniest way of selling an idea. Being a visual medium, if you can't tell it visually then you should get another art director" (Interview by Rich Cheatham, 1 Nov. 1980, Doheny Library.

49. Michael J. Toolan's observations on the relative importance of event, character, and setting to the novel are useful to our discussion of decor in film: "Less fundamentally essential to narrative than event and character . . . the establishment of an identifiable setting is a strong psychological preference in most readers. We like, in our reading of narratives, to know where we are, and look for clear spatiotemporal indications of just where and when a thing happened." He makes this further point consonant with our treatment of decor and genre: that the "specificity requirement seems relative to genre, story type" (*Narrative: A Critical Linguistic Introduction* [London: Routledge, 1988], 103).

50. There were two previous films based on Dashiell Hammett's novel: the 1931 *Maltese Falcon* starring Ricardo Cortez and Bebe Daniels and the 1936 *Satan Met a Lady* starring Warren William and Bette Davis.

51. The intertitle that precedes the first sequence of the film establishes the generic historicity of the narrative and its landscape, as well as the genre's dominant ideology: "This is a story of the Winchester Rifle Model 1873. The gun that won the West. To cowman, outlaw, peace officer or soldier, the Winchester '73 was a treasured possession. An Indian would sell his soul to own one."

52. See David Thomson's analysis of the decor of *The Big Sleep* in a rare article on the narrative function of constructed scenery ("The Art of the Art Director," *American Film* [Feb. 1977]: 12–14).

Chapter 3 Set as Punctuation

1. Cited in Schatz, *The Genius of the System*, 421.
2. In *"Mildred Pierce* and the Second World War" (in *Female Spectators: Looking at Film and Television*, ed. E. Deidre Pribam [London: Verso, 1988], 12–30), Linda Williams responds to what she considers reductive readings of the film by other feminist critics. She calls World War II the "absent referent" (25). The only signs of the war are fleeting references to the "duration" and to working in a defense plant. Williams also comments on the film's elision of the Great Depression, which in the novel is one of the factors that explains Veda's materialism.
3. Citing an extreme example, Paul Leni describes the effect of lighting on the varying decorative intensity of a single set in *Die Verschwörung zu Genua* [*The Conspiracy in Genoa*], a film he designed and directed. The set becomes an element of action as it is modified in seven different scenes, "each time underlining the *Stimmung* [mood] of the characters and actions at a given moment." The set is shown filled with light, half dark with "nervous shadows," as a simple background, with a single table illuminated, etc. The lighting effects change the character of the room. At the conclusion, "the room goes dark. The walls are eliminated—they die, fall into darkness. That is space as event, image as action" ("L'Image comme action," *Cinémato-graphe* [Feb. 1982]:8, reprinted from *Kunst und Film* 2/1921, reproduced from catalogue *Hätte ich das Kino!*, Schiller-Nationalmuseum, Marbach a.N., 1976).
4. Albert LaValley refers to the other "tough, resilient, lower-class and lower-middle-class women" who make "their way up in life" in Warner Bros. films of the 1930s, albeit in milieus less glossy than that of *Mildred Pierce* (Albert J. LaValley, *Mildred Pierce*, ed. with an introduction by Ranald MacDougall, Wisconsin/Warner Bros. Screenplay Series [Madison: University of Wisconsin Press, 1980], 10).
5. The split generic allegiance of *Mildred Pierce* has attracted the attention of a number of critics. In *"Mildred Pierce,"* Williams cites, among others, Joyce Nelson, *"Mildred Pierce* Reconsidered," *Film Reader* 2, ed. Patricia Erens and Bill Horrigan (Evanston: Film Division of Northwestern University, 1977), 65–70; Pam Cook, "Duplicity in *Mildred Pierce*," in *Women in Film Noir*, ed. E. Ann Kaplan [London: British Film Institute, 1978), 68–83; Janet Walker, "Feminist Critical Practice: Female Discourse in *Mildred Pierce*," *Film Reader* 5 (Evanston: Film Division of Northwestern University, 1982), 164–172; Andrea Walsh, *Women's Film and Female Experience, 1940–1950* (New York: Praeger, 1984), 121–131; and LaValley, *Mildred Pierce*. Pam Cook refers to Steven Farber, "Violence and the Bitch Goddess," *Film Comment* (Nov.–Dec. 1974):8–11, and John Davis, "The Tragedy of Mildred Pierce," *Velvet Light Trap* 6 (1972):27–30. See also Adriana Rivera, "The Ideological Function of Genres in *Mildred Pierce*," *Imagenes* 3, no. 1 (1987):16–18.
6. The City Pier at Santa Monica in the published script (LaValley, *Mildred Pierce*).

7. The Hawaiian Cafe in the published script (LaValley, *Mildred Pierce*).

8. Cited in David Deschner, "Anton Grot: Warners Art Director 1927–1948," *Velvet Light Trap* 15 (Fall 1975):19. Grot's notions about designing mysteries were widespread among his colleagues and constitute a set of conventions about which William Cameron Menzies commented just a few years before: "If the mood of the scene calls for violence and melodramatic action, the arrangement of the principal lines of the composition would be very extreme, with many straight lines and extreme angles. The point of view would be extreme, either very low or very high. The lens employed might be a wide angled one, such as a twenty-five millimeter lens which violates the perspective and gives depth and vividness to the scene. The values or masses could be simple and mostly in a low key, with violent highlights" ("Pictorial Beauty in the Photoplay," 166).

9. Following the general trend of glamorizing the material, the upright piano indicated in the final script becomes a baby grand (LaValley, *Mildred Pierce*, 97).

10. LaValley offers a useful analysis of the transformation of James M. Cain's novel *Mildred Pierce* into the film we know, through approximately eight treatments and screenplays by six different writers. Only toward the end of this process does the beach house replace Lake Arrowhead as the site of Mildred's tryst with Monte. "This is not so much an idyll for Mildred as Arrowhead seemed, but the entrance into a more complex, entangled world" (*Mildred Pierce*, 38).

11. The precise locations of the restaurants and most of the houses are drawn from the published script (LaValley, *Mildred Pierce*). While the film shows the differences, it does not specify the neighborhood.

12. See Rivera, "The Ideological Function of Genres," and Cook, "Duplicity in *Mildred Pierce*."

13. These same functions will be reconsidered in subsequent chapters, where the structural markers of opening and closing and of narrative crisis are reflected in sets of higher design intensity, and where genre, character, and theme are transposed at higher decorative pitches.

14. "I thought it should be quite tall, that it loom over the crowd, and that it be both quite modern and ominous" (Trauner, *Décors de cinéma*, 46).

15. Ciment and Jordan, "Entretien avec Alexandre Trauner," 14, 15.

16. *Directed by Vincente Minnelli*, 194.

17. See fig. 108.

18. Thomson, "The Art of the Art Director," 18.

19. Interview by Charles Affron, 21 June 1989, Los Angeles.

20. This was Jenkins's first screen credit. For the sake of camera movement, it was customary to build oversized sets and photograph them so their dimensions appeared in normal scale. Jenkins states that Wyler was happy to work in the sets of *Best Years*, "the first time I ever worked in sets that were the same size as they'd be in real life" (Corliss and Clarens, "Designed for Film," 45).

21. Writing about the mountain set devised for *Sergeant York*, cinematographer Sol Polito describes the advantages of using large constructed sets over location sites, a tendency he traces to the Spanish galleon built for *Captain Blood* ("The Mountain Comes to Mohammed," *American Cinematographer* [June 1941]:264).

22. *Agee on Film*, 271. Also, see chapter 1.

23. The picture, in fact, began without a production designer. In a memo addressed to production manager Richard L. Johnston about the work of Josef von Sternberg (who directed some sequences of *Duel in the Sun*), Selznick complains that Sternberg is not doing what William Cameron Menzies usually does: "The lack of a production designer has given him a terrific opportunity to fill this function but . . . he is not filling it" (*Memo from David O. Selznick*, 347). Joseph McMillan Johnson, the head of the art department for Selznick, took on that function later and received the credit.

24. This is the cover image of Albrecht, *Designing Dreams*.

25. Boris Leven describes the impact of his design: "After spending eleven unsuccessful days in Texas in search for an appropriate location for the film, I got back to the studio with several ideas floating in my head, but one of them intrigued me most. . . . I quickly made a small sketch of that idea. A large Victorian house standing all by itself on a Texas prairie. I showed this sketch to Stevens. He took it and without saying a word left the room. Minutes passed. He returned, came close to me and put his big hand on my shoulder. 'Pardner' he said, 'This is the best damn thing that happened to this film!' We built this big Victorian house on a prairie in Marfa, Texas" (Letter to Patrick Downing, 16 Oct. 1982, Margaret Herrick Library).

26. The configuration of the newsroom of the *Washington Post* in *All the President's Men* recalls the office in *The Apartment*, particularly when Woodward and Bernstein, typing out their story, are shown alone in its expanse.

27. The social topography and the individual houses are more explicitly characterized in the novel upon which the film is based, Henry Bellamann's *Kings Row* (New York: Simon and Schuster, 1941): "These were social boundaries. Every step away from these clearly marked precincts took one a step downward in the well-defined and perfectly understood social order of Kings Row" (29). "Madame von Eln's house was as individual as she was herself. . . . People exclaimed when they saw it, 'Quaint! Charming!' "(27–28). The Towers house, important in the film's decorative scheme, has nothing of Bellamann's description: "In the middle of the next block he squinted at a dingy house set in the midst of tangled shrubbery and swarming vines. The place was neglected and in bad repair. The narrow porch roof sagged like the back of an old work horse, and the floors of the side galleries were greenish with moss and damp" (33).

Chapter 4 Set as Embellishment

1. Ciment and Jordan, "Entretien avec Alexandre Trauner," 19.
2. Shooting on this set, built at the Victorine studio in Nice, began on August 17, 1943, and was terminated three days later when the Allied forces landed in Sicily. When production resumed in February 1944, the storm-damaged set had to be largely rebuilt.
3. Others are three films released in 1941–1942: *Via delle cinque lune*, based on a short story by Matilde Serao; *I promessi sposi*, based on Alessandro Manzoni's celebrated novel; *Piccolo mondo antico*, based on Antonio Fogazzaro's best-known work. *Un colpo di pistola*, also released in 1941, was based on an Alexander Pushkin short story.
4. A principal target of François Truffaut's celebrated article "Une Certaine Tendance du cinéma français" (*Cahiers du Cinéma* [Jan. 1957]:15–29), was Claude Autant-Lara, the director of *Douce*, *Sylvie et le fantôme*, and *Le Diable au corps*, who began his career as an art director. Among the films he designed, in whole or in part, were Marcel L'Herbier's *L'Inhumaine* and Jean Renoir's *Nana*.
5. *My Work in Films*, 10.
6. Doré's illustrations were the principal influence on a number of other important film designs, including, thanks to the intervention of Jean Cocteau, those of *La Belle et la bête* (Alekan, "La Volonté de perfection," 64). Anne Hollander offers this explanation of Doré's influence: "His paintings are uninteresting; but he had a magnificent gift for sensational composition in black and white, based on spatial depth and light rather than on detail and line or abstract surface interest, as if he were conceiving film frames. And like the old illuminations, Doré's pictures were offered in books, personally aimed at each viewer. What they lack in action they make up for in satisfying stolid realism—visions and monsters look feasible, as if designed so that a studio workshop could handle them" (Anne Hollander, *Moving Pictures* [New York: Knopf, 1989], 428).
7. "Musical Comedy Design for Stage and Screen," in *Scene Design for Stage and Screen*, ed. Orville Larson (East Lansing: Michigan State University Press, 1961), 197.
8. Anne Hollander observes that this film "emulates Rembrandt etchings and chiaroscuro Biblical scenes with great success, even though some of the costume details are slightly wrong. The movie offers a Dutch world through the eyes of Rembrandt's contemporaries as well: Steen and Saenredam supply the neutral interiors and exteriors, as if we were seeing life through the ordinary representational conventions of Rembrandt's milieu, and only perceiving private emotional moments in his distinctive mode" (*Moving Pictures*, 450–451).
9. Trauner recounts that, like Meerson, he had come to Paris to be a painter. He replaced a friend at the Epinay studio and met Meerson, who was, at the time, at work on *Sous les toits de Paris*. "It turned out that Meerson and I spoke more of painting than of film" (*Décors de cinéma*, 16). Vincent Korda, too, began as a painter. In fact, he and Trauner attended the Ecole des Beaux-Arts in Budapest at the same time (Ibid., 11).
10. Meerson's prestige did create a true succession, the French school of design inseparable from the larger movement known as "poetic realism" that we discuss in chapter 3. Its chief figures are Trauner (whose relationship to the director Marcel Carné is often compared to Meerson's relationship to Feyder or to René Clair), Max Douy, and Léon Barsacq.
11. See Barsacq, *Caligari's Cabinet*, 78.
12. "Les Décors de Lazare Meerson," in *Jacques Feyder ou le cinéma concret*, ed. Comité National Jacques Feyder (Brussels: ASBL, 1949), 51.
13. See Bandini and Viazzi, *Ragionamenti sulla scenografia*, 69.
14. Korda's imitation of Meerson is obvious in this notion of larger-than-life interiors and smaller-than-life exteriors. We take the measure of this design stratagem by the relative size of the *Night*

Watch. In *Rembrandt*, the painting is swollen by at least one-third relative to its size as we admire it on the walls of Amsterdam's Rijksmuseum, thus allowing Korda a soaring setting for the painting in the crucial scene of its unveiling.

15. The manipulation of archaic models of illustration is taken further in M-G-M's 1936 production of *Romeo and Juliet*. Following the credits, we see first what we perceive to be a tapestry depicting a terrace filled with human figures, then the animation of the tapestry into a stage upon which the Prologue delivers the opening lines of the play. Following his speech, we return to the stasis of the tapestry. In the next shot, the camera approaches a painting of Verona, viewed from above, that becomes the five-acre reconstruction of the city's Piazza San Zeno and its surrounding neighborhood. The two-dimensionality of tapestry and painting are deployed both to highlight cinema's capacity for serving up the illusion of the third dimension and to remind audiences that *Romeo and Juliet* is a narrative rooted in traditions of "serious" art. This opposition of two- and three-dimensionality is, however, not unique to Cukor's version of *Romeo and Juliet*. In devising the celebrated opening of *Henry V*, Laurence Olivier and his colleagues may have remembered the M-G-M *Romeo and Juliet* (see chapter 5); the credits of *Hangover Square* appear over an etching-like image of the square we see a few minutes after the film opens; Böcklin's painting *The Isle of the Dead* is the background for the credits of the Val Lewton production to which it lends its name. These are a few among numerous examples of this convention.

16. Robert Boyle gives some sense of the importance of the research department to the designers of his day: "We had access to all the research in the world. In those days too, every studio had a magnificent research library. What became of those I'll never know. Some of them just disappeared, became producers' libraries in their homes. . . . The studios have fallen into the hands of people who don't know what a library is. . . . That's the tragedy now, that nobody recognizes that these things have value. But anyway, we would take the reality of the research and we would twist it into what we thought was France, what we thought were the roofs of Paris. Because in those days, anybody who went to Europe lived in a garret, *Sous les toits de Paris*" (Interview by Charles Affron, 21 June 1989, Los Angeles).

17. Hambley and Downing, *The Art of Hollywood*, 54.

18. Ibid.

19. These cinematic reproductions were among the most highly prized items at the 1970 auction of M-G-M property.

20. Much of the information on the reconstruction of Versailles is taken from a lecture, "*Marie Antoinette*: Hollywood and History," given by Richard Barsam at the Frick Collection, New York City, 15 Nov. 1980.

21. Steen, *Hollywood Speaks!*, 234.

22. Quoted in Hambley and Downing, *The Art of Hollywood*, 54.

23. Director Sidney Franklin's annotated script of *Marie Antoinette* (Doheny Library) is a rare archival document in that it makes extensive reference to decor through handwritten annotations about each set. His notes most often refer to scale and quantity: for example, "Hall of the Knights 'Shoot this on spiral staircase. . . . Add columns at top of staircase and pan her in.' "

24. *Marie Antoinette* illustrates Anne Hollander's contention of an affinity between the subject matter of history painting and what she calls the "costume epic" (Hollander, *Moving Pictures*, 27–28).

25. This liberality extends to revered texts that might well stand without it: *Romeo and Juliet*, for example, another sumptuous vehicle for Norma Shearer. In an effort to sell Shakespeare to the general public, the film's lavish sets were the object of unusual publicity. See chapter 7.

26. Donald Albrecht has this view of the mutual attraction between modernism and cinema: "In addition to its novelty and connotations of affluence and progressiveness, modernism was attractive to moviemakers on aesthetic grounds: Like modern architecture, film design was fundamentally a manipulation of the elements of space, light, and movement. A number of key film producers, directors, stars, and art directors who were aware of the influence that the cinema had come to wield on its vast audience were, in fact, able to develop a film aesthetic that fostered architectural experimentation" (*Designing Dreams*, xii).

27. This is Albrecht's description of that scene: "In the beautifully fluid sequence that introduces the apartment, cinematographer William Daniels's camera glides along this diagonal axis [described in preceding paragraph] and draws the viewer gracefully through the semicircular glass wall of the foyer, into the living room. After travelling for some distance, the camera finally stops with a gently curving motion, bringing into view the entrance of Garbo from the terrace, beyond which lies infinite space, an illusion created by the lights of distant skyscrapers on the

horizon. For the sequence that takes place in the apartment, lighting, materials, and finishes are carefully chosen to indicate unequivocally the luxury of the setting. Metallic finishes dominate: the black-and-silver facets of the piano, the satiny sofa in an indirectly lit niche of mirrors, and the metal-and-glass curtain wall softened only by vertical panels of sheer drapes. Even Garbo herself is brought into the harmony of the decor, her every move made incandescent by the myriad reflections of her silvery dress, while the curving lines of a metal tubular chair (reminiscent of Mies's MR chair) trace her seductively languid contours. (Two decades later, Judy Garland would pay similar homage to Mies's Barcelona chair when in *A Star Is Born* (1954) she removed its back cushion and played its leather straps like the strings of a harp.) Rarely have fashion, architecture, and star persona been combined into so crystalline an image" (Ibid., 95).

28. Wright himself was first approached to design the film, but his fee, $250,000, was considered too high. The film was finally designed by Edward Carrere. For references to the parallels between the film's fiction and Wright's work within the postwar architectural controversy, and to the architectural community's fiercely negative response to *The Fountainhead*, see ibid., 168–174.

29. King Vidor Papers, Special Collections, Research Library, UCLA.

30. Enrico Guazzoni, a fellow Italian, painter, set designer, and director of *Brutus, Agrippina, The Maccabees,* and *Quo Vadis?*, had ventured "deliberately into three-dimensional scenery" at about the same time (Barsacq, *Caligari's Cabinet,* 15).

31. Ibid.

32. Ramirez, *La arquitectura en el cine,* 149.

33. An entire issue of *Bianco e nero,* May–Aug. 1975, entitled "Pastrone e Griffith: L'ipotesi e la storia," ["Pastrone and Griffith: Hypothesis and History"], is dedicated to this subject.

34. Kevin Brownlow, *The Parade's Gone By* (New York: Bonanza Books, 1968), 53.

35. It can be argued that Griffith owes to Pastrone strategies for lighting interiors and for camera movement, particularly as it advances the narrative (Davide Turconi, "G.P. & D.W.G.: Il dare e l'avere," *Bianco e nero* [May–Aug. 1975]:37–38).

36. David Thomson has this comment about Belshazzar's court: "Perhaps for the first time, a set is the subject of a scene. Sheer spectacle exerts itself in the exhilarating tracking-crane shot that Griffith took from an anchored balloon to illustrate the magnificence of his set. There is no plot in this shot, only the wish to plunge the viewer into a Babylon that no doubt complies with whatever history recalls, but which is also obstinately American, manufactured, and twentieth century" ("The Art of the Art Director," 14). The gloss at the bottom of an intertitle reads: "This hall over a mile in length imaged after the splendor of an olden day."

37. In *Cabiria,* elephants appear three times: the real elephants of Hannibal, and statues of elephants both in the Temple of Moloch and in the palace of Hasdrubal.

38. Alan Nadel, in his ingenious reading of the 1956 *The Ten Commandments* as a reflection of the political ideology of the Eisenhower years, comments on the depiction of Egypt as a function of "three chief sites of conflict, each corresponding to a socioeconomic class in postwar America. The Egyptian court signifies upper management, or the country club set; the Goshen hovel of Moses's family, the working class; and the 'suburban patio' of Baka the master builder, middle management. Even Baka's outdoor fire suggests the barbecues that adorned middle-class patios" ("God's Law and the Wide Screen: *The Ten Commandments* as Cold War 'Epic,'" *PMLA* [May 1993]:420–421). Nadel goes on to examine the relationship between these decors and the value systems that, he argues, they represent.

39. The 1925 arena has elicited comment for the technical means with which it suggested great size: "Although the sets were vast, especially the Circus Maximus with its enormous sculptured figures, its apparent scale in the film is created by one of the best early examples of foreground model shots, complete with moving miniatures to simulate the massed ranks of excited onlookers" (Hambley and Downing, *The Art of Hollywood,* 54). "Having designed miniatures which would combine with the full-size set in much the same way as a glass shot, they [Gibbons, A. Arnold Gillespie, Andrew MacDonald] added a triumphant master stroke; a set of galleries with ten thousand tiny people, all of whom could stand up and wave. The camera photographed miniature and full-size stand together" (Brownlow, *The Parade's Gone By,* 413).

40. The sequence was shot in the Roman Arena of Verona.

41. M-G-M's *Julius Caesar* serves as an unusual counterexample to the colossal; its reconstructions of Rome are on a human, nonheroic scale and are only minimally picturesque. Nonetheless, *Julius Caesar* was the third most expensive of the six films produced at M-G-M in 1952 (out of a total of forty-six) whose budgets for art direction exceeded $100,000 (M-G-M archives, Margaret Herrick Library). Even when Shakespeare's text provides an occasion for spectacle,

the film resists. Of the stadium, a set almost obligatory in the colossal film, we see the gate and the stairs that lead to the upper levels, but never the arena itself. The forum, the crucial site for the orations of Brutus (James Mason) and Mark Antony (Marlon Brando), crowds speakers and listeners into a relatively shallow space bounded by construction scaffolding and an un-adorned podium at the door of the Senate chamber. Art director Edward Carfagno attributes the austerity of the film's design to its director, Joseph Mankiewicz, who wanted to "eliminate the bric-à-brac" typical of films set in ancient Greece or Rome (Interview by Charles Affron, 21 June 1989, Los Angeles). Carfagno worked on the lavish *Quo Vadis?*, as well; he preferred the spare lines of *Julius Caesar* (David Deschner, "Edward Carfagno: MGM Art Director," *Velvet Light Trap* [Spring 1978]: 33).

42. P. L. Mannock, "And They Took a Sphinx to Egypt," *London Herald*, 12 Dec. 1945.
43. Marjorie Deans, *Meeting at the Sphinx: Gabriel Pascal's Production of Bernard Shaw's Caesar and Cleopatra*, foreword by George Bernard Shaw and Gabriel Pascal (London: Macdonald, 1946), 94.
44. Ibid., 112.
45. De Mille's *Male and Female, Manslaughter, Adam's Rib, The Ten Commandments* (1923), and *The Road to Yesterday* preceded *Noah's Ark*.
46. The staging of this disaster is a marvel of illusion, its models expertly integrated with full-scale structures. Kevin Brownlow reports that the prodigious effect of realism cost the lives of several extras (Brownlow, *The Parade's Gone By*, 324).
47. The *New York Times* reports that the $30,000 temple miniature was eighty square feet in area and sixty feet in height (23 Nov. 1948). Barsacq adds that the temple sequence cost $150,000 and a year's work. The seventeen-foot-high idol was made to appear one hundred feet tall (*Caligari's Cabinet*, 188).
48. The precatastrophe part of the sequence was staged on the *Queen Mary*. The revolving set was built to the same dimensions: 118′ × 60′ × 28′ high (L. B. Abbott, *Special Effects: Wire, Tape, and Rubber Band Style* [Hollywood: ASC, 1984], 184).
49. Both films were produced by Irwin Allen, who specialized in disaster and science-fiction films (*The Big Circus, The Lost World, A Voyage to the Bottom of the Sea*).
50. The 138-story building was translated by two models: the first, of the whole building, was seventy feet high and built to a scale of one-half inch per foot; the other, representing the top forty stories, was built to a one-and-a-half-inch scale (Abbott, *Special Effects*, 190–192).

Chapter 5 Set as Artifice

1. Letter to Patrick Downing, 16 Oct. 1982, Margaret Herrick Library.
2. Siegfried Kracauer, *From Caligari to Hitler: A Psychological History of the German Film* (Princeton: Princeton University Press, 1947), 68–69.
3. "In relation to the conventional expectations of most viewers, the expressionist settings of *Caligari* are excessive and transgressive; they are perhaps the first and most important way in which the film deviates from the realist norms of classical narrative cinema. They seem insistently to force their attention on us, to refuse the subordination of 'background' to narrative action and character demanded by classical cinema" (Mike Budd, "The Moments of Caligari," in *The Cabinet of Dr. Caligari: Texts, Contexts, Histories*, ed. Mike Budd [New Brunswick: Rutgers University Press, 1990], 12).
4. *Excelsior*, 5 May 1922, quoted in Raymond Bachellot, Daniel Bordet, and Anne-Claude Lelieur, *Paul Iribe* (Paris: Denoël, 1982), 162.
5. *The Art of Hollywood*, 46.
6. *The Haunted Screen: Expressionism in the German Cinema and the Influence of Max Reinhardt*, trans. Greaves Roger (Berkeley and Los Angeles: University of California Press, 1965), 115.
7. The uncredited Herman Rosse collaborated with Hall on *Frankenstein*.
8. See chapter 3.
9. Richard Sylbert, the production designer of *Dick Tracy*, explains his attraction to this style: "We knew we needed the Expressionistic 1938 feeling that would convey the moon and the stars and the darkness. We needed a generic quality. You couldn't say, 'That's a Ford' or 'That's New York,' because you would spoil everything. . . . These are not buildings, these are icons of buildings. . . . I looked at German Expressionist paintings and Dick Tracy Sunday supplements" (Vincent LoBrutto, *By Design: Interviews with Film Production Designers* (Westport, Conn., and London: Praeger, 1992], 61).
10. Corliss and Clarens, "Designed for Film," 29.

11. "The Style of Fairbanks' *The Thief of Bagdad* was determined long before any cameras rolled. The decision to make Bagdad a city of whiteness and light, spectacular but not solid, a city that was a backdrop to action and fantasy, not a city in which people really lived, was reached by Fairbanks and his consulting artists, by designer William Cameron Menzies and cameraman Arthur Edeson" (Everson, *American Silent Film*, 304–305).

12. Corliss and Clarens, "Designed for Film," 29.

13. Beverly Heisner describes the suitability of Menzies's sets to Fairbanks's acting style: The "relatively unadorned backgrounds serve as perfect foils for Douglas Fairbanks' acrobatic and balletic leaps and stunts" (*Hollywood Art*, 45).

14. Jean Cocteau counteracts the realism of speech in the enchanted castle of his *La Belle et la bête* [*Beauty and the Beast*] by having the protagonists (Josette Day and Jean Marais) move in ways often closer to mime than to conventional comportment—in slow motion, sometimes gliding over the floor, in a measured pace that echoes the measured delivery of their lines.

15. Reviewer Herb Lightman comments on the relationship between the "other world" of Peter, "a man who was both poet and flier," and the designs of Alfred Junge (Herb A. Lightman, "Two Worlds in Technicolor," *American Cinematographer* [July 1947]:237).

16. Ibid.

17. See also *Dante's Inferno, Heaven Can Wait, Angel on My Shoulder*.

18. "The Imagination of Disaster," in *Against Interpretation and Other Essays* (New York: Farrar, 1966), 216.

19. Janet Staiger uses *Blade Runner* as one of the principal examples of the dystopic in a subgenre of science fiction she calls "future noir." "Integral to all these dystopias is a bleak criticism of utopian versions of high modernist architecture and modern cityscapes, exterior structures which house corrupt economic and social institutions" ("Future Noir: Contemporary Representations of Visionary Cities," *East-West Film Journal* [1988]:41). Production designer Lawrence G. Paull describes his approach to the film: "I brought in just about my entire architectural research library, and we went from Egyptian to Deco to Streamline Moderne to Classical, from Frank Lloyd Wright to Antonio Gaudi" (LoBrutto, *By Design*, 171). Giuliana Bruno's discussion of pastiche in *Blade Runner* also applies to *Metropolis* with its juxtapositions of the machine-age aesthetic, the Gothic, and the exotic. "Pastiche, as an aesthetic of quotation, incorporates dead styles; it attempts a recollection of the past, of memory, and of history. The result of this architectural pastiche is an excess of scenography" ("Ramble City: Postmodernism and *Blade Runner*," in *Alien Zone: Cultural Theory and Contemporary Science Fiction Cinema*, ed. Annette Kuhn [London and New York: Verso, 1990], 187).

20. This extraterrestrial object was originally to be a tetrahedron. Special effects supervisor Con Pederson states, "The tetrahedron didn't look monumental or simple or fundamental. It tended to express diminution more than impressive scale. And there would be people who would think of pyramids" (Jerome Agel, ed., *The Making of Kubrick's 2001* [New York: Signet, 1970], n.p.).

21. Annette Michelson situates the narrative crux in the display of this suite. "The sudden contraction into these limits, projects us from galactic polymorphism into an extreme formality, insinuating, through the allusion of its décor, the idea of History into Timelessness. It shocks. . . . An Idea of a Room, it elaborates the notion of Idea and Ideality as Dwelling" ("Bodies in Space: Film as 'Carnal Knowledge,'" *Artforum* [Feb. 1969]:60).

22. Harry Horner, "First Night on Stage 21," *Theatre Arts* (Dec. 1947):31.

23. Through costume and makeup, the Chorus (Leslie Banks) corresponds to popular conceptions of Shakespeare's own appearance. In Kenneth Branagh's 1989 version of *Henry V*, the Chorus (Derek Jacobi) enters a movie sound stage in twentieth-century attire.

24. *On Acting* (New York: Simon and Schuster, 1986), 271.

25. Ibid., 273–274.

26. Katherine herself is no longer played by the actress we saw in the courtship scene but by the actor we saw in the woman's costume in the backstage sequence, shortly after the film's opening.

27. André Bazin states, "In making his film out of a play by showing us, from the opening, by a cinematic device that we are concerned here with theatrical style and conventions instead of trying to hide them, he relieved realism of that which makes it the foe of theatrical illusion" (*What is Cinema?*, ed. and trans. Hugh Gray [Berkeley and Los Angeles: University of California Press, 1967] 1:88). Demonstrating the film's ideological project as well as its stylistic virtuosity, Dudley Andrew offers an analysis of the film's various sources in French and Dutch art (*Film in the Aura of Art* [Princeton: Princeton University Press, 1984], 131–151).

28. Rick Altman corrects the conventional view that there is a radical split between the numbers

and the narrative of what he calls "the show musical": "Because it is continuous visually with the real world as well as thematically with the stage world, the backstage middle-world serves to establish an unexpected continuity between the diametrically opposed realms of reality and art" (*The American Film Musical* [Bloomington and Indianapolis: Indiana University Press, 1987], 206).

29. Rick Altman comments further on the narrative relevance of the conclusive numbers of *Footlight Parade*. The first, "Honeymoon Hotel," is a "song about the love relationship, transferring the lovers from the narrative to the stage"; the second, "By a Waterfall," "redefines the overt thematics of the first song in graphic terms"; "Shang'hai Lil," the third, "breaks down the separation between production personnel and performers," thereby revealing "the general strategy typifying the closing moments of the backstage musical" (Ibid., 230–231).

30. Joseph Urban was responsible for stage editions of the *Ziegfeld Follies* from 1915 until 1931, as well as other shows produced by Ziegfeld. He also designed New York's Ziegfeld Theatre. Urban's film work was concentrated on the sumptuous productions for Marion Davies's 1920s films.

31. Richard E. Ziegfeld and Paulette Ziegfeld, *The Ziegfeld Touch*, foreword by Patricia Ziegfeld (New York: Abrams, 1993), 174.

32. The song was featured in the *Ziegfeld Follies of 1919*. "Although Ziegfeld had introduced the staircase lined with women back in 1916, it was only after this number in 1919 that the staircase became identified with Ziegfeld" (Ibid., 250).

33. Designer and teacher John Koenig notes: "It is the designer's job to make it possible for the director to shoot the set in such a way that not only will the sketch be shot as indicated, but also closeups and medium shots. Therefore, when you look at the 'Pretty Girl is Like a Melody' number from *The Great Ziegfeld*, notice that set. The last thing you see is a long shot, but what you have seen in the meantime is a very teasing indication of what it might be. That is, they give you nothing but medium and close shots, and only at the very end do you get a sense of what the entire structure looks like. In that way it is a very good design, and also the apotheosis of musical comedy sets ever since it was built" (Lecture, 11 Jan. 1938, typescript in library of Museum of Modern Art, New York, 41–42).

34. See Charles Affron, *Cinema and Sentiment* (Chicago and London: University of Chicago Press, 1982), 140–143, for an analysis of the conflict between appearance and talent in *Ziegfeld Girl*.

35. Tony Thomas and Jim Terry, *The Busby Berkeley Book*, with Busby Berkeley, foreword by Ruby Keeler (Greenwich, Conn.: New York Graphic Society, 1973), 134.

36. *Showstoppers: Busby Berkeley and the Tradition of Spectacle* (New York: Columbia University Press, 1993), 131. Rubin points out "a certain divergence between Berkeley's film style and the Ziegfeld tradition. Berkeley's conception of spectacle does not usually depend as much on elaborate and ornate settings; the settings of his numbers tend to be more abstract and even streamlined" (114).

37. *American Film Musical*, 227–228.

38. *Designing Dreams*, 133–134.

39. Croce mentions the technical improvement in film stock that allowed the photographing of predominantly white sets: "Cameramen like Sol Polito at Warners, Gregg Toland at Goldwyn, and J. Roy Hunt and David Abel at RKO exploited maximum contrasts in black and white photography to produce a rich visual mood for musical sequences" (*The Fred Astaire and Ginger Rogers Book* [New York: Galahad, 1972], 25). Contrary to Croce, Howard Mandelbaum and Eric Myers locate the origin of the "bit white set" at M-G-M in the late 1920s: "Arc lighting had been used in the past, which necessitated rendering the white parts of the set in pink or green. The effect on the finished film would otherwise have been blinding. With the newly developed incandescent lighting, true white could become the predominant element in a set. In addition, the new changes in film stock (from orthochromatic to the more sensitive panchromatic) lent the image a crisp glossiness ideal for Deco sets" (*Screen Deco: A Celebration of High Style in Hollywood* [New York: St. Martin's, 1985], 34).

40. Gerald Mast speculates on the rapport between Astaire himself and the shape of the Eiffel Tower in the set Carroll Clark created for the "Top Hat, White Tie, and Tails" number of *Top Hat*: "Why the Eiffel Tower in a number on a London stage, in a film which makes no reference to Paris? Perhaps that tower, like Astaire, represents a synthesis of linearity and circularity. The Clark design emphasizes this suggestion with curving lines, rising to its pinnacle, trimmed with fancifully semicircular scalloped latticework instead of the rectangular grillwork the tower actually displays. Or perhaps the tower, like Astaire, represents a synthesis of old and new. This late nineteenth-century structure consciously rejected the ponderous solidity of earlier archi-

tectural design. Or perhaps the tower, like Astaire, is an edifice of air, anchored below but soaring above, solid yet ethereal. Or perhaps the Eiffel Tower is ultimately a monument to itself, one of a kind, nothing else like it—exactly like Astaire himself" (*Can't Help Singin': The American Musical on Stage and Screen* [Woodstock, N.Y.: Overlook, 1987], 154).

41. See chapter 3 for our discussion of the Beragon mansion in *Mildred Pierce*.

42. The Silver Sandal was inspired by New York's Silver Slipper, located on West 48th Street. *Swing Time*'s other nightclub, Club Raymond, is a "composite of Hollywood's Clover Club and Rockefeller Center's Rainbow Room." John Harkrider, who was responsible only for the set for the "Bojangles of Harlem" number, was given credit for the whole Silver Sandal (Croce, *Fred Astaire and Ginger Rogers*, 112).

43. Clair, cited in R. C. Dale, *The Films of René Clair: Exposition and Analysis* (Metuchen, N.J., and London: Scarecrow Press, 1986), 1:174.

44. Ibid., 174–175.

45. Ibid., 175–176.

46. Oliver Smith, primarily a Broadway designer, creates a likeness of Jo Mielziner's sewer set used in the original stage production. Preston Ames, who designed *Brigadoon*, states: "I don't want to see the play. . . . I'd like to get it with my thoughts in mind. Yet in the 40s, for musicals, it was the practice to base the sets on the Broadway versions" (Interview by Hugh Fordin, 1972, Doheny Library).

47. Designer Jack Smith stated: "I went to Tiepolo, one of my favorite artists. . . . I drew a sketch. It was too modern. I revised it to make it more decadent. Minnelli was always a great admirer of decadence, used correctly" (Interview by Hugh Fordin, July 1972, Doheny Library). Rick Altman cites the credit sequence of *Yolanda and the Thief*, with its mixture of the "shallow and unrealistic" and the "fully three-dimensional," as a device that introduces "increased reality" into the "contrived world of the musical" (*American Film Musical*, 78).

48. The 1959 *Li'l Abner* owes its stylized decor to its comic-book-via-Broadway-musical provenance.

49. "The Truth about this Film," *The Tales of Hoffmann*, souvenir booklet (Bristol and London: n.d.), n.p.

50. Virginia Wright Wexman comments on the correlation of character and environment in *Sunset Boulevard*: "The film's introduction of her [Norma] identifies her with her decrepit mansion, as she first appears gazing at Joe through its windows. This identification is strengthened as the action proceeds by shots that equate her tile floor with a spider web and her rat-infested empty swimming pool with her decaying career" (*Creating the Couple: Love, Marriage, and Hollywood Performance* [Princeton: Princeton University Press, 1993], 149–150).

51. The filmmakers indulge in a significant bit of ironic, studio-referential decor. Next to the telephone in the apartment of this lowly assistant director is a miniature model of the statue of Dagon, from Cecil B. De Mille's *Samson and Delilah*.

52. One is *Hold Back the Dawn*, with a script by Billy Wilder and Charles Brackett, two of the writers responsible for *Sunset Boulevard*.

53. The Washington Square set for *The Heiress*.

Chapter 6 Set as Narrative

1. In his book on "cinematurgie," Marcel Pagnol begins his consideration of decor with a discussion of the three unities. He cites unity of place as the one most susceptible to violation by the cinema, a violation he welcomes as truly liberating: "The instant set change has finally freed us from the burdens of theatrical servitude" (*Cinématurgie de Paris*, 135). In film, no explanation is needed each time the character enters or leaves the stage. One can begin at the height of dramatic action simply by changing the set.

2. See Norman Gambill, "Harry Horner's Design Program for *The Heiress*," *Art Journal* (Fall 1983):223–230; Harry Horner, "Designing *The Heiress*," *Hollywood Quarterly* (Jan. 1950): 1–7; Barbara Bowman, *Master Space: Film Images of Capra, Lubitsch, Sternberg, and Wyler* (New York: Greenwood, 1992), 129–130.

3. "The Production Designer," 155. Using a Dantesque analogy, Donald Lyons describes Catherine's three principal ascensions: "Early on, in the throes of passion for Morris . . . she flies up and down, a Paradise; deserted on elopement night, she bleakly and brokenheartedly trudges up, in Purgatory; finally, smirking with self-satisfied hate, she glides coolly up to the accompaniment of the returned and still-greedy Morris's pounding at the door—she has neatly turned the tables, but hate is Hell" (Donald Lyons, "Theaters of Cruelty," *Film Comment* [Nov.–Dec. 1993]:20).

4. Lillian Hellman, *The Little Foxes*, in *Four Plays* (New York: Modern Library, 1942), 166–167.

5. Charles Higham, *The Films of Orson Welles* (Berkeley and Los Angeles: University of California Press, 1971), 49.

6. Two important porch scenes fell victim to the radical reediting of the film following Welles's departure to work on another project (Robert L. Carringer, *The Magnificent Ambersons: A Reconstruction* [Berkeley and Los Angeles: University of California Press, 1993], 163–172, 217–219).

7. "There were good reasons for Welles's decision to shoot the interiors of the mansion in traveling shots. The point was to make the audience feel the spacious innards of the place, to make them experience as directly as possible the grand solidity of the Amberson wealth—an effect which cannot be achieved by cutting back and forth between relatively static compositions" (James Naremore, *The Magic World of Orson Welles* [New York: Oxford University Press, 1978], 119). Some of Welles's elaborate staging of this scene was lost in the reediting. "His shooting plan involved a series of backward-moving camera shots that traversed the third floor of the Amberson mansion, where the ballroom was located, along a circular course, twice. The RV [release version] not only destroyed the rhythm of this plan but also rendered the physical layout of the space incomprehensible" (Carringer, *The Magnificent Ambersons*, 77). The layout is, indeed, unclear, but the sense of interconnectedness between the playing areas survives.

8. A four-and-one-half-minute-long shot, cut from the film, moved around the first floor and then mounted the steps to Isabel's room; another shot (severely truncated in the released version of the film) navigated through no fewer than eight rooms. "Each time the camera was in a room, the camera saw four walls and a ceiling" (Higham, *The Films of Orson Welles*, 51–52).

9. The Amberson staircase was reused in many subsequent RKO productions, most memorably in *Cat People* (Thomson, "The Art of the Art Director," 14).

10. Carringer, *The Magnificent Ambersons*, 245. Some of the sets for the Amberson mansion were reused for the old house George and Mary Bailey occupy in Frank Capra's *It's a Wonderful Life* (Naremore, *Magic World of Orson Welles*, 112).

11. François Truffaut, *Hitchcock*, with Helen G. Scott (New York: Simon and Schuster, 1967), 94.

12. In two of Peter Greenaway's other films, *The Draughtsman's Contract* and *The Belly of an Architect*, narrative is explicitly rooted in issues of design.

13. *How Green Was My Valley* won the Oscar for Best Picture and for Art Direction. The *New York Times* reports that 150 men spent three months constructing an eighty-acre set that included six hills (7 Sept. 1941). Philip Dunne, its screenwriter, credits William Wyler, the first director assigned to the film, with a significant input in "the pre-production phase: casting, building of sets" (*How Green Was My Valley: The Screenplay for the Darryl F. Zanuck Film Production Directed by John Ford*, introductory essay by Philip Dunne [Santa Barbara, Calif.: Santa Teresa, 1990], 15).

14. Beverly Heisner describes this set accurately: "The village's long street, lined with blocks of uniform workers' housing, climbed a steep hill to the colliery at the top, perched like a Gothic cathedral above the town and like a cathedral, the dominant factor in the lives of the inhabitants. The men trailing to work and returning from it on the steep hill, sometimes singing and sometimes bone-weary silent, is a motif woven throughout the film. The miner's houses (their lives) are built upon the hill in which they spend most of their waking hours" (*Hollywood Art*, 194). According to Philip Dunne, the decision to shoot so much of the film on and near the street was dictated by the outbreak of World War II. The initial project was to have been shot on location in Wales, in color. The stand-in California hills could not supply the requisite green, hence black and white, and a minimum of "nature" shots (*How Green Was My Valley*, 20).

15. *Street Scene* opens one hot summer evening; act 2 begins the next morning; the action closes that afternoon. *Dead End* begins one morning and ends late the same evening.

16. Day's set conspires, of course, to support the characteristic mise-en-scène of director William Wyler. Particularly in his collaborations with cinematographer Gregg Toland, Wyler's signature is recognizable in staging in depth and in effects achieved by eschewing camera placement that simulates eye-level position.

Chapter 7 Judgment and Prize

1. For the judgments of researchers and scholars, see chapter 1 and appendix B.

2. 5 March 1937, in Graham Greene, *Graham Greene on Film: Collected Film Criticism 1934–1940*, ed. John Russell Taylor (New York: Simon and Schuster, 1972), 136.

3. 23 Oct. 1936, in ibid., 109–111.

4. 8 April 1946, in Agee, *Agee on Film*, 363.

5. 20 July 1946, in ibid., 208.

6. See chapter 5. John McCarten, whose reviews in the *New Yorker* almost never make reference to production values, is unusually expansive with regard to the art direction of *Henry V*: "The freshness of *Henry V* is hugely enhanced by sets that do not depend for their effectiveness on humdrum realism. Foregrounds that look as tangible as the earth under your feet blend into backgrounds that might well be used to illustrate a fairy tale" (22 June 1946:40–42).

7. 14 Dec. 1946, in Agee, *Agee on Film*, 232.

8. Nov. 1946, in *The Golden Screen: Fifty Years of Films*, ed. George Perry, introd. by Dirk Bogarde (London: Pavillion Books, 1989), 60.

9. April 1947, in ibid., 67. Many of Junge's sets are mentioned, positively if briefly, in the British press of the 1930s. *Roadhouse*: "Lavish and spectacular settings make intriguing settings" (*Today's Cinema*, 26 Nov. 1934). *The Iron Duke*: "Seldom in a film have such vast and wonderful settings been seen, a triumph of art director's skill" (*Sunday Referee*, 2 Dec. 1934). *Sailing Along*: "The settings are superb . . . the settings are an entertainment in themselves" (*Cinema*, 2 Feb. 1938). *Gangway*: "Settings on an ornate scale" (*Daily Film Renter*, 13 Aug. 1937). *King Solomon's Mines*: "Both settings and scenery are excellent" (*Manchester Guardian*, 22 July 1937).

10. March 1949, in *Golden Screen*, 82.

11. 30 Sept. 1948.

12. 30 Sept. 1948.

13. 2 Oct. 1948, 90.

14. 23 Oct. 1948.

15. 23 Oct. 1948 (both reviews).

16. Eric Newton, "Film Décor," *The Year's Work in the Film: 1949* (London: Longmans, Green, 1950), 60.

17. 25 Oct. 1948, 101.

18. "In Love with Ballet," *Observer*, 25 July 1948.

19. July 1948, in *Golden Screen*, 75.

20. Paul Holt, "*Jew Süss*," *London Daily Express*, 3 Oct. 1934.

21. William Foss, "The Film That Cost Britain £125,000," *Sunday Chronicle*, 7 Oct. 1934.

22. *Los Angeles Herald and Express*, 26 Dec. 1934; *New York Herald Tribune*, 28 Dec. 1934; *Los Angeles News*, 26 Dec. 1934; *New York Motion Picture Daily*, 13 Oct. 1934; *New York Times*, 5 Oct. 1934; *New York Daily News*, 5 Oct. 1934.

23. "£125,000 Picture without a Soul," *Reynolds Illustrated News*, 7 Oct. 1934.

24. John Betjeman, "*Jew Süss*," *London Evening Standard*, 6 Oct. 1934.

25. C. A. Lejeune, "*Jew Süss*: A Costly Experiment in Horror," *Observer*, 7 Oct. 1934. Lejeune specifically objects to the fact that *Jew Süss* is an indictment of pogroms. She contends that *The House of Rothschild* had already "argued the case against pogroms reasonably well. With all the sympathy in the world for the oppressed Jew, I fancy that there are other problems worthy of being tackled at some expense by our native film industry." Even in 1934, before the Holocaust, Lejeune's callous remark is shocking.

26. See chapter 4 for our discussion of *calligrafismo* and our redefinition of the calligraphic.

27. "Retrospettive: *Addio giovinezza!*, *Sissignora*, *Gelosia*, *Le Sorelle Materassi*, *Il cappello del prete*," *Cinema* (May 1950):314.

28. Richard Winnington, "Big, Pretty, Dull," *Northern Chronicle*, 24 April 1948; Sirol Hugh Jones, *Time and Tide*, 13 July 1948.

29. *New York Times*, 28 April 1948; *New York Herald Tribune*, 28 Apr. 1948.

30. 10 May 1948, 81.

31. See chapter 1.

32. 4 April 1951, 6.

33. "Foot and Mouth," *Daily Express*, 19 April 1951.

34. *New York Times*, 5 April 1951.

35. 23 April 1951, 110.

36. *New York Herald Tribune*, 5 April 1951.

37. *New York Times*, 23 Nov. 1945.

38. 10 Dec. 1945, 97.

39. *Hollywood Reporter*, 17 Oct. 1945, 10.

40. 22 Oct. 1945.

41. *Newsweek*, 3 Dec. 1945, 100; *New York Herald Tribune*, 23 Nov. 1945; and *New York Daily Mirror*, 23 Nov. 1945, are the surprising exceptions.

42. *New York Daily News*, 21 Nov. 1945.

43. See chapter 5.
44. 15 Feb. 1954, 97, 98.
45. 22 Feb. 1954, 102.
46. *Pictures Will Talk: The Life and Films of Joseph L. Mankiewicz* (New York: Scribner's, 1978), 262.
47. *Time*, 14 Nov. 1955; *New York Times*, 4 Nov. 1955; *New York Herald Tribune*, 4 Nov. 1955; *New Yorker*, 5 Nov. 1955, 119; *Newsweek*, 7 Nov. 1955, 117–118.
48. 13 Sept. 1954, 109.
49. 4 Oct. 1954, 103.
50. *New York Times*, 17 Sept. 1954. Neither McCarten of the *New Yorker* (24 Sept. 1954, 61–62) nor Guernsey of the *New York Herald Tribune* (17 Sept. 1954) mentions the stylized sets.
51. *Directed by Vincente Minnelli*, 130.
52. "Film Décor," 59.
53. May 1948, in *Golden Screen*, 72.
54. 27 Sept. 1948, 87–88.
55. *The Nation*, 28 June 1948, in Agee, *Agee on Film*, 389. Agee's thinking about the nexus of decor and text is consistent in his negative criticism of the sets of another adaptation of a prestigious play, Shaw's *Caesar and Cleopatra*: "They are often pleasantly gaudy, sometimes beautiful, and never, I think, primarily objectionable; yet to some extent, by their massiveness and their violence of complexion, they cloy one's attention and thus slow up the mind and the dialogue" (*The Nation*, 17 Aug. 1946, in ibid., 213).
56. In 1937, each studio was guaranteed a nomination in the category. This opened the nominations to some of the less powerful studios, such as Republic and Hal Roach (Mason Wiley and Damien Bona, *Inside Oscar: The Unofficial History of the Academy Awards* [New York: Ballantine Books, 1986], 696, 699). It also generated a proliferation of nominations. The number escalated from just seven in 1936 to twelve in 1937. The total of nominations reached a high of seventeen in 1940 (thirteen in black and white and four in color), the first year separate awards were given for the art direction of color films. It was not until 1945 that the nominees were reduced to a manageable five for color and five for black and white, and thereafter sometimes descended to three or even two in each category.
57. In appendix D, we support our findings with tables and a detailed analysis of the data.
58. See appendix E for a discussion of canon formation based on a correlation between the Academy Awards, the Producers Guild "landmark" designations, and critical reception.
59. Cited in Richard Shale, ed., *Academy Awards: An Ungar Reference Index*, foreword by Fay Kanin (New York: Ungar, 1982), 121.
60. Cited in Wiley and Bona, *Inside Oscar*, 3.
61. Ibid., 689.
62. Ibid., 693.
63. Cited in Emanuel Levy, *And the Winner is . . . : The History and Politics of the Oscar Awards* (New York: Ungar, 1987), 23.
64. Joseph McBride, *Frank Capra: The Catastrophe of Success* (New York: Simon and Schuster, 1992), 37.
65. Levy, *And the Winner Is*, 292.
66. Encomiums for Day's designs come from practitioners (Boyle, Leven), historians (Hambley, Downing, Albrecht), and theoreticians (Eisner, Cappabianca).
67. *Adventures of Tom Sawyer, Our Town, Thief of Bagdad* (1940), *The Pride of the Yankees, For Whom the Bell Tolls, Address Unknown*.
68. Cited in Wiley and Bona, *Inside Oscar*, 701.
69. See chapter 3.
70. *Experiment Perilous, Frenchman's Creek* (award winner for color), *The Keys to the Kingdom, National Velvet, The Picture of Dorian Gray, San Antonio, A Thousand and One Nights*.

Appendix B Histories of Set Design

1. Ann Lloyd, *The History of the Movies* (London and Sydney: Macdonald Orbis, 1988); Gianni Rondolino, *Storia del cinema* (Turin: UTET, 1988); Douglas Gomery, *Movie History: A Survey* (Belmont, Calif.: Wadsworth, 1991); Kristin Thompson and David Bordwell, *Film History: An Introduction* (New York: McGraw-Hill, 1994).
2. 304–305, 313, 307.
3. (New York: Charles Scribner's Sons, 1990), 118–122.
4. Louis Giannetti, *Understanding Movies*, 3d ed. (Englewood Cliffs, N.J.: Prentice-Hall, 1986),

266–282; Joseph Boggs, *The Art of Watching Films* (Palo Alto: Mayfield, 1985), 106–109; Dennis DeNitto, *Film: Form and Feeling* (New York: Harper & Row, 1985), 73–74.

5. Gerald Mast, *A Short History of the Movies* (New York: Macmillan, 1986); Thomas W. Bohn and Richard I. Stromgren, *Light and Shadows* (Palo Alto: Mayfield, 1987); David A. Cook, *A History of Narrative Film* (New York and London: Norton, 1990); David Bordwell and Kristin Thompson, *Film Art: An Introduction* (New York: McGraw-Hill, 1990), 91–95.

6. Born in Russia in 1906, Barsacq studied decorative arts and architecture in Paris until 1926. He was assistant to set designers Perrier and Andrejew, among others, and worked with the directors Baroncelli, Duvivier, Pabst, Renoir, Grémillon, Carné, and Christian-Jaque. Barsacq's credits include *La Marseillaise* (directed by Jean Renoir, 1938), *Lumière d'été* and *Pattes blanches* (directed by Jean Grémillon, 1943 and 1948), and *Les Diaboliques* (directed by Henri Clouzot, 1955).

7. *Designing for Moving Pictures* (London and New York: Studio Publications, 1941), republished as *Designing for Films* (London and New York: Studio Publications, 1949).

8. (Paris: IDHEC, n.d.).

9. "Note per una storia della scenografia cinematografica," in *Scene e costume nel cinema*, ed. Mario Verdone (Rome: Buzzoni Editore, 1986), 127–138.

10. "Lo sviluppo della scenografia cinematografica," *Bianco e nero* 12 (1952):24–39.

11. (Bloomington and Indianapolis: Indiana University Press, 1993), 367–376.

Appendix C Carlo Enrico Rava and Italian Film Journals of the Fascist Period

1. The series of articles, "La casa nel film [The House in Film]," appeared in *Domus*, a bimonthly publication, from November 1937 to October 1938. Between May and August 1939, Rava had a second series in the same periodical on essentially the same subject, "Architettura e arredamento nel film italiano [Architecture and Interior Decoration in Italian Film]." Through all of 1941, Rava's third series, "Il gusto negli interni di film [Taste in Interior Decoration in Film]," was published in a monthly column on set design featured in *Stile*, a magazine whose full title can be translated as "Style in the Home and in Interior Decoration."

2. *Cinema*, a biweekly publication that appeared between 1936 and 1943 (and was revived between 1948 and 1956), was the best-known Italian periodical of the time. The articles in *Cinema* are in general very well informed; the magazine was printed on fine paper and generously illustrated. Mussolini's son, Vittorio, was its editor-in-chief beginning in 1938, and, for a time, Rudolph Arnheim, P. M. Pasinetti, and Michelangelo Antonioni were on its editorial board. Most surprisingly, *Cinema* continued to survey American film through 1943, a year in which there were late reviews of, for example, *The Wizard of Oz* and *The Women* and a feature article on King Vidor. More than fifteen serious articles on set design, far in excess both in quantity and quality of a comparable run of any major film journal ever, appeared in *Cinema* between 1936 and 1943. These include interviews with art directors, analyses of the decor of individual films, and pieces on questions of praxis and aesthetics. One, in particular, signed by a writer who published under the pseudonym G. Vi, is of interest here. Vi takes position against the tradition of Italian set design and in favor of the American aesthetic. He argues that while some may think that spectators do not pay much attention to decor, busy as they are following the narrative and observing the performances, in fact a good story, good directing, and good acting will not suffice to overcome a false design ("Verità negli ambienti," *Cinema* [25 April 1938]:268). Truthful sets hold the film together, at least for the time the spectator is in the movie theatre, before he or she has the chance to reflect on the probability or improbability of the plot. Unconvincing sets generate unease, uncertainty, and ultimately disbelief. Vi continues in praise of Hollywood for the care and detail of its decor, even when—and here he joins in a conventional European refrain—everything else about American film rings false. The true image of America is translated, in Vi's view, not by the scriptwriter, nor by the actor or actress, but by American set designers. How is that? Because, unlike Italian set designers, American art directors shaped by the studio system are free of the craving to be original, to introduce into their work their own tastes and aesthetic judgments. They are thus released to address the concrete, everyday reality that translates time and mores and constitutes the principal fascination of film. According to Vi, and here he separates from Rava, the role of the set designer in film is not really very different from that of, say, the grip: the set designer is definitely an artisan, not an artist. Above all, the set designer is not an educator of the public taste. Decor's standard, for this writer, is not the ideal, but the real.

3. "La casa nel film," *Domus* (Nov. 1937):30–32.

4. The set designer's role as educator of public taste was announced in writings published

throughout the 1920s and the 1930s, both in Europe and in the United States. Among those who claimed for decor the Aristotelian ideal of the pleasing inseparable from the useful were the critic and theorist Léon Moussinac and the art director William Cameron Menzies. Moussinac rails against the inauthenticity and bad taste of recent French film decor. He urges contemporary directors to follow the example of their colleagues who, through collaboration with great contemporary decorators, sought to educate the public taste to the difference between banality and imitation and genuine originality and authenticity: L'Herbier with Autant-Lara, Delluc with Francis Jourdain, and Raymond Bernard with Mallet-Stevens ("Intérieurs modernes au cinéma," *Cinémagazine* [2 Feb. 1921]:5–8). Some years later, in a 1929 lecture delivered at the University of Southern California, William Cameron Menzies credits movies directly with the increased attention to design evident in American products of all sorts—typewriters, clothing, furniture, automobiles. Film, according to Menzies, had been successful in accomplishing the useful function ascribed to it earlier by Moussinac: the education of public taste. "I know for a fact that many designers and illustrators see motion pictures for the inspiration and pictorial ideas they get from them. The pictorial history of the photoplay is a history of the development of public taste for beauty on the screen. This taste has been developed by tasting. One artist, in his efforts, has outdone the other, and the public continues, as always, to demand more and more. The artist who succeeds today must give a wee bit more than his predecessors. Through cumulative progress the motion picture, with its tremendous resources, physical and human, will continue to blaze the trail for all other pictorial arts, and will assure our recovery from what has been referred to as 'the ugliest age in our history'—1850–1900" ("Pictorial Beauty," 163).

5. "La casa nel film," *Domus* (Nov. 1937):30–32.

6. "La casa nel film," *Domus* (Oct. 1938):64.

7. "Architettura e arredamento nel film italiano," *Domus* (March 1939):64.

8. "Architettura e arredamento nel film italiano," *Domus* (May 1939):64.

9. "Architettura e arredamento nel film italiano," *Domus* (Aug. 1939):64. Donald Albrecht cites the example of Guido Fiorini, a distinguished modernist architect admired, even imitated, by Le Corbusier among others. "From 1933 . . . Fiorini devoted himself largely to the cinema as a professor at Rome's famous film school, Centro Sperimentale di Cinematografia, and as a set designer, most notably for grand historical spectacles. By the late 1930s, even sets that would have called for modern decor only a few years earlier were given by Fiorini a historical flavor: his neo-classical department store interior for *I grandi magazzini* (1939), for example, features classical columns and entablatures" (*Designing Dreams*, 107). Albrecht suggests that this turn in Fiorini's aesthetic, from the international modernism of his work as an architect in the 1920s to the national classicism of his work as a set designer in the 1930s, was a concession to the aesthetic favored by the regime. How then are we to understand Rava's evolving message? For Albrecht, Italian cinema of the early 1930s, and more generally European cinema of the time, had engaged in an "apolitical appropriation of architectural modernism" and "had come to value modern architecture for its stylishness rather than on any ideological grounds" (Ibid., 71). For Rava, architectural modernism in film was decidedly political, and Fascist to boot, internationalism notwithstanding.

Appendix D The Art Direction Oscar and Awards in Other Countries

1. Ted Bentley Hammer, *International Film Prizes: An Encyclopedia* (Hamden, Conn.: Garland, 1991).

Appendix E A Canon for Art Direction

1. "Landmark Films," *New York Times*, 22 March 1991.

Selected Bibliography

Abbott, L. B. *Special Effects: Wire, Tape, and Rubber Band Style.* Hollywood: ASC Press, 1984.

Agee, James. *Agee on Film.* New York: Wideview/Perigee, 1958.

Albrecht, Donald. *Designing Dreams.* New York: Harper & Row, 1986.

Alekan, Henri. "La Volonté de perfection n'existe pas, n'existe plus ou existe peu." *Le Technicien du Film et la Technique Cinématographique,* no. 211 (15 Jan.–15 Feb. 1974):43–45, 64.

Altman, Rick. *The American Film Musical.* Bloomington and Indianapolis: Indiana University Press, 1987.

André, Jean, Max Douy, Bernard Evein, Pierre Guffroy, Willy Holt, François De Lamothe, Theo Meurisse, Rino Mondellini, Jacques Saulnier, Alex Trauner, and Georges Wakhevitch. "Les Décorateurs du cinéma français défendent leur profession." *Le Film Français,* no. 1415–2430 (12 Nov. 1971):12–13.

L'Architecture-décoration dans le film. Proceedings of the Second International Meeting of the Schools of Film and Television, organized by the IDHEC, during the Cannes Festival, April–May 1955. Paris: Institut des Hautes Etudes Cinématographiques, 1955.

Arnheim, Rudolph. "Dettagli che non sono dettagli." *Cinema* 1 (10 March 1937):180–182.

Bandini, Baldo, and Glauco Viazzi. *Ragionamenti sulla scenografia.* Milan: Poligono Società Editrice, 1945.

Barsacq, Léon. *Caligari's Cabinet and Other Grand Illusions: A History of Film Design.* Ed. and rev. Elliott Stein. Foreword by René Clair. Trans. Michael Bullock. Boston: New York Graphic Society, 1976.

———. *Le Décor de film.* Paris: Editons Seghers, 1970.

———. "Le Décor." In *Le cinéma par ceux qui le font,* ed. Denis Marion, 191–207. Paris: Arthème Fayard, 1949.

———. "Les Décors de Lazare Meerson." In *Jacques Feyder ou le cinéma concret,* ed. Comité National Jacques Feyder, 47–52. Brussels: ASBL, 1949.

———. "Etude sur le décor." *Arts,* no. 493 (8 Dec. 1954).

———. "Le Rôle du décor dans le film." *La Cinématographie Française,* no. 1390 (Oct. 1950).

———. "Le Silence est d'or." *Ciné-club,* no. 1 (1947).

Bertrand, Paul. "The Set Designer." *Unifrance Film,* no. 20 (Oct. 1952):3.

Bianco e nero, April 1955. Special Issue on Art Direction in Italy.

Bordwell, David, Janet Staiger, and Kristin Thompson. *The Classical Hollywood Cinema: Film Style and Mode of Production to 1960.* New York: Columbia University Press, 1985.

Brownlow, Kevin. *The Parade's Gone By.* New York: Bonanza Books, 1968.

Cappabianca, Alessandro, Michele Mancini, and Umberto Silva. *La costruzione del labirinto: la scena, la maschera, il gesto, la cerimonia.* Cinema e Informazione Visiva. Milano: Gabriele Mazzota Editore, 1974.

Carrick, Edward [Edward Craig]. *Designing for Moving Pictures.* "How to Do It" series. London and New York: Studio Publications, 1941. Republished as *Designing for Film*. London and New York: Studio Publications, 1949.

Carringer, Robert L. *The Magnificent Ambersons: A Reconstruction*. Berkeley and Los Angeles: University of California Press, 1993.

Chatman, Seymour. *Coming to Terms: The Rhetoric of Narrative in Fiction and Film*. Ithaca, N.Y.: Cornell University Press, 1990.

Ciment, Michel, and Isabelle Jordan. "Entretien avec Alexandre Trauner." *Positif*, no. 223–224 (Oct.–Nov. 1979): 4–19, 46–56.

Cook, Pam. "Duplicity in *Mildred Pierce*." In *Women in Film Noir*, ed. E. Ann Kaplan, 68–82. London: British Film Institute, 1980.

Corliss, Mary, and Carlos Clarens. "Designed for Film: The Hollywood Art Director." *Film Comment* 14 (May–June 1978): 26–60.

Cossa, Ubaldo. "Scenografia, problema vitale." *Cinema*, no. 126 (25 Sept. 1941): 198–199.

Croce, Arlene. *The Fred Astaire and Ginger Rogers Book*. New York: Galahad Book, 1972.

Douy, Max. "Long Live Movie Sets." *Unifrance Film*, no. 51 (Oct.–Dec. 1959): 17.

Dunne, Philip. *How Green Was My Valley: The Screenplay for the Darryl F. Zanuck Film Production Directed by John Ford*. Introductory essay by Philip Dunne. Santa Barbara, Calif.: Santa Teresa Press, 1990.

Durand, Philippe, ed. "Le Décor." Robert Bresson, Carl Dreyer, Georges Franju, Jean-Luc Godard, Elia Kazan, Buster Keaton, Nicholas Ray, Alain Resnais, Léon Barsacq, Jean Pelegri, Pierre Kast, Michel Mardore, Jacques Joly, Jean d'Eaubonne, Jean Bastaire, Pierre Renaud, Yves Kovacs, Lotte Eisner, Gilbert Salachas, Jean Collet, Jean-Charles Pichon, Henri Pevel, and Anne Villelaur. *Image et Son*, no. 175 (July 1964): 71–83.

Eisner, Lotte. "Lo sviluppo della scenografia cinematografica." *Bianco e nero* (1952): 24–39.

———. *The Haunted Screen: Expressionism in the German Cinema and the Influence of Max Reinhardt*. Trans. Greaves Roger. Berkeley and Los Angeles: University of California Press, 1965; Paris: Le Terrain Vague, 1965.

Epstein, Jean. "Le Décor au cinéma." *Revue Mondiale*, 1 March 1923.

Everson, William K. *American Silent Film*. New York: Oxford University Press, 1978.

Gibbons, Cedric. "The Art Director." In *Behind the Screen: How Films Are Made*, ed. Stephen Watts, 41–50. New York: Dodge Publishing, 1938.

Hambley, John, and Patrick Downing. *The Art of Hollywood: A Thames Television Exhibition at the Victoria and Albert Museum*. London: Thames Television, 1979.

Harmetz, Aljean. *Round Up the Usual Suspects: The Making of "Casablanca"—Bogart, Bergman, and World War II*. New York: Hyperion, 1992.

Harvey, Stephen. *Directed by Vincente Minnelli*. The Museum of Modern Art. New York: Harper & Row, 1989.

Hay, Peter. *MGM: When the Lion Roars*. Atlanta: Turner Publishing, 1991.

Heisner, Beverly. *Hollywood Art: Art Direction in the Days of the Great Studios*. Jefferson, N.C., and London: McFarland, 1990.

Higham, Charles. *The Films of Orson Welles*. Berkeley and Los Angeles: University of California Press, 1971.

Hollander, Anne. *Moving Pictures*. New York: Knopf, 1989.

Horner, Harry. "The Production Designer." In *Filmmakers on Filmmaking*, ed. Joseph McBride, 149–61. The American Film Institute Seminars on Motion Pictures and Television, vol. 2. Los Angeles: J. P. Tarcher, 1983.

Kazan, Elia. *A Life*. New York: Knopf, 1988.

Korda, Vincent. "The Artist and the Film." *Sight and Sound* 3 (Spring 1934): 13–15.

Laurent, Hugues. *La Technologie du décor de film*. Paris: IDHEC, n.d.

LaValley, Albert J., ed. and with an introduction by. *Mildred Pierce*. By Ranald MacDougall. Wisconsin/Warner Bros. Screenplay Series. Madison: University of Wisconsin Press, 1980.

Leven, Boris. Letter to Arthur Knight, Margaret Herrick Library, Los Angeles, 1961.

———. Letter to Patrick Downing, Margaret Herrick Library, Los Angeles, 1982.

Levy, Emanuel. *And the Winner is . . . : The History and Politics of the Oscar Awards*. New York: Ungar, 1987.

LoBrutto, Vincent. *By Design: Interviews with Film Production Designers*. Westport, Conn., and London: Praeger, 1992.

Lourié, Eugene. *My Work in Films*. San Diego: Harcourt Brace Jovanovich, 1985.

Mandelbaum, Howard, and Eric Myers. *Forties Screen Style: A Celebration of High Pastiche in Hollywood*. New York: St. Martin's Press, 1989.

———. *Screen Deco: A Celebration of High Style in Hollywood.* New York: St. Martin's Press, 1985.

Marchi, Virgilio. *Introduzione alla scenotecnica.* Siena: Ticci Editore, 1946.

Menzies, William Cameron. Interview. *Cinématographe,* no. 75 (Feb. 1982):28–34.

———. "Pictorial Beauty in the Photoplay." Lecture, 10 April 1929. In *Introduction to the Photoplay,* ed. John C. Tibbetts, 162–180. Shawnee Mission, Kans.: National Film Society, 1977.

Moussinac, Léon. "Intérieurs modernes au cinéma." *Cinémagazine,* no. 6 (25 Feb. 1921):5–9.

Myerscough-Walker, R. *Stage and Film Decor.* London: Pitman, 1945.

Naremore, James. *The Magic World of Orson Welles.* New York: Oxford University Press, 1978.

Newton, Eric. "Film Décor." In *The Year's Work in the Film: 1949,* 55–61. London: Longmans, Green, 1950.

Pagnol, Marcel. *Cinématurgie de Paris.* Paris: Editions Pastorelly, 1980 [1966].

Powell, Dilys. *The Golden Screen: Fifty Years of Films.* London: Pavillion Books, 1989.

Quenu. "L'art de la décoration au cinéma." *Cinémagazine,* 26 Dec. 1924.

Ramirez, Juan Antonio. *La arquitectura en el cine: Hollywood, la edad de oro.* Madrid: Hermann Blume, 1986.

Rava, Carlo Enrico. "Architettura e arredamento nel film italiano" series. *Domus,* March, May–June, Aug. 1939.

———. "L'architettura scenica nel cinematografo." *La rassegna italiana* (April 1937):269–277.

———. "La casa nel film" series. *Domus,* Nov. 1937, Jan., March, May, Aug., Oct. 1938.

———. "Della fotografia come elemento fantastico (in margine ad 'Architettura e cinematografo')." *Domus* (Nov. 1939):39–42.

———. "Funzione e importanza della scenografia." *Primi piani* (April 1942):26.

———. "Il gusto negli interni di film" series. *Lo stile nella casa e nell'arredamento,* Jan.–April, July–Dec. 1941.

———. "Scenografia: elemento formativo del gusto." *Bianco e nero* (31 Oct. 1937):11–20.

Relph, Michael. "Designing a Colour Film." In *Saraband for Dead Lovers: The Film and Its Production at Ealing Studios,* ed. Michael Balcon, 76–84. London: Convoy Publications, 1948.

Rivera, Adriana. "The Ideological Function of Genres in *Mildred Pierce.*" *Imagenes* 3, no. 1 (1987):16–18.

Rotha, Paul. "The Art Director and the Composition of the Film Scenario." *Close Up* 6 (May 1930):377.

Rubin, Martin. *Showstoppers: Busby Berkeley and the Tradition of Spectacle.* New York: Columbia University Press, 1993.

Schatz, Thomas. *The Genius of the System: Hollywood Filmmaking in the Studio Era.* New York: Pantheon Books, 1988.

Selznick, David O. *Memo from David O. Selznick.* Ed. Rudy Behlmer. New York: Viking, 1972.

Souriau, Anne. "Fonctions filmiques des costumes et des décors." In *L'Univers filmique,* ed. Etienne Souriau, 85–100. Paris: Flammarion, 1952.

Steen, Mike. *Hollywood Speaks!: An Oral History.* Interview with Preston Ames, 225–239. New York: Putnam, 1974.

Tashiro, Charles Shiro. "'Reading' Design in *The Go-Between.*" *Cinema Journal* (Fall 1993):17–34.

Terrana, Claudio. "Scenografia come realtà e scenografia come illusione." *Bianco e nero,* no. 5/6 (Sept.–Dec. 1979):65–97.

Thomas, Kevin. "Art Director Carré: Perspectives of a Proud Craftsman." *Los Angeles Times,* 6 Feb. 1977, 36–37.

Thomson, David. "The Art of the Art Director." *American Film* 2 (Feb. 1977):12–20.

Trauner, Alexandre. Interview. With Jacques Kermabon. *L'Avant-Scène Cinéma,* no. 374 (Oct. 1988):17–18.

———. *Décors de cinéma.* With Jean-Pierre Berthomé. Paris: Jade-Flammarion, 1988.

Verdone, Mario. "Hein Heckroth." *Bianco e Nero* 12 (1952):40–54.

Wiley, Mason, and Damien Bona. *Inside Oscar, the Unofficial History of the Academy Awards.* New York: Ballantine Books, 1986.

Williams, Linda. "*Mildred Pierce* and the Second World War." In *Female Spectators: Looking at Film and Television,* ed. E. Deidre Pribam, 12–30. London: Verso, 1988.

Unpublished Interviews Cited

Ames, Preston. Interview with Hugh Fordin, July 1972. Doheny Library, Los Angeles.

Boyle, Robert. Interview with Charles Affron, 21 June 1989. Los Angeles.

Brown, Hilyard. Interview with Rich Cheatham, 1 Nov. 1980. Doheny Library, Los Angeles.
Carfagno, Edward. Interview with Charles Affron, 21 June 1989. Los Angeles.
Michelson, Harold. Interview with Charles Affron, 20 June 1989. Los Angeles.
Pye, Merrill. Interview with Hugh Fordin, July 1972. Doheny Library, Los Angeles.
Smith, Jack Martin. Interview with Hugh Fordin, July 1972. Doheny Library, Los Angeles.
Smith, Oliver. Interview with Hugh Fordin, 27 Sept. 1972. Doheny Library, Los Angeles.
Zuberano, Maurice. Interview with Charles Affron, 20 June 1989. Los Angeles.

Index of Names and Titles

Page numbers for illustrations are in **italics**. Except in instances of possible confusion, persons listed elsewhere in the indexes are indicated only by last name in the film credits. A.D. credits include production designer, art director, and, where available, other art direction personnel. These do not, however, account for the many persons who failed to receive official credit for their work.

Index of Production Designers, Art Directors, and Related Personnel

Charles Affron is Professor of French at New York University and has written on the affective response to cinema, on screen acting, and on Federico Fellini. **Mirella Jona Affron** is Professor of Cinema Studies at The College of Staten Island/CUNY and at the Graduate School/CUNY, and has written on French and Italian cinema.